The Next Generation

The  Generation Next

Contemporary Expressions of Faith

Patricia C. Pongracz *and* Wayne Roosa

WILLIAM B. EERDMANS PUBLISHING COMPANY
GRAND RAPIDS, MICHIGAN / CAMBRIDGE, UK

MUSEUM OF BIBLICAL ART
NEW YORK, NEW YORK

This catalog accompanies the exhibition
The Next Generation: Contemporary Expressions of Faith,
on display at the Museum of Biblical Art (MOBIA)
August 20–November 13, 2005

Published jointly 2005 by

Museum of Biblical Art
1865 Broadway at 61st Street
New York, New York 10023
PHONE 212.408.1500
FAX 212.408.1292
EMAIL info@mobia.org
www.mobia.org

and

Wm. B. Eerdmans Publishing Co.
255 Jefferson Ave. S.E., Grand Rapids, Michigan 49503 /
P.O. Box 163, Cambridge CB3 9PU UK
www.eerdmans.com

Printed in the United States of America

The exhibition was curated by Patricia C. Pongracz,
Chief Curator, Museum of Biblical Art,
and Wayne Roosa, Professor of Art, Bethel College,
St. Paul, Minnesota

EDITOR Patricia C. Pongracz
PROJECT MANAGER Ute Keyes
CONTRIBUTING EDITOR Kenneth Benson
CATALOG DESIGN Kara Van Woerden
EXHIBITION DESIGN Lou Storey
PRINTING The Stinehour Press, Lunenburg, VT

Library of Congress Cataloging-in-Publication Data

Pongracz, Patricia C., 1969–
    The next generation : contemporary expressions
    of faith / Patricia C. Pongracz and Wayne Roosa.
      p. cm.
    ISBN 0-8028-2947-3 (hardcover : alk. paper)
    1. Bible--Illustrations--Exhibitions. 2. Christian
art and symbolism--Exhibitions. 3. Spirituality in
art--Exhibitions. 4. Art, American--21st century--
Exhibitions. 5. Art, Canadian--21st century--
Exhibitions. I. Roosa, Wayne. II. Museum of
Biblical Art. III. Title.

N8028.R66 2005
704.9'482'090511--dc22

                          2005040061

Unless otherwise noted, all biblical quotations
are taken from the Revised Standard Version
(Old Testament Section, Copyright 1952,
New Testament Section, Copyright 1946,
by the Division of Christian Education of
the National Council of the Churches
of Christ in the United States of America).

Has art that reflects the narratives, rituals, and symbols of the Judeo-Christian religious traditions disappeared with the advent of modernism? Ask any number of art historians specializing in modern and especially contemporary art, and the answer will be an unambiguous "Yes." After all, modernism purposefully rejected a host of traditional artistic functions and symbols, that of interpreting and serving religion among them. Whether one subscribes to the thesis that in modern times art is the new religion (and the museum, its temple), or that art is simply created for its own sake, all religious connotations, functions, and symbols have either become irrelevant or they just cannot find a place within any reasonable interpretation of the artwork.

Simply put, common art historical wisdom teaches us that modern and contemporary fine art is not religious. Surely, there still are some artists today who tackle religious subject matter without rebuff or controversy, but their art is derivative, reflective of a tired tradition, deeply suspect, or at least problematic. And in any case, such art is outside the canon of modernism. Much of contemporary art with religious content does unfortunately fit that rather unflattering description, and follows a tradition where faith tends to be confused with, and often totally replaces, artistic talent and creativity. Such works, while interesting to the cultural anthropologist, do not belong in either museums or the art historical discourse.

Yet we at the Museum of Biblical Art believe that there is more to contemporary creativity and religion than is commonly thought. Religious patronage of the arts has all but disappeared, and the trajectory of fine art has moved away from serving religious beliefs and rituals — and yet artists continue to interpret the meanings and symbols of the Bible in powerful ways (albeit in admittedly smaller numbers). This is precisely what *The Next Generation: Contemporary Expressions of Faith* — the first of what we hope will become the MOBIA contemporary art triennial exhibition — sets out to illustrate. Whether the works on display narrate the ancient stories in contemporary language or abstract and synthesize them to match our sensibilities, they take their place — as is beautifully analyzed in Wayne Roosa's introductory essay — in the long tradition of biblical art. And as we acknowledge how different they are from many of their historical counterparts, we believe that there are still lessons to be learned from looking at contemporary interpretations of Jewish and Christian religious traditions.

With this exhibition, we invite you to be a part of the dialogue that is at the heart of the mission of the Museum of Biblical Art, whose premise is that contemporary works of art that speak to art and religion as duality and dialogue are worth another (art historical) look. The long relationship between art and religion did not die with the advent of modernism, yet its substance and its manifestations have both changed dramatically. What we need now is to explore how that relationship has changed, and how — or even if — art that speaks to religion can still be relevant in the contemporary art world.

This exhibition would not have been possible without the generous support of the American Bible Society; we thank you for your foresight and for taking the gamble of backing a museum dedicated to art and the Bible in the heart of New York City. Like any such project, the exhibition is a collaborative effort of many individuals and institutions. My gratitude goes to the artists represented in the exhibition, whose stunning works illustrate better than any words the relationship between faith and visual representation. To all the lenders, we thank you for agreeing to part with these works for the duration of the exhibition. Special thanks also go to Sandra Bowden, President of Christians in the Visual Arts (CIVA) and MOBIA trustee, and to the CIVA family for their help and support in the early stages of planning.

I am most indebted to MOBIA Chief Curator Patricia Pongracz and to Professor Wayne Roosa of Bethel College for creating a conceptual framework for the exhibition, and for the writing and editing of the catalog. Roosa's insightful essay helps us fully understand the multi-layered meanings and rich traditions of religious iconography, and places the featured artists within the narrative of the history of art. Thanks also go to the rest of my staff — MOBIA Exhibitions Manager Ute Keyes, who continues to wear many hats without wrinkling any, and Exhibitions Coordinator Idyl Mohallim. This book was shaped by graphic designer Kara Van Woerden's creative talent, and its accuracy was insured by contributing editor Kenneth Benson. To all of them, and everybody else to whose hard work, talent, and dedication this exhibition is due, my deep gratitude.

The Next Generation: Contemporary Expressions of Faith features the works of forty-four artists actively inves-
tigating Judeo-Christian themes within the terms of contemporary art. This group reflects, on a small scale,
the variety inherent in explorations of such themes and their meanings today. *The Next Generation* developed
in response to a set of seemingly simple questions addressing the state of the field at the beginning of the
twenty-first century. Working from the very broad question of "Exactly what *is* contemporary Judeo-
Christian art?," the Museum of Biblical Art wanted to get a sense of some of the basics surrounding the
production and broad patronage of this art. Namely, we wanted to know (or more accurately, to begin to
comprehend) what Judeo-Christian art looks like, who makes it, who sees it, who supports it, and who
exhibits it. In short, we wanted to understand the context of the genre — a topic/issue that scholars and
artists alike have been addressing in various ways and with increasing frequency during the past ten years.[1]

      The issues surrounding the making of contemporary Judeo-Christian art (not to mention
the discussion of it) can be nuanced and complex, and, like most questions involving cultural contexts,
defy simple explanations or categorizations. The sheer breadth of the subject matter (as well as the tensions
that are often evoked by matters of religion, even in the supposedly "secular" United States) makes coming
up with a clear, concise definition a difficult — if not torturous — task.[2] Theodore L. Prescott, one of the
artists in our exhibition, aptly likens defining "Christian art" to the "intellectual equivalent of entering a
briar patch," enumerating some of its multiple meanings:

*"Christian art" can variously mean: 1) work with obvious Christian subject matter like biblical narratives; 2) work whose
worldview or spirit is Christian; or 3) work that is made for a Christian audience, to be used in some Christian way —
usually liturgically. If these possibilities aren't confusing enough, sometimes people simply mean that Christian art is art
made by Christians.*

Prescott examines the construction of artistic identities and critical perceptions of artists working with
Judeo-Christian themes. In raising the issue of who controls identity and who determines perception, he

illuminates another critical point of tension undergirding the discussion: what exactly *is* the role of faith (actively lived and practiced) in contemporary Judeo-Christian art — if any — and who gets to decide?[3]

Though a single exhibition cannot answer such questions definitively, consideration of them is critical to understanding the cultural context in which contemporary Judeo-Christian art is made today. *The Next Generation* demonstrates how — in painting, collage, sculpture, film, photography, mixed-media, computer-aided design, and installation art — artists continue to draw from both the rich visual heritage and the traditions of Judeo-Christian art, interpreting, combining, and at times redefining its symbolism for a twenty-first-century audience. The selection of art in *The Next Generation* speaks directly to MOBIA's point of entry into this vital discussion. Seeking works for the exhibition, we partnered with Christians in the Visual Arts (CIVA) to publicize our call. With its home office located at Gordon College in Wenham, Massachusetts, CIVA is a national network of artists and scholars united in their recognition that religious faith is a legitimate area of inquiry for the contemporary artist.

Spurred by a 1977 conference organized by Professor Eugene Johnson and hosted by his institution, Bethel College, in St. Paul, Minnesota, CIVA has grown into a sustained national community of Christian artists and scholars since its official founding in 1979. Over the past twenty-five years, CIVA has instituted a number of programs to foster and sustain communication among its members, including: biennial conferences and juried exhibitions (many of these recorded in the "About the Artists" section of this catalog); a newsletter (*CIVASeen*); a series of traveling exhibitions (of both contemporary art and art of the past); and a biennial membership directory.[4]

Though drawn largely from the ranks of CIVA, the artists in *The Next Generation* display different levels of experience and visibility within the larger art world, as well as a diversity of styles, media, and training, a diversity that one would expect to find within any broadly defined group. Jurors Wayne Roosa, Ena Heller, and I chose works mirroring this rich diversity. As the curricula vitae illustrate, some are established artists with long exhibition histories, the recipients of critical recognition in their fields; others are recent graduates counting *The Next Generation* among their first exhibitions; and still others occupy a ground somewhere in between. Of the forty-four artists participating in our exhibition, thirty-six are current or former members of CIVA. Fifteen of the artists are professors at colleges or universities, and sixteen identify themselves as artists first. The rest hold various positions as educators, administrators, or in jobs connected with art (a custom framer and an illustrator, for example), and one is a full-time pastor.

In an effort to provide a fuller portrait of both the artists and their creations, the entries accompanying the works include a statement about the specific work on display (not to be misread as a general statement about the artist's art or beliefs), as well as details of educational background and current professional affiliation. The artists' resumes — featuring selected awards, exhibitions, collections in which the art is held, and bibliographical references — are recorded in an appendix. This primary material is invaluable because it allows the artists to speak to us directly about the role that faith may play in the creative process. Read together, the resumes also begin to suggest larger trends relating to the current production and display of Judeo-Christian art. The exploration and exhibition of these larger trends is central to MOBIA's mission and future.[5]

1 Recent exhibitions examining contemporary Judeo-Christian art accompanied by catalogs include: *100 Artists See God* (San Francisco: The Contemporary Jewish Museum, 2004; traveling); *Like a Prayer: A Jewish and Christian Presence in Contemporary Art* (Charlotte, NC: Tryon Center for Visual Art, 2001); *Faith: The Impact of Judeo-Christian Religion on Art at the Millennium* (The Aldrich Museum of Contemporary Art, Ridgefield, CT, 2000); and *Anno Domini: Jesus Through the Centuries*, (Edmonton: The Provincial Museum of Alberta, Edmonton, AB, Canada, 2000).

Recent publications include Eleanor Heartney, *Postmodern Heretics: The Catholic Imagination in Contemporary Art* (New York: Midmarch Arts Press, 2004); and Neil MacGregor, *Seeing Salvation: Images of Christ in Art* (New Haven: Yale University Press, 2000).

Since 1989, *Image*, a journal of the arts and religion, has regularly examined the work of contemporary literary and visual artists whose work embodies "a spiritual struggle that seeks to strike a balance between tradition and a profound openness to the world" (www.imagejournal.org). In addition, St. Louis University's Museum of Contemporary Religious Art (MOCRA) was founded in 1993, "dedicated to the ongoing dialogue between contemporary artists and the world's faith traditions" (mocra.slu.edu).

2 The tension between art and religion in the United States has been the subject of much discussion. See, for example, two recent anthologies: *Crossroads: Art and Religion in American Life*, edited by Alberta Arthurs and Glenn Wallach (New York: The New Press, 2001); and *Reluctant Partners: Art and Religion in Dialogue*, edited by Ena Heller (New York: The Gallery at the American Bible Society, 2004).

3 Theodore Prescott, "Who do you say I am? Artist and Christian: Two Identities, One Person?," in *It Was Good: Making Art to the Glory of God,* edited by Ned Bustard (Baltimore, MD: Square Halo Books, 2000): 142. Also see Prescott's historiography of Christian scholarship, p. 143 and following.

4 For a history of CIVA, see *Faith and Vision: Twenty-five Years of Christians in the Visual Arts*, edited by Sandra Bowden and Cam Anderson (Baltimore, MD: Square Halo Books, 2005). I am grateful to Sandra Bowden, President of CIVA, for sharing the manuscript draft of this work with me.

5 The artists' resumes make clear that the studies examining the state of Judeo-Christian art noted above are but a small part of a much larger, well-established, though primarily regional contemporary tradition — one which to my knowledge has never been systematically studied. Reading through the resumes, characteristics of the tradition begin to emerge. Often, the resume's record of an artist's participation is the sole documentation of an exhibition, outside of the institution that organized it, making the resumes an invaluable tool for assessing current trends. And throughout, a number of institutions appear regularly in the exhibition histories, suggesting a network of venues — be they independent galleries, galleries and museums at religiously affiliated colleges and universities, or museums — that consistently exhibit contemporary Judeo-Christian art. Beginning in the spring of 2005, MOBIA will launch a formal, systematic study of the display of Judeo-Christian art in the United States.

Dancing in the Dark,
Waltzing in the Wonder:
Contemporary Art about Faith
Wayne Roosa
Professor of Art,
Bethel College

There may be in literature, music and the arts lineaments, spoors of a presentness prior to consciousness and to rationality as we know them. . . . We must read *as if*.
—George Steiner, *Real Presences*

Faith tends to heal if we realize it is a "walking in darkness" and not a theological solution to mystery.
—Flannery O'Connor, *Mystery and Manners*

Art is — among many things — visual. It is fundamentally visual, resting on sensory phenomena, materials, and perception. Even the most radically conceptual art still depends upon the artist's subversion of sight's conventions to make us "see." Faith is — among many things — invisible. It is fundamentally about what is believed but not seen. As one of the New Testament authors put it, "Faith is the assurance of things hoped for, the conviction of things not seen."[1] And yet, in proper paradoxical fashion, the fourth-century monk Abba Bessarion could rightly say about the life of faith, "The monk should be all eye," even as the nineteenth-century artist Odilon Redon could complain that with Impressionism, art had become too much about the eye, declaring that, "Monet is only an eye."[2]

In their essence, both art and faith are modes of discourse between what the physical senses detect in reality and what the mind believes about reality beyond the report of the senses. The senses supply the data that the mind's reason construes into sense. Even the word "sense" bears this paradox within itself, pointing as it does both to the mess of undifferentiated sensory experience and to the rationalizing of that experience into an abstract order, as in "making sense of." But once reason has ordered the data, the more holistic task of what to make of it all — what to believe — begins. Even those who think they have stopped with reason go on, in fact, to take leaps of faith that cannot be empirically proven.

One of the great dialogues, then, comes when art and faith cease to be parallel modes of discovery and turn toward each other, each enabling the other. When this dialogue is vigorous, art and faith serve as each other's lenses, but also as each other's conscience. The psyche must test the senses no less than the senses must keep the psyche honest.

What Martin Buber once said about Hasidic Judaism applies broadly here.

In most systems of belief the believer considers that he can achieve a perfect relationship to God by renouncing the world of the senses and overcoming his own natural being. Not so the Hasid. Certainly "cleaving" unto God is to him the highest aim of the human person, but to achieve it he is not required to abandon the external and internal reality of earthly being, but to affirm it in its true, God-oriented essence and thus so to transform it.[3]

This earthy, embracing concept of spirituality is born out in the scriptures of the Jewish faith, scriptures chock-full of raw and existential stories unfolding around a piety that is highly graphic because it is always embodied in the terms of flesh and earth.

Similarly, the Catholic writer Flannery O'Connor, one of the clearest voices to articulate the symbiotic dynamic between art and Christian faith, contended that "everything has its testing point in the eye, an organ which eventually involves the whole personality and as much of the world as can be gotten into it."[4] Drawing upon her experiences as a woman growing up in the Deep South, the Christian scriptures, and her battle with lupus, an autoimmune disease, O'Connor was a person who deeply embraced the mysteries of faith and a belief in the larger reality of a supernatural world. But in her view, it was the very existence of that larger spiritual reality which shored up and substantiated the value of the material world under our fingernails. Like Buber, she saw these two realms as a continuum — a dialogue — racked with violence and full of grace.

Working out of a theology and a poetics that were deeply incarnational and firmly sacramental, O'Connor dared to claim that "the beginning of human knowledge is through the senses, and the fiction writer begins where human perception begins. He appeals through the senses, and you cannot appeal to the senses with abstractions. . . . The world of the fiction writer is full of matter . . . [not] unfleshed ideas and emotions."[5] Given this stance, O'Connor argued that artists genuinely interested in the spiritual will therefore be committed to "all those concrete details of life that make actual the mystery of our position on earth."[6]

This enfleshed aesthetic, which understands the terrible and fecund specificity of the senses as being interwoven with the mystery of the spiritual, is not a bad starting point for thinking about the artworks in *The Next Generation: Contemporary Expressions of Faith*. We find in the artists represented in the exhibition a diversity of stylistic and conceptual visions, but a unity of interest in the question of how "all those concrete details" are joined to spirit, making "actual the mystery of our position on earth."

God in the Details

For some of these artists, the "concrete details" are deeply tied to daily domestic life. Several artists in the exhibition explore that odd duality in which domestic spaces and mundane objects — places and things usually taken for granted — can suddenly be glimpsed differently for one brief moment. What was familiar becomes uncanny, and what one took for granted suddenly yields an epiphany. The domestic interior and mundane object is thus experienced simultaneously as concrete detail and metaphor, providing several of these artists with the vehicle needed to imply contiguous realities.

In *Winter Conversation*, for example, Joel Sheesley depicts a slightly oblique view of the hall and dining room in his own home (entry 1). On the wall is a large reproduction of the *Portinari Altarpiece* by the Northern Renaissance master Hugo van der Goes (fig. 1). The house interior is filled with a cold, diffuse light, which is reflected through the windows off of the whites and blues of the snow outside. This same winter light glances off of the glass covering the print, such that a reflection of the front window and the house across the street supplants the center panel of the altarpiece, obscuring the Holy Family, the shepherds, and the Magi adoring the Christ child. In turn, the silhouettes of two women sitting on the living room couch in front of the reflected window block out the sun, allowing part of the original print to fill in their contours. The flat cutout shape of one of the women now contains a first-century angel kneeling with hands folded in prayer, and the shape of the other's head is now shrouded in royal blue and is graced with flowers symbolizing both the Virgin Mary and Christ's Incarnation.

FIGURE 1
Hugo van der Goes
Portinari Altarpiece,
ca. 1476–79
Tempera and oil on panel

In this brief visual moment, two contemporary women are simply themselves, sitting in a living room. But they also become the Annunciate Angel and the Virgin Mary of van der Goes's fifteenth-century altarpiece, which in turn references the first century. What is ancient and what is contemporary merge. Faith always involves both a remembering through tradition and an identification of the contemporary believer with the spiritual exemplar of the past. In this case, speaking visually, the remembering is literal and the identification complete. The present reality of these women and their home exists, as it were, as a kind of palimpsest. That is, the visuality of their twenty-first century setting is dominant, but the traces of an earlier fifteenth-century setting are still evident, and these in turn contain references to the first century. Each earlier period "shows through" and informs our reading of the modern, such that, like a palimpsest, Sheesley's image of contemporary domesticity and faith bears within itself a complex history of traces. This is an analogue of the structure of faith, which is borne within a contemporary person's being, but is premised upon ancient, originating events long sustained by the traditional imagery that transports those events into the present. All of this is enhanced as Sheesley connects a first-century holy moment with a Chicago suburb by using the same anachronism used by Hugo van der Goes, who placed his patrons' portraits in the wings of his altarpiece, dressed in fifteenth-century fashion, witnessing a first-century event.

This visual/spatial device allows Sheesley to create an image of something that happens constantly within our mental and cultural spaces. That is, as he puts it, *Winter Conversation* records a simple visual phenomenon and at the same time invites the viewer to consider the "collision of worlds this optical phenomenon suggests."[7] Like Emily Dickinson's "certain Slant of light . . . Where the meanings" are, Sheesley finds a contemporary suburban interior near Chicago, a religious altarpiece painted in the fifteenth century in northern Europe, and the founding moment of Christianity suddenly reshuffled in the mind by a cold day's winter light. This simple fleeting moment becomes a humble occasion for contemplation.

But all of this is only one thing that Sheesley has painted. All of this is what the viewer sees when looking *into* the painting. Something else becomes visible when looking *at* the painting. While this is a painting of a series of planes and objects receding into a domestic interior, it is also a painting of a state of mind, a moment's epiphany. It holds in suspension a very brief moment of recognition that our lives are made from the layers of meaning and history that form us. And yet like a thought that slips away so quickly, this visual moment is only a transient reflection that will change either slowly as the sun moves, or instantly as the family member/viewer seeing it walks on down the hall. The painting underscores just how temporal our lives here are; they are like a transparent reflection passing in the glass. What gives us substance, permanence, is the larger ground upon which we have our being — the historical depth, the cultural heritage, the partaking in faith that fills in our contours — joining us to a larger story. And what gives us significance is our capacity to "see" that, to believe and connect with what is greater than ourselves, even as we drift down the hallway.

Sheesley's work stands within a long tradition of painting, especially that coming out of northern Europe, in which artists delight in the rich visual phenomenon of daily life, finding there a sense of *presence* in the odd play of light and juxtapositions. The interest here is in a subtle presence as opposed to the overt or dramatic dogma of religious themes. In many ways, this is more appealing to our contemporary sensibility, which often finds the buried psychological hint more credible than the outward, dogmatic declaration. Indeed, for a twenty-first century artist interested in these issues, there can be a kind of exhaustion felt in the countless renditions of overt Christian images. Sheesley's love of the latent or submerged *presence* satisfies in a more oblique manner. As such, his work raises a key aesthetic problem for artists interested in spirituality and faith. The challenge is to discover freshness against the tremendous weight of tradition.

This aesthetic problem is handled more bluntly by the late American poet Jane Kenyon in her poem "Dutch Interiors." Because her poem extends our exploration of the issue in ways that will illuminate other artists in the exhibition, it is worth considering here.

Christ has been done to death
in the cold reaches of northern Europe
a thousand thousand times.

                            Suddenly bread
and cheese appear on a plate
beside a gleaming pewter beaker of beer.

Now tell me that the Holy Ghost

does not reside in the play of light
on cutlery!

A woman makes lace,
with a moist-eyed spaniel lying
at her small shapely feet.
Even the maid with the chamber pot
is here; the naughty, red-cheeked girl. . . .

And the merchant's wife, still
in her yellow dressing gown
at noon, dips her quill into India ink
with an air of cautious pleasure.[8]

The artistic dilemma is in how to find a freshness within a still rich but well-used genre. Kenyon so intelligently takes on the powerful tradition of portraying the Christian faith through the overt religious subject matter of Christ, finds it spent (*a thousand thousand times*) as a vehicle for stating the transcendent, and so turns to the interior domestic scene. There, while three women go about their business within the room, the humbleness of an ordinary meal of bread, cheese, and beer suddenly flickers with light, suggesting the subtle presence of the Spirit. This kind of embedded sign serves Kenyon nicely, for it allows her not only to imply the same sense of presence that Sheesley evokes, but also to place the divine inside a more complex human narrative latent with things we do not necessarily associate with spirituality. While we easily accept the woman making lace, things get a bit more dicey when Kenyon leads us to "the maid" by way of a "moist-eyed spaniel" at the lace maker's "small shapely feet." Such sensuous and suggestive concrete details carry some unnamed subplot, picked up by the maid carrying the chamber pot reeking at this late morning hour.

Pressing the narrative further, the poem keeps company with the Holy Ghost residing in the light glinting off of the cutlery right alongside a maid who is "red-cheeked" and "naughty." What is naughty and causing her to blush is not said, though the line trails off as knowingly as the look on the girl's face. Clearly, there is more to the pot, to the night preceding its filling, and to the merchant's wife being still in her nightgown at noon, dipping her quill with a lingering "air of cautious pleasure."

This conjoining of bodily realities, desire, and domestic settings with God's implicit presence is, I would dare to argue, true to the textured character of the biblical narrative that underwrites the Jewish and Christian faiths. It is what Buber and O'Connor called for. In keeping with this attitude, we find the next work, a large collage by Mary Fielding McCleary titled *Allegory of the Senses*, to embody an equally engorged but slightly more haunted use of the domestic interior (entry 2).

Upon first appearances, the viewer encounters a well-appointed living room occupied by a middle-aged man and woman, both seated, and a teenage boy standing while talking on the phone. The man sits on a couch holding a book, his head and shoulders turned toward us. He cranes his neck around and looks out of the corners of his eyes as if to glance at something that has interrupted his reading. The woman, sitting on the arm of a stuffed chair and playing with a dog, turns her head in the direction of the teenage boy, but looks distracted, as if she is lost in thought or absent-minded boredom. And the teenager, his body facing the fireplace, turns his head in the viewer's general direction, as if he has been interrupted during his phone conversation.

The overall effect of the grouping is one of normal domestic activity momentarily interrupted or transfixed. The three people seem to belong together, and yet the various pauses in their activities create a kind of suspension or waiting, implying a tension or even a discomfort in each other's presence. Although it makes sense to imagine that the same thing has interrupted each of their activities, the fact is that each person seems quite isolated from the others. It is more as if some vague disquiet has come over them as they go about their business.

All around the figures are the objects that one might expect within a domestic interior: flowers in a vase, knickknacks, books, cutlery, a plate, and a drinking glass, on table, bureau, and mantel. Closer inspection of these objects, however, fixes one's attention on each of them, as they are well chosen to convey a secondary level of meaning. Thus, in echo of the human figures that pause and suspend normality, these objects cause the eye to halt, wondering about the meanings they imply.

On one level, according to McCleary, this is merely a family portrait.[9] She, her husband, son, and their family dog pose in the familiar comfort of their living room, seated amidst the objects they have collected and enjoy. One could easily be satisfied with this as both the subject matter and the content of the image, were it not for the abundance of oddities tucked into this ordinary — albeit sensuous — scene. For one thing, the top of the man's bald head bears a strange eye, the kind found on vintage teddy bears, where the black pupil rattles around over the white, the whole encased in a clear plastic bubble. And the book he holds has another eye on its cover. Indeed, the entire four-by-six-foot collage is littered with these unblinking eyes across its surface. At first they seem randomly placed, as the viewer finds one here, and then another there. But the mind quickly realizes that they have been placed in a regular geometric grid, where they play against the more organic flow of forms in the world behind them. In effect, the grid creates a transparent plane of consciousness, a kind of omnipresence of God that permeates and yet floats just outside of the room, like a visual equivalent of the mystery of monotheism: God as wholly Other and yet as immanently involved in the world.

It is not exactly that the *presence* evoked by the plane of eyes is what has interrupted the family. And yet there is a fine psychological analogue between the way that the eyes arrest the viewer's perception of a normal, seamless reality, and the way that the people within that reality are not quite at home there. It is as if a kind of unexpected self-consciousness has been inserted within the otherwise uniform fabric of being. A kind of slippage in the very fabric of things, one that disrupts and perhaps haunts, is evoked here. Martin Buber once described the condition of being human as being marked by a "twofold" quality. Humans, he wrote, "are that species of life which, instead of being content like the rest with the perception of things and conditions, began to perceive its own perceiving as well."[10] Whereas *an animal in the realm of its perceptions is like a fruit in its skin; man is . . . in the world as a dweller . . . who knows as one knows a house in which he lives. . . . Man is like this because he is the creature through whose being "what is" becomes detached from him. . . . It is the peculiarity of human life that here and here alone a being has arisen from the whole, endowed and entitled to detach the whole as a world from himself and to make it an opposite to himself, instead of cutting out with his senses that part he needs from it, as all other beings do, and being content with that.*[11]

This twofold condition, by which we live as bodily creatures within our domestic spaces (like "an animal in the realm of its perceptions" as "a fruit in its skin") and yet also live self-consciously detached from our spaces and even our very being (like a dweller who knows the "house in which he lives"), is the source of self-conscious disquiet. In the context of discussing faith, it is the awareness of our being here, and yet of our being incomplete or separate from God. And in the context of discussing art about faith, it is the making of art that signifies our self-consciousness about being "twofold." McCleary's collage embodies, as we have seen, several layers of such self-consciousness or tensions. These disjunctions, which are caused by realizing that the space here is inhabited, that the "skin" of domesticity is ruptured by detachment, impose upon the viewer an awareness that the spiritual and the physical are contiguous realities, simultaneously separate yet interwoven.

This disjunction is sharply exacerbated when the viewer considers the objects within the room. For these objects also bear a disjunction within themselves. That is, they appeal simply to the senses as part of the room's decor. But they are also allegorical, each having a symbolic meaning beyond itself. As physical things, they report what the eye sees as sensory data from reality; but as symbolic objects, they point to the order of meaning that the mind constructs out of the report of the senses. In the slippage between sensual fact and symbolic meaning lies the function — the translation — of allegory.

Like Jane Kenyon's "Dutch Interiors," McCleary's ordinary interior, so ripe with concrete details, becomes charged with the mystery of our position on earth. For example, on the cover of the novel held by the father, there is a foreshortened Superman flying over tall buildings, one supposes "with a single leap." Just above Superman's extended arm is one of the vintage teddy bear eyes, a disembodied stare as large as his head. The novel itself is a now-obscure work by Bruce Marshall published in 1945, its title barely legible in the collage on the book's spine: *The World, the Flesh and Father Smith*.[12] Searching the Internet for a review or summary of this little-known novel, one can click on one of the Google links bearing the book's title, which takes one to a website dedicated to tracking down quotations both correctly and incorrectly attributed to G.K. Chesterton. Among the quotations covered there, one will find the following:

"A man knocking on the door of a brothel is knocking for God."

The website's experts then clarify the source of the quotation: "Variously ascribed to Chesterton, St. Francis, and St. Augustine, we have discovered that the only documented source of this quotation is the book *The World, the Flesh, and Father Smith* by Bruce Marshall (1945). And the quote is really: '. . . the young man who rings the bell at the brothel is unconsciously looking for God' (p. 108)."[13]

The idea of a young man enjoying the pleasures of the flesh as a substitute for spiritual completeness is an old *vanitas* theme. And of course on a larger level, McCleary's *Allegory of the Senses* is a *vanitas* work. It deliberately celebrates the body's five senses and all of the beautiful things in the world that delight them. The lilies in full bloom appeal to smell, the crackers and wine to taste, the telephone to hearing, the plaster hand on the table and all the tactile surfaces to touch, and the artwork in the coffee table book, as well as the visually lush color everywhere, to sight; all of these are conveyed in McCleary's chosen medium of collage, which joyfully embraces thousands of fascinating objects and fragments obsessively gathered together. This obsessiveness itself underscores the fact that the very ground of being in the physical world is an astonishing array of sensory fragments constituting a gluttonous feast for the senses.

There is enormous sensual pleasure in looking at McCleary's work. But like all *vanitas* pieces, the lure of that beauty is both a goodness and a bait. We take it in until we encounter the many references to the decay, corruption, and death that are interlaced with what is delicious. Thus, while the eyes of God stabilize reality with the mathematical order of their geometric grid, there is also a more random scattering of black moths throughout the composition, suggesting the disorder of all that devours. The vase of lilies extends precariously over the table's edge, crows eat the ripening corn in the Audubon print on the wall, and the hand on the table is frustrated by its frozen inability to use the pencil, suggesting the limitations of knowledge and the arts.

Perhaps even more poignant are the small ceramic collector's plates on the mantel. These reach beyond the terrible — but natural — realities of decay and mortality by evoking a sense of decadence and vanity. They are decorated with reproductions of allegorical scenes about the senses by the eighteenth-century French Rococo painter Fragonard. This references the devotion to sensual pleasure in the court of Louis XVI, a time of corrupt political power, luxury, sensuality, and sexual intrigue. That court was violently destroyed by the French Revolution, which brought moral judgment against the aristocracy. While this little allegory inside of an allegory adorns the eighteenth-century mantel upon which the plates sit, a tiny airplane banks into its approach just outside the narrow tower of windows near the woman's head. So, a subliminal reference to impending disaster whispers outside of the interior space, as we blithely enjoy our material wealth, while the black moths flutter everywhere within. Herein lies the bottom line of our "twofold" self-consciousness, for we all realize almost continually that death is imminent, and yet our appetites defer the inevitable through the pleasures of the senses.

Like many other *vanitas* paintings in the history of art, McCleary's *Allegory of the Senses* bears another layer of symbolism. This one is redemptive. For woven in amongst the beautifully sensuous objects and the warnings of decay are numerous signs of salvation. The carved wood eighteenth-century mantel bearing the collector's plates, for example, contains clusters of grapes and wheat, both Eucharist symbols of incarnation and salvation. And, in the still-life motif on the table, the viewer is moved from apple seeds, suggesting the Fall, through the Passover meal implied in the matzo crackers, to the Eucharist of bread and wine established by Jesus, whom the gospel writers referred to as the Paschal Lamb. Next to the meal's remnants, the coffee table book is open to portraits of the face of Christ. Executed in McCleary's collage technique, these literally become miniature mosaics for contemplation. McCleary also employs kitsch items bearing symbolically weighty meanings, placing a small plastic church on the mantel between the Fragonard plates, and a small crèche illuminated by a lamp-cum-star on the bureau just beneath the devouring crows.

Accompanying all of this complex imagery are three strings of words from three different texts, running around the border. With her usual humor and insight, McCleary brings together lyrics from a popular 1930s song and words from the Bible. One string of words is from a song by Howard Dietz (music) and Arthur Schwartz (lyrics), "Dancing in the Dark." The song's refrain goes

Dancing in the dark,
Till the tune ends
We're dancing in the dark,
And it soon ends.
We're waltzing in the wonder
Of why we're here.
Time hurries by, we're here
And gone,
Looking for the light
Of a new love
To brighten up the night.
I have you, love,
And we can face the music together,
Dancing in the dark.[14]

The song's tender, soft nihilism of "eat, drink, and be merry for tomorrow we die" is the solution — the salve — that the senses offer to our disquiet. But then McCleary juxtaposes "Dancing in the Dark" with a second text, one taken from the New Testament. This offers a different salve — a salvation — to our distress. The text comes from Paul's second letter to the Christians living in ancient Corinth. It reads, "While we look not at the things which are seen, but at the things which are not seen; for the things which are seen are temporal, but the things which are not seen are eternal."[15]

These words act as a chorus, providing a commentary on the visual events on stage. They posit the visible, material world and the invisible, spiritual world as opposites. We are here and we dance; it soon ends and we are gone. The things that are seen are temporal, but the things that are not seen are eternal. One is a more worldly, existential response, the other a more religious, theological response to the shocking brevity of life and to the sadness of ending our conscious pleasure in being. To the senses, to the immediate intensity of experience, the realm of McCleary's living room is the greater reality. Better to knock on the door of the brothel, with its guarantee, than to trust in the abstraction of faith's beyond. But then to faith, there is the hope of more. Despite every corny formulation of the dilemma, this choice of viewpoints has long been one of the central human questions.

It is to the crux of this dilemma that the third text in McCleary's collage speaks. That text is taken from the first of three letters written by the Apostle John: "That which was from the beginning, which we have heard, which we have seen with our eyes, which we have looked at and our hands have touched—this we proclaim concerning the Word of life."[16] What John writes about is, of course, the Christian idea of the Incarnation. For the Christian faith, it is the Incarnation—God become flesh, gendered in time and space—that is the conduit and continuity between the world of our senses and natural being and the world of God and spirit. This is what the theologian Paul Tillich called "the scandal of particularity." In this scandal, all that the senses contain and convey is caught up into discourse with all that the abstractions of faith and the transcendent promise. Here, the paradox between sense and faith, eye and epiphany is held in a beautifully wrought aesthetic tension. We now feel the force of Buber's notion that resolution is found not by "renouncing the world of the senses and overcoming [our] own natural being," but rather by affirming them in their "true, God-oriented essence" and thus so transforming them. It is fitting that such ideas be expressed by artists because of all the human languages, it is the physical, visual arts that most directly manifest the connection between raw matter, the senses, ideas, and meaning. Indeed, the visual arts are, in a lesser way, deeply "incarnational," in that they understand how spirit and meaning are distinct from—and yet inseparable from—the world of matter.

Part of the richness of this exhibition is that it addresses the themes of faith across a spectrum of media and generations. For example, Sheesley and McCleary explore the ideas discussed above within the terms of oil painting and collage, as grounded in the visual traditions that began in the Renaissance. And it is within the terms true to that tradition that these artists have expressed ideas about what is sensory and transitory in relation to what is spiritual and eternal. Both appeal powerfully to the tactile reality of the visual world through the devices of naturalistic color, light and shadow, and the illusion of perspective, presenting a stable and rational world seen as if through a window. Both then leverage off of our confidence in that way of picturing the world in order to evoke an invisible reality, or presence, contiguous to it. The result is that we feel we are able to contemplate "the mystery of our position on earth" from the stable vantage point of a rationally constructed world of "concrete details."

But can the artist really touch the mystery of what is unknown from the controlled stability of what is well known? We easily take pictorial structure for granted, thinking only about what is depicted, and forgetting that the pictorial devices of depiction are themselves a way of signifying the order that the senses and the mind have negotiated "to make sense" of reality. There is a certain irony here, in our thinking that we can contemplate what is beyond our control by way of a pictorial language that puts us in a position of control.

Other artists in the exhibition have taken a different approach to such questions. In his piece *4 or 5 Trees*, for example, Gregory King inverts the basic terms of the Renaissance tradition through his use of video as a medium (entry 3). In this black-and-white work, a hand-held camera leads the viewer through a glass conservatory with a group of tall palm trees growing up into its dome. The camera moves slowly, turning around through an arc of 360 degrees, while appropriately minimalist music accompanies the camera's movement, and occasionally a voice-over speaks in fragments about the space. The camera angle is either straight up into the canopy of trees and the architectural vaulting of the dome, or straight down into water, which reflects the trees and the structure above. Either way, the viewer is slightly disoriented in the way one is, for example, when walking straight forward while looking overhead at the clouds above. The shifting quality of the hand-held camerawork is reinforced by the shimmering patterns of light breaking through the leafy canopy and the reflections of what is overhead in the water's surface. The overall effect is one of drifting through an architectural space as if one were a cross between an explorer and a dreamer. The visual experience evokes a strong sense of memory, but also of a mystical vision received through nature and sacred space.

In general, the visually disorientating effect of *4 or 5 Trees* is lyrical, even comforting. But the gentleness of the work should not obscure the radicalness of King's vision here. In the pictorial structure of Renaissance perspective, the viewer is essentially a "knowing" eye that exists outside of the pictorial space, looking into the image's world with a kind of omniscience or control. But here, in keeping with the inherent nature of video, King uses a hand-held camera in constant movement through the conservatory to relocate the viewer's eye "inside" the work's space. Both the viewer and the world seem to move in relationship to one another, making us aware that our human vantage point—though powerful and rich—is not omniscient or fixed. It is, in reality, limited and temporal. We do not really grasp the world from the "outside," despite our powers of abstracting and ordering sensory experience into intellectual systems.

In King's hands, the nature of video is especially well suited to this point. Video is literally a temporal medium. It is not merely a matter of the artist adapting to an intriguing new technology, but rather of finding a medium whose inherent nature is more accurately an analog to the nature of human experience. Duration is one of video's fundamental moorings. In *4 or 5 Trees*, duration and its correlate, motion, essentially supplant one-point linear perspective as the central orienting pictorial device. King's piece lasts only five minutes and fifty-five seconds. Since it is a filmic medium, one must watch it proceed moment by moment. In King's hands, the flow of time and the shifting vantage point of the hand-held camera become the crucial platform from which the question of how the eternal, played against the temporal, might be glimpsed.

In other words, King defies our assumptions about the natural givenness of perspectival pictorial structure. He makes the spatial base on which the image rests one that is moving and unstable. No longer is the viewer (or more accurately, the assumption that the viewer's mind makes absolute sense out of seeing) an external static point, the site where vision looks onto a fixed world. And, therefore, no longer is the viewer's eye omniscient. Now the *viewer* becomes a shifting point internal to the work, and the mind must triangulate between the eye, objects in space, and perception as motion within a world that is fully 360 degrees and perceivable through duration. It could be argued that this overall visual structure is closely related to human experience and the problem of knowing. Here, the medium of video is disconcertingly akin to the "medium" of being human. Despite the mind's abstract ability to think our being— that is, to average the experience of the senses and to rationalize from that a universal, stable vantage point projected as identity—the body's senses and the mind's restless activity are really quite fluid, shifting constantly through space in time.

King has characterized his interests as an artist by saying that at "the core of my work is the desire to engage perception, to visually interpret the fundamental material and spiritual dimensions of the world, [and] to navigate the possibilities of how these are distinct and yet intertwined."[17] To get at this, he sees art as an "act of poetically transforming the infinitely complex interactions between humanity and the environment" and as a way to engage the "imagination in time." He seeks through this process to "focus one's ability to observe . . . the environment as a physical and metaphysical entity." Here, like Sheesley and McCleary, King reveals his interest in what Sheesley has so aptly described as finding a visual experience that invites the viewer to consider the "collision of worlds [that] this optical phenomenon suggests."

FIGURE 2
Juan Sánchez Cotán
Quince, Cabbage,
Melon, and Cucumber,
ca. 1602
Oil on canvas

In King's case, that collision is far more ephemeral than it is with Sheesley or McCleary. One feels this immediately through the evocative text of the voice-over in King's video. Its language summons up a deep memory of a real space experienced as a mystery, to the point that the memory of it transforms the space into a sacred holy of holies that should not be entered. A few lines excerpted here will give the overall impression: "I was thinking about it again the other day . . . I can't remember the name . . . I used to go there pretty often . . . It was set back from the street by a courtyard garden . . . The winding path, the stone gazebo, and four or five trees . . . I never went inside . . . It was clear to me that I should keep it as it was in my imagination . . . The most peaceful place."

While Sheesley, McCleary, and King all create complete interior spaces flush with objects, space, light, and complexity, Christine Huck and George Wingate pluck single objects of domestic life out of such places, isolating them in small still lifes that are both intimate and yet powerful in their ability to evoke presence.

The greatest still lifes in Western art history tend to fall into one of two categories. Most accessible are the "maximalists," those lush and dazzling pieces that are packed from edge to edge with an abundant wealth of textured and variegated objects — the works of Jan Breugel, Chardin, William Harnett, John Peto, and Janet Fish come to mind. The other category follows an opposite strategy, isolating only a few objects, or even a single one, against a simple ground. These "minimalist" still lifes must find all their expressiveness within the limited properties of a few elements. Here, success rests on two crucial ingredients: one being the poignant placing of isolated objects in relationship to one another, to the edges, and to that exact place in foreground or depth that causes them to resonate within the painting; the other being the richness of the painting itself, the nuances of color harmonies, the textured buildup of brushstrokes, and the weight of light playing over form and surface. Still lifes in this vein are usually small and intimate, so that the viewer must come in close to engage with the painting. One thinks here of the works of Juan Sánchez Cótan (fig. 2), Zurbarán, Manet, Cézanne, Giorgio Morandi, and Philip Guston.

Christine Huck and George Wingate both favor the minimalist tradition. It allows for a kind of visual silence, a meditation that draws us through the seductive beauty of the sensual surface into the presence of the object, in which we feel a palpable solidity of being. For Huck, this is manifest in the power of the isolated object. For her, the worn and battered object is a kind of surrogate portrait. She celebrates the evidence of use, experience, and wear borne by the object as a means of expressing both suffering and beauty. In *Portrait # 32*, for example, she floats a well-used faucet in a field of blue-white paint that eliminates all spatial depth or sense of reality (entry 4). In a way, the flat, slightly luminous pale ground gives an iconic feel to the object. But the faucet is in fact so richly constructed by thick brushstrokes that despite its understated color, it has real weight and a palpable opacity.

Within this blue-white ground, Huck places the faucet at a slight angle in space, so that a nice tension is created between a straight frontal view (which reinforces the hint of a spiritualized or iconic image) and a fully relaxed three-quarters view (characteristic of a naturalistic portrait). In addition, her way of rendering the faucet strikes another important balance. That is, her realism is meticulous in that it records nicks, worn-off chrome plating, and the reflections of light. But at the same time, she avoids the kind of sharp-focus photo-realism that can become too much about retinal information-cum-abstract formalism. Instead, Huck's realism favors a loose enough way of painting, one which generalizes the object to just the right degree. Consequently, the object's sculptural or three-dimensional form is preserved, giving the image a quality of gravitas.

Huck is certainly aware of the Western still life tradition. But in terms of influences, she cites Edward Hopper first.[18] Hopper's sense of the isolation and alienation of people and objects is echoed in Huck's metaphoric portraits of single objects. As she puts it in her artist statement, "I am interested in painting these objects as portraits and see them as metaphors representing humanity in its broken, down-trodden, but also beautiful reality. . . . There is beauty in the places where people do not tend to look."[19] At this point, however, it seems to me that Huck departs from Hopper's vision, because for her, the pathos of this idea has a theological reality that Hopper did not share. "What beauty is apart from God?," she asks in her artist statement. "Any delight, any good thing, any sweet spilling of pleasures comes from him. Out of nothing. Out of dirt. Take the cracks and burns of life, he will draw beauty out of even that."

If the sense of portraiture or narrative association found in Huck's metaphoric use of common objects is present in George Wingate's *Tangerine: Two States*, it is only as a latent or deeply fused element (entry 5). For Wingate, the beauty and value of the still life object lies in its own, simple, and inherent *being there*, not in what references beyond itself are conjured up. His artist statement, which is as terse as his still life paintings, reduces his goals down to an equally concentrated idea: "My paintings are my celebration of the beauty and the mystery of the commonplace. We strive so often for the significant that we devalue the most dear."[20]

At the end of Plato's *Republic*, all of the heroes are given a chance to choose a new life. The great warrior-traveler Ulysses, after all of his epic exploits, wisely chooses the simple option of being a farmer. What he has understood, it seems, is that what is great lies most deeply within what is humble. He now prefers a state of *being present* within nature to a state of *active narrative* within a life of heroic deeds. Although still life is itself a far more humble genre than Homer's epic poetry, there is a nice resonance here, as we will see. Wingate's preference for "the beauty and the mystery of the commonplace," as well as his implication that, in fact, beauty and mystery may only be accessible when we abandon our need to be significant, is borne out by the sheer juicy painterliness of *Tangerine: Two States*. The two pieces of fruit, present in two states — peeled and unpeeled, nude and clothed — almost vibrate with the intelligent tensions Wingate has created within the composition. Placed just off center, the larger unpeeled tangerine slightly crowds the right edge, while its delectable peeled counterpart enjoys a wide margin to the left. Their placing within the three horizontal bands of the ground creates a subtle ambiguity between a flat decorative feeling and a three-dimensional presence in space. Wingate's sensuous use of thick brushwork and his modulations of color give *Tangerine*'s surface what the painter James Winn calls "a fine lickability." And this is exactly to the point, for Wingate's ability to stimulate multiple senses, within such a finely tuned composition, is precisely why we feel such a rich *presence* embodied in these "most dear" but utterly commonplace objects.

To some readers, it may seem a far stretch to speak of *Tangerine* (or Huck's faucet) in the same paragraph as Plato's *Republic* and the hero of Homer's *Odyssey*. But, in fact, there is a rich still life tradition that has always understood the metaphysical presence latent within the humble objects of the world. The obvious example is the frequent use of a skull placed amongst beautiful things in *vanitas* still lifes, warning the viewer against trusting too much in the physical world. But there also exists a subtler, and ultimately more potent, attitude toward the still life, which concentrates the overtly symbolic or narrative associations more deeply *into* the objects and their composition. No one has articulated this idea better than did T.S. Eliot in his essays defining Metaphysical poetry. He argued that the best work was neither "philosophical poetry nor poetic philosophy." Rather, "poetical work of the first intensity [was] work in which the thought is so to speak *fused* into poetry at a very high temperature."[21] Such work, Eliot believed, "fuses a unity of the medium (its nature and possibilities) with thought, emotions, and the senses." It is able "to make mind, body, ears, tongue, eyes, and complexion join together in the same moment of experience."[22]

This notion of the unity felt within the simply expressed commonplace object has a strong counterpart in the history of still life painting. In painting, of course, the "poetry" is a matter of form, composition, color, surface, and object. For at least three-and-a-half centuries, artists have commented upon why, within such an ostensibly humble genre, the simple visual strategy of the minimalist still life seems to be so rich with possibilities. As early as the 1630s and '40s, the Spanish painter and theorist Francisco Pacheco articulated this dynamic in his lectures to his students, including Velázquez.[23] A profoundly devout Catholic, Pacheco taught his students to attend carefully to nature, its colors, shadings, textures, and so on. But he also taught them to attend equally to the underlying geometry of nature's forms, for in that geometry, Pacheco argued, the artist discovers the deeper ordered harmony of God's presence within creation. This attitude is certainly what underlies the powerful intensity achieved in the still lifes of Pacheco's contemporaries Juan Sánchez Cótan and Zurbarán.

This same kind of theological metaphysics was carried forward much later by Cézanne, who was also a devout Catholic. Though Modernist formalism since Roger Fry has denuded Cézanne of his theological dimension, it was precisely that dimension that he acknowledged in a famous letter to Emil Bernard (May 26, 1904). Whereas Cézanne's spiritual sense was far more embedded within naturalism, Bernard was active in the more overtly Catholic dimension of the Symbolist movement at the turn of the twentieth century. In his letter, Cézanne was speaking out of his larger aesthetic agenda — his desire to "to do Poussin over again according to nature" — when he advised the younger Bernard to spend much time before nature, but also to "treat nature by the cylinder, the sphere, the cone, everything in proper perspective so that each side of an object or plane is directed towards a central point. Lines parallel to the horizon give breadth, that is a section of nature or, if you prefer, of the spectacle that the *Pater omnipotens aeterne Deus* spreads out before our eyes."[24] As the painter Archie Rand has observed, this inclusion of a Latin phrase for God, the *omnipotent and eternal Father*, is hardly a casual idiom, given Cézanne's lifetime devotion to attending Mass and Bernard's own deep involvement (with Maurice Denis) in a neo-Catholic aesthetic linked to Symbolism.[25]

In short, the still life that examines a single or limited number of objects in a shallow but palpable space allows for a sustained meditation. The sensuous surface and appeal of the object is celebrated, even as the volumetric, sculptural *presence* of its form is deeply felt. We are made conscious of the sheer existence of the object in space. In the academy of the seventeenth century, the genre of still life was considered the least profound. Yet in the hands of some artists, the genre's very insignificance becomes the occasion of its greatness, for it takes the specific, singular object, especially as a small and unimportant component of reality, and shows us an astonishing beauty and a presence that is infused with creation's details.

Such an understated metaphysics moves us because we find beauty and presence there, in a place utterly free from the pomp and ego of the "great" themes of history painting. Like the enlightened Ulysses, who chooses farming over war, and like the resurrected Jesus on the shore, who chooses to reveal his triumph over Death to his disciples by cooking fish and offering them breakfast, the still life of the humble object attains beauty by shucking off greatness.

Before leaving this section of artists who deal with presence by celebrating the humility of domestic things, we should consider one more artwork, a piece that at first glance seems to be an unlikely bedfellow with the works of Huck and Wingate. The work is Doris Hutton Auxier's *Solitude: First Temptation* (entry 6). Although her images are abstract and very different from those of either Huck or Wingate, let alone Sheesley or McCleary, what Auxier shares with these artists is a beginning point in the concrete details of reality, followed by an intense aesthetic meditation. She starts with "detritus that has been sheared from its original organic source."[26] These small fragments of daily reality, which might be as simple as a lock of hair cut from a friend's head, become the starting point of the work.[27] Her idea of "solitude" involves an intentional withdrawal from the noisy, brute crush of life's struggles and the culture wars for the purpose of "crying out to God" and listening for the Spirit. As Auxier says in her artist statement, her *Solitude* pieces came from "a year of my soul's withdrawal to a still, silent place where even that which has been discarded becomes sacred and refueled with God's presence and breath."

The word "solitude" conjures up images of a hermitage or a saint's pilgrimage into the wilderness. The artist's counterpart to these is the withdrawal into the studio, but also into the objects or images that allow the heart to focus in a meditation. Auxier's meditation on discarded fragments is not so much a meditation on beauty, as is Wingate's *Tangerine*, as it is a meditation on suffering. The sense that by deeply valuing, even ensconcing — indeed, almost fetishizing a discarded thing, until it is symbolically redeemed by being incorporated layer by layer into a work of art which has aesthetic value — also belongs to the still life tradition discussed here. The final result is highly abstract, but it is not non-objective, not a purely formal exercise. Auxier's *Solitude: First Temptation* is profoundly connected to life, from its death as a flayed or shorn scrap and subsequent rebirth in a work of art, to its final state as "a silent death mask or icon that holds within it the ancient, current, and future voice of its creator."

Thinking for a moment about Sheesley, McCleary, King, Huck, Wingate, and Auxier together, there is a kind of common ground to their conceptual interests despite their aesthetic diversity. That ground is a shared sense of *presence* encountered within the sensuous richness of place, objects, and materials. The evocation of presence is, indeed, one of the central thematic qualities running throughout many of the works in *The Next Generation*. While the artists discussed above discover something about "the mystery of our position on earth" as grounded in the particularities of "concrete details," other artists, as it were, invert the equation. They seek to visualize a more expansive ground of mystery in which concrete details exist.

In her triptych *Reflections on a Poet God,* for example, Theresa Couture relies on the abstract qualities of an artwork to embody what she sees as essential mysteries (entry 7). The work's three-part structure is organized with a verticality at its center and a horizontal expansiveness extending on each side. This basic structure nicely implies both a sense of ascending (transcendence) and a lateral movement outward (nature's horizontality). Each panel of Couture's triptych exists as a vast and dark space. Each of the spaces is ambiguous and mysterious, although not amorphous. For within the three brooding, brown-black realms, there are subtle geometric divisions and vertical "zips" or bands that give order to what would otherwise be dark abysses without form. Then, hovering within each dark field is a luminous "object" or "place," or perhaps even better, a luminous "event." Each of these "events" exists within a smaller, dark rectangle that floats above (or inside) the dark ground of the larger panel.

All of this is what the viewer sees at a distance. But if he or she moves in for a closer inspection — really enters into these realms — more specific elements become visible. In the left panel, titled *Between the Space and the Echo*, for example, the horizontal ground is divided into two sections, one a smaller, almost black square to the left, and the other a wider, better lit rectangle to the right. At the junction of these two sections floats a third dark rectangle, in which the luminous "event" hovers. When seen up close, the viewer discovers that these sections of dark color are really made up of fragments that are coalescing into a "world." In the left panel, the ground contains obscure patterns, suggestive of grids, maps, or manuscripts, all overlaid with more organic patterns of darker color. There is a sense of a world latent in or even underwriting the space. And in the smaller rectangle near the center, an illuminated series of planes, more like sheets or pages, furls around a center. The surfaces of the pages — which are illuminated with light — are blurry. But they seem to bear registers, as in a musical score or a manuscript. In their midst, as if emanating from them, is a luminous disk that rests on a kind of open woven sphere. The sphere is made out of strips of musical staffs with notes, winding around in space, interspersed with a grid pattern and bits of pink and yellow color. The overall sense is of a sphere or a world in formation within a brooding, infinite space.

The feeling that we are witnessing something in formation, something moving and emerging, is underscored by the panel's title, *Between the Space and the Echo*. And indeed, the left panel feels extremely spatial. In contrast, the right panel, while also stressing a sense of something in formation — something "between" states — has a much flatter quality. This is fitting, since the luminous event within it references language, or perhaps the page of a book. Here, an ancient-looking calligraphy, like a rune or a

Hebraic letter, seems to act within the larger, brooding realms of the panel. This, too, is underscored by the panel's title, *Between the Word and the Entry*.

Taken together, this laterally expansive pair of panels implies that a kind of music of the spheres and the spoken word act as generative forces alive within an enigmatic void. Clearly, given our context of art about faith, the panels are evocative of creation narratives. Couture's notion of God as Poet, speaking some ur-language and singing music, lends great mystery to the work.

It is not quite that Couture is seeking to illustrate a creation narrative. Rather, her imagery bears, in a visual way, the ambiguity that is named in the opening lines of Genesis and the Gospel of John as "the beginning." In the account of creation in Genesis, this is a place where the earth existed but was without form and void, where the darkness was upon the face of the deep, and "the Spirit of God was moving over the face of the waters." And in John's Gospel, this is a "place" of even greater mystery, for what existed in the beginning is solely the Word, the *logos*. The Word, wrote John, was both "with God" and "was God," and the agent by which all things were created.[28] It is this ur-world — over and in which the Spirit of God moves and creates, or within which the *logos* gives order — that Couture's three brooding panels evoke.

But Couture does not attempt to *illustrate* such a place of primordial energy, as might a diorama in a science museum. Rather, she is interested in evoking a sense of mystery, of emanation, where life and meaning pulse, as if emerging from a ground of being we cannot understand or master. As she says in her artist statement, "What is most captivating to me about the arts is that they give substance to an intensely engaging perception that everything of consequence in life is hidden. Everything that really matters is a mystery: the cycles of nature, the rhythms of our bodies, the capacity to have ideas and to make things, the expanses of the human heart, the convergences of all things true, good, and beautiful. Life's major challenge is to welcome mystery. The way of art is to approach mystery through indirection and metaphor."[29]

Although Couture evokes these matters through a highly abstract visual idiom, she does not really posit a vague or purely abstract spirituality. There is a significant difference between broadly universal, ungrounded notions of "spirituality" and the concrete understanding of "Mystery" within the Judeo-Christian tradition. This presents an artistic challenge to the visual artist. On the one hand, the language of non-objective abstraction nicely implies the ineffability of the Divine, avoiding what is corny or too literal. But on the other hand, in the Judeo-Christian tradition, which is deeply grounded in the high value of creation and a sacramental mentality, God certainly is invisible Mystery, but yet is never generic.

Indeed, in all three panels of Couture's triptych, a kind of event is taking place, hovering within the reaches of darkness. These "events" are portrayed with a visuality that endows them with concrete detail and substance, even though what is being portrayed is highly abstract. In each of the two wings, there is a sense of a concrete thing or place, perhaps still being formed, with calligraphic characters bearing the quality of an ancient script and musical notations floating as if they were the active agents — the very atoms — giving shape and substance to the event. The center panel likewise has something at its heart, this time centered. That something is an apparitional "book," its transparent pages open with an outpouring of the familiar runic typography floating up from its gutter. And interspersed within the transparent layers of the pages are curving planes the color of pinkish flesh. Couture suggests a kind of primordial language here, a Word or *logos* that creates, orders, and informs nature out of the void. One might compare this to a literary equivalent, such as an evocative passage in Norman Maclean's short story "A River Runs Through It." In the story, the older son asks his preacher father what he is reading as they sit by a river rushing past, and the father replies,

"A book. . . . "

 Then he told me, "In the part I was reading it says the Word was in the beginning, and that's right. I used to think the water was first, but if you listen carefully you will hear that the words are underneath the water."[30]

The question of which is first (or most profound) — the ever-shifting flow of the water, or the eternal, generating order of the *logos* underneath the water — is one that is raised by Couture's work. Hers is a more abstract and poetic way of asking the question that Francisco Pacheco and Cézanne raised. Namely, what is the actual relationship between the transitory flux of light and water and sensation that our senses report about reality's gorgeous surface, and the ordered structure that the mind finds in a deeper "sense" of underlying geometry, form, and logic underneath the report of the senses? Exactly where, or how, the joint within these things lies seems always somehow to be "between" the separate elements. It is Mystery. And Couture captures that sense of mystery visually, but also linguistically in her titles, which stress the "between" of "space and echo," and "word and entry." Within her triptych format, of course, the twin realms of "the between" actually have a third realm at their junction. There, literally in what we might imagine as the *between* that exists inside all lesser "betweens" is the center panel, titled *Kenosis*. This Greek word means a pouring out, an emptying, or a humbling. In Christian theology, the *kenosis* refers to the Incarnation, in which God takes on human flesh. This is what Saint John speaks of in his gospel — the passage that Maclean's preacher father was reading by the riverbank — which says not only that "In the beginning was the WORD," and that "all things were made through him [the Word]," but also that "the Word became flesh and dwelt among us."[31] This sort of sacramental sensibility is the New Testament's understanding of the mysterious relationship between the temporal and the eternal. For Christians, God's entering the created world by way of Christ's Incarnation is the touchstone, the "joint" that fixes the "between" on which the realms of matter and spirit hinge.

In exploring the mystery of *kenosis* visually, Couture places the image of a spiritual book at the center of her work. In doing so, she brings into sight, as well as into metaphor and sign, the idea of "Book." Whether thinking of "The Book" in the broadest possible terms, as in what is written, tradition, and authority (as Jacques Derrida does in "Edmond Jabès and the Question of the Book"), or more specifically in terms of the enormous importance of the Bible in the history and culture of the West, the theme of "The Book" is enormously rich and shaping.[32] It is also a central one to the artists in the exhibition.

"Book" is literally linked to the physicality of the book, as in the Pentateuch, the Torah, the Midrash, and the Bible as Old and New Testaments. But conceptually, it is linked as well to Word, Logos, Language, and Naming as mysteriously foundational to reality. Another artist who takes on this conceptually large domain is Ellie Murphy in her *"In the beginning was the Word" . . . (Binary Triptych)* (entry 8). Like Couture, Murphy uses a triptych format, encompassing an extensive sense of open space and suspending specific linguistic characters as creative agents operating within that space. In Murphy's case, as a sculptor, she uses literal space, in which she marks off three divisions or planes with a series of horizontal rails from which she hangs multiple strands of digital characters (ones and zeroes) formed out of clay.

The result is a "world" demarcated, as it were, out of a larger "universe" of the unending space all around us. The three spatial planes of this world, zigzagging through open space, are each articulated by the strings of language dangling within them. As one of what Murphy calls her "digital sculptures," *Binary Triptych* implies a structural relationship between matter, space and time, and language. The language used here is the electronic binary system of ones and zeroes used in computer programming. But just as our own genetic coding is made up of strings of fundamental information bundled into (translated into) the larger physical phenomena we call body and experience, so these suspended strings of ones and zeroes translate into the opening verses of the Gospel of John. In binary language, the three sections spell out John 1:1: "In the beginning was the WORD" (first panel), "and the Word was with God" (second panel), "and the Word was God" (third panel).

The sense that Reality is an encoded structure inseparably bound up with, on the one hand, sensory experience and cultural meanings through symbolic language, and, on the other, with God as creator and Presence, is nicely embodied in Murphy's work.

If Couture and Murphy express this cluster of ideas and meanings by way of using extensive open space inhabited by articulate linguistic signs referencing the *logos*, then sculptor Theodore L. Prescott's steel and marble monolith, *Tabula Rasa II*, carries the subject forward in yet a different way (entry 9). Prescott compresses everything into a minimal form, in which structures and materials eloquently express a rich set of meanings in terms of themselves. Here, the meanings are immanent or inherent within the matrix of forms and materials.

Also referencing The Book, Prescott describes his piece as having "the form of a book or tablet, and a substance (marble) with a long history of being used in public address."[33] But in this case, there is no specific typographical marking. "The text is the material of the stone itself, whose normal opacity is contrasted with its potential translucency." And rather than employ a vast extension of space, the intensity of the monolithic form internalizes immensity into its vertical presence and the depth of the surface qualities of the work's two materials, steel and marble. The irregularly shaped opening in the "tablet" of the marble, acting much like the "luminous events" of object and ancient-looking calligraphy in Couture's work, forces open the otherwise self-contained perimeters of the shaft, evoking an Otherness beyond its own world.

In addition, the purity of the materials and forms carries with it a serene — even a silent — Presence that summons the viewer to meditation. And, as is called for in a state of meditation, the contemplative person must set aside distractions and be able to listen. One of the meanings of the phrase "tabula rasa" is "the mind in an empty state before receiving outside impressions." Once again, we encounter the paradoxes inherent in both art and faith. For in Prescott's piece, it is precisely the refined, delicate, and sensuous experience of form and surfaces that brings the viewer into quietude; but then it is that quietude which detaches the self from the report of the senses, emptying the mind of its preconceived ordering. It is this state of prepared openness that ultimately allows one to listen fully and to receive.

The ideas explored by Couture, Murphy, and Prescott are so imaginatively fertile that other artists in the exhibition have embodied them in surprisingly different ways. Both John Reid Perkins-Buzo and Roger Feldman, for example, employ the idea of reality as a spatially open structure generated by a logic (from *logos*, word + *ikos*, -ic) of forms or elements within which humans encounter a sense of Presence or Being. But these two artists extend the importance of *being* within those spatial and temporal structures in a radically interactive way. That is, both artists embrace the viewer's own being — literally the viewer's presence, body movements, and passage through a span of time — as inherently part of their artwork. We saw how Gregory King, in *4 or 5 Trees*, made the viewer's point of view an integral component of his work. But now, Perkins-Buzo and Feldman, working three dimensionally, go a step further, such that the viewer's actions and movement through their artworks actually help to complete the pieces.

This is most literally the case with Perkins-Buzo's interactive multimedia video projection piece *The Portal* (entry 10). This work involves a large, luminous projection field on the wall of the gallery, onto which is projected an ever-changing grid pattern. The grid pattern is generated by a small video camera placed at the base of the projection field. When viewers approach or pass by the field, the camera takes moving images of them, then feeds the images through a computer program that translates them into shifting patterns of pixels on a large grid, which are then projected as abstract image patterns onto the field of the wall. The translation of the images of the viewers can range from the fairly representational to the radically abstract and geometric. The "logic" that translates the naturalistic appearance of viewers into pixel grids on a wall is based on the population algorithms of mathematician John H. Conway's "Game of Life."

Put too simply, in the "Game of Life" a large grid constitutes a world. Each cell constitutes a place for one life. Each cell on the grid has eight neighboring cells. A cell is either switched on or off. When on, it is alive, when off, it is dead. Each pattern of *alive* and *dead* makes up the life of a generation. Patterns change constantly according a set of rules. Essentially, all eight of a given cell's surrounding neighbors are checked to see if they are on or not. Depending on the number of live cells surrounding it, a given cell will either be born, survive a while longer, or die. A given cell, for example, is switched off and dies when the count of live cells surrounding it is less than two or greater than three. If the count is exactly two or exactly three, a given cell survives, and so on. As in a society, the fate of each cell is connected with its relationship to the other lives all around it.[34] The changing of patterns within the grid world constitutes a kind of history of generations, thus simulating life over a duration of time.

In Perkins-Buzo's *The Portal*, the viewer moving in front of the camera sends new input into the system, and therefore the viewer's choices affect the life patterns that occur within the perimeters of the software's *logos*. In other words, the image that is the artwork on the gallery wall is determined partly by the viewer's choices to move, leap, or dance, and partly by how these movements are translated within the limitations of the pixel grid and the binary language of the computer program's logic. In essence, this means that the viewer exists simultaneously outside the world of the artwork (as a kind of omniscient viewer/creator) and inside the world of the artwork (as an image of the viewer/creator's will translated into the electronic pixel structures inherent in being within that world's possibilities).

The viewer, in a sense, approximates God, moving before the face of the luminous projection field, a field that, until acted upon, is without form and void. The grid-patterned images moving lyrically around the luminous field bear, as it were, the stamp of the viewer's movement. That is, although the projected images do not look like the viewer (this would be too anthropomorphic), they nonetheless are "in the image" of the viewer (albeit in the terms of a pixilated language or "word") because they were generated in response to the viewer's movements. Thus, the individual cells in the grid, analogous to individuals in a populated world, have a life. They are born, they survive, and they die in accordance with the will of the viewer's movements.

In Perkins-Buzo's *The Portal*, the viewer's presence and actions so thoroughly determine the piece, that the viewer is simultaneously creator and creature, transcendent and immanent. The mystery of God's actual involvement within the events of time-space history, as well as the mystery of what Genesis means in its creation narrative by saying (reading selectively), "In the beginning God created the heavens and the earth. The earth was without form and void . . . and the Spirit of God was moving over the face of the waters. . . . So God created man in his own image, in the image of God he created him; male and female. . . . "[35]— the mystery of all of this is richly evoked by *The Portal*.

For Perkins-Buzo, this high-tech correspondence — between the viewer outside the created world and the ever-changing patterns of life inside the created world — bears a powerful analogy with the Scripture's narrative (one recalls late-nineteenth-century Symbolist theories of Correspondence suggesting Divine Presence in the world). He writes

The Portal, *an interactive multimedia installation, concerns the emergence of life from the* tohu bohu *[empty void] of non-existence under God's constant creative impulse. . . . As people walk, dance, hug, or play in front of the screen, it bursts with colors and patterns, some of which they recognize as drawn from themselves, and others that are entirely abstract. In response to the installation, many people feel the urge to move and dance, delighting in its playfulness. To me, this is their way of celebrating God's continued creative presence in their lives. It is a presence often elusive, sometimes difficult to recognize, yet always responsive as we come to deepen our relationships with God.*[36]

Although a very different kind of piece, Roger Feldman's *Current* also requires the kinetic presence of a viewer to complete its meaning (entry 11). Adopting a large triptych format (nearly 4 x 12 feet), *Current* presents the viewer with three large panels. With its wood-grained surface, the center panel suggests a continual flowing, which is echoed in the lushly colored patterns painted on the flanking mortar panels to each side. Placed slightly off-center on the wood-grained panel is a drawing of an architectural structure consisting of several curved planes standing upright, which cast shadows onto the otherwise flat expanse of wood grain, while color flows like run-on patterns to the outer edges of the work. The architectural structure seems to occupy perspectival space, given the shadows that it casts. It feels as if one could walk through it. But the ground on which the structure stands tilts up flat, running expansively to the work's twelve-foot width, as if the structure were only a constantly shifting pattern without three-dimensional depth or solidity. The spatial ambiguity is increased by an ambiguity of scale, as the architectural structure could be miniature, or it could be as large as Stonehenge on the English plains.

To fully appreciate *Current*, it is helpful to know something about Feldman's art in general. Typically, his sculptures are three-dimensional architectural constructions built on a large scale. The small structure in *Current*, for example, if built, would enable a viewer to walk through its labyrinth-like space as a kinetic-spatial experience. That idea is central to Feldman's aesthetic. As he says in his artist statement, "Since 1976, my three-dimensional installations have explored the fundamental relationship between visual and kinesthetic perception. I create works to be walked on, moved through. . . . Auditory aspects emerged, and I have included them in the work from the beginning. All of these perceptual processes have been orchestrated to lead to experiential metaphor."[37]

What Feldman calls "experiential metaphor" involves the artist's acceptance of the viewer's experience of passing though his forms, spaces, and colors as being an intrinsic part of the work. Or more radically, it involves accepting that experience as somehow being the completion of the work. This grants freedom to the viewer, as each individual makes what he or she will of what the artist as creator has structured. Thus, the kinetic element is part of Feldman's medium, though not fully under his control. It is what causes "psychological responses . . . [that] help to reinforce the symbolic value of the sequence of movements."

The idea is that human spatial experience and action belong to our sense of presence and sacred space. Although our understanding of the Divine as eternal may conjure up a naive notion of God as "fixed," our human consciousness of the Divine can only be a glimpse received while in motion, for we are temporal. Both our existence and our perception of Reality beyond ourselves inherently involve, as it were, a view from the window of a moving car, in a passage through Reality's "currents." Any notion of faith grounded in the Judeo-Christian tradition must value matter and the spatial-temporal dimensions of the created world as belonging to the spiritual. Thus, Feldman's spatial-kinetic meditations correct the Gnostic temptation to think of the sacred or the spiritual as primarily intellectual. In a way comparable to Gaston Bachelard's study of how we experience intimate space, Feldman joins our experience of space, with its ambiguities of interior/exterior, rooted/flowing, intimate/infinite, in order to evoke a sense of wonder about our being here.[38] He achieves this by allowing the viewer's participatory actions to be the element that completes his architectural installations.

Another artist who uses open space, a sense of suspension, and movement in relation to the viewer's body to evoke mysterious presence is Laurie Wohl (entry 12). Wohl's medium is textiles and weaving. There is an enrichment in this, for the deep meanings inherent in cloth—in garments, coverings, veils, tapestries, and vestments—certainly belong to the sacred and to mystery. In *Veil of Light: The Protecting Veil*, Wohl suspends a circular framework from which long bands of cloth hang down. This articulates a cylindrical space, making reference to a sacred architecture of domes, chapels, and stained glass windows. But in Wohl's case, the characteristics of cloth evoke something more ethereal than stone, referencing "wings, trees, prayer shawls, veils, ladders, falling waters."[39]

The space created by the bands of cloth is only loosely contained because the bands themselves are not woven together. They are, rather, what Wohl calls "unwoven spaces." The range of colors suggests showers of light as much as anything with solidity. And worked into the fabric descents are beads, alluding to both meditation and the liturgical practice of prayer within sacred spaces, including "rosaries, worry beads, and the beaded doorway curtains of Mediterranean countries."

Wohl's evocation of a veil of light plays well in relationship to David Blow's digital work *Lightness of Being* (entry 13). Though working in a different medium and with different imagery, Blow here shares with Wohl a sense of suspension within a light-saturated open space. He gets at this with a pattern of rhythmically circling birds, their outspread wings allowing them to float within the image's white field. Blow has said that he is "interested in the spiritual emotions of peace, solitude, comfort, and joy, as well as color, rhythm, shape, and pattern."[40]

To get at this, Blow has selected five different images of large birds in flight. Two sail with wide, outstretched wings in a position that makes them flatten out against the flat plane of the white ground. Two others fly at angles to that plane, giving a sense of three-dimensional depth to the sky. And the fifth flies at a slightly less acute angle, establishing a gradation between pure flatness and depth. Blow then uses a computer program to repeat the five images many times, spacing them in an all-over, run-on pattern. In addition, some of the birds fly from left to right, some from right to left, while others tip towards a diagonal path of motion.

The result is an overall pattern that feels simultaneously static (opposite directional motions tending to hold each other in check) and yet almost frenetic (multiplicity of directions and angles suggesting randomness). Tension is furthered by Blow's careful spacing of the birds. Being more or less equidistant from one another, a pattern that fills the space is created, resolving — like an ancient Roman mosaic — the eye's *horror vacuii*. And yet, given that the birds are in motion, and are all on practically the same plane, the possibility of collision is inevitably implied. In the end, what is achieved is a sense of rhythmic patterning that navigates between feeling "natural" and feeling "artificial." As Blow puts it, he finds here "the magic of a time found in nature" reconciled with "the technological changes that are taking place in our culture," this "while maintaining my love for the beauty of our natural environment." Blow argues that through the use of the computer, he can "bring the viewer into my vision of universal harmony between nature, man, and technology. Aesthetically, I am seeking to show the harmony between the natural environment and the electronic one."

One can appreciate Blow's goal of wanting aesthetics to help him find a way of reconciling nature with man's technological dominion over it. This is, in fact, one of the most pressing problems of modern times. Yet, in spite of Blow's optimism, it seems to this writer that as an image, *Lightness of Being* is more haunting than harmonious. For what at first feels like a liberating suspension in free flight becomes, after longer viewing, a fixed repetitive pattern that runs on forever, admitting no escape by individual deviation. To say this is not to fault the artist. It is, rather, to acknowledge the deeper honesty of materials, images, and creative process that every artist knows. For the terrible dilemma of reconciliation that Blow takes on here is far larger and stronger than is art's capacity of resolution.

Running through the works of Couture, Murphy, Prescott, Perkins-Buzo, Feldman, Wohl, and Blow, there is a broad theme of divine presence, as well as an engagement between concrete and spiritual realities by way of *logos,* language, form and pattern, and motion within space and time. In this context, there is another artist in *The Next Generation* whose work ought to be considered as a kind of conclusion to this broad theme. That artist is Bruce West. In a certain way, his work can also stand as a counterpoint to the approach of the others. His two photographs in the exhibition, *Reverend Dennis's Golden Chair, MS*, and *Entrance to Margaret's Grocery, MS*, represent a larger body of work documenting the art, architecture, and preaching of the Reverend H.D. Dennis, who lives in the Mississippi Delta (entry 14).

As West tells us in his artist statement, Rev. Dennis is "a self-proclaimed preacher, architect, and artist, who has been converting his wife's grocery store into his own very unique church for the past twenty years."[41]

At first glance, West's relationship to the seven artists just examined may seem unclear or even specious. But the connection is actually very straightforward, although as we will eventually see, it is not a simple one. The connection is most evident in *Entrance to Margaret's Grocery, MS.* This photograph literally depicts a portal inviting the viewer into a sacred space. Though a converted store may not have the same kind of mystery as, for example, the spaces in Couture's *Reflections on a Poet God*, it is sacred nonetheless. Rev. Dennis's conversion of a secular space into a sacred one is, as West observes, "an inspired labor of love involving the construction of several towers (some over two stories tall), the creation of an Ark of

FIGURE 3

Howard Finster
***THE LORD WILL DELIVER HIS PEOPLE ACROSS JORDAN, AND THE MOON BECAME AS BLOOD, THER SHALL BE EARTH qUAKES,* 1976**
Enamel on fiberboard

the Covenant containing tablets inscribed with the Ten Commandments, the invention of new religious iconography, and very elaborate painting and decoration." In the photograph, the entrance into the holy space is charged with brightly colored patterns and religious language. The viewer actually enters by passing over the name of GOD, followed (under Rev. Dennis's own feet) by the greeting, "ALL IS WELCOME / THE HOUSE OF / PRAYER / PASTOR / REV. HD. DENNIS."

Although achieved within a thoroughly folk idiom, Rev. Dennis's sacred space is no less an interweaving of word, space, faith, and the viewer's bodily participation than is the work of Couture, Murphy, Perkins-Buzo, or Feldman. And it is the use of the folk idiom that raises interesting questions within the context of this theme. Artists like Theresa Couture explore such ideas within a generally elegant and sophisticated aesthetic, one associated with the mainstream contemporary art world and the training they received in MFA graduate programs. West introduces a different aesthetic into the mix. This aesthetic is not, however, West's aesthetic. It is the aesthetic of the Reverend H.D. Dennis, made visible to us through the auspices of Bruce West's own aesthetic.

Dennis's aesthetic comes out of the tradition of folk, self-taught, and visionary art. Over the last four decades, this folk tradition began to be discovered—and increasingly appreciated—by the mainstream of contemporary art lovers. Within this tradition there are many remarkable artists who directly engage religious themes and spiritual experience. Examples of the most widely known would include the Reverend Howard Finster (fig. 3) and Sister Gertrude Morgan (fig. 4). Clearly, the art of Rev. Dennis belongs to this genre; as the noted architect and MacArthur Fellow Samuel Mockbee has written of Margaret's Grocery, "Its crude materials and methods of construction place it in an ethereal state of being and perpetual state of beauty."[42] Although we now realize that this aesthetic actually has its own long and sophisticated history, one that has been passed down the generations through its own cultural means of training, there is still a powerful sense of the "difference" or "otherness" of this tradition to eyes accustomed to viewing mainstream contemporary and traditional Western art.[43]

FIGURE 4
Sister Gertrude Morgan
Jesus is my air Plane,
ca. 1970
**Tempera, ballpoint
pen and ink, and pencil
on paper**

What appeals in this kind of work is the sense of immediacy, directness, and even child-like freshness. Mockbee's linking of "crude materials and methods of construction" to the aesthetic and spiritual qualities of an "ethereal state of being" and a "perpetual state of beauty" raises important questions concerning the very subject of the exhibition. For though we may love to think of the creator God as Poet, that does not mean that the Poet's dialect would be one of elegance. What if, as Flannery O'Connor suggested, God's real presence, grace, and epiphany were more often found in the shock of the crude and the grotesque? Indeed, from a spiritual or divine perspective, is there not something suspicious about a cultural hierarchy that places folk art as "low" and MFA art as "high"?

Even more problematic is the fact that what appeals to the sophisticated viewer about so-called self-taught folk art is exactly the crudeness of its visionary character. Implicit here is a sense that for the highly educated, often jaded self-consciousness of the modern/postmodern viewer of art, innocence has been lost. The child-like capacity to believe is difficult to attain within the rational, critical atmosphere of modernity. And it is easy to feel that a kind of direct, open, innocent eye has better access to faith than does our own. A deep yearning for authenticity, even as our historicist, self-conscious, deconstructed, and ironic "selves"

stay alert to the possibility of being tricked, remains a powerful force. West himself openly admits to this deep longing when he says, "I have come to realize that one of my primary motivations for pursuing my photographic work in Mississippi . . . grows out of a personal desire to reconnect with a greater sense of spirituality and religiosity in my own life. My photographs affirm the possibility of a more spiritual and enlightened sensibility."

What arrests our attention and spirit is the aesthetic immediacy of Rev. Dennis's visionary art. It is made out of an unabashed surrender to faith, religious experience, and a sense of calling very different from the motives prevalent in the contemporary gallery and the art-collecting scene (this, despite the irony that today, "outsider" art is both highly collectible and very expensive). The sheer visual inventiveness of such work feels aesthetically fearless, innocent, and liberated. These qualities inspire

Mockbee's claim that ethereal states of being and perpetual beauty can emerge out of crudeness. Surely, part of the reason for this is that we immediately feel that these are not works that we could have invented ourselves. They feel truly "other," as opposed to "self" invented. And it is this promise of an encounter with something truly "other" on which the hope of genuine faith rests. Again, as one of the authors of the New Testament wrote, "Faith is the assurance of things hoped for, the conviction of things not seen."

At this point in the discussion we have fallen into an aesthetic, cultural, and spiritual danger. For one thing, the capacity of the so-called crudeness of visionary art to embody a more authentic spiritual reality may well be due to the fact that it is "crude" only to those of us not raised and educated within the social context of, say, the Mississippi Delta. Do we romanticize the "other"? But more importantly, we must remind ourselves that with West's two photographs, we are not in fact looking at visionary, self-taught art. We are looking at highly sophisticated photographs *about* visionary art made by a culturally sophisticated artist with MFA training. The context of our discussion here illuminates the subtle complexity latent in West's photographs.

The point is not made to pull the viewer back from any freshness of religious experience that he or she has felt before West's works. Rather, it is made because by becoming aware of the complex phenomena going on when we view them, we gain a more profound understanding of the deep issues operating in this exhibition of art about faith within the context of twenty-first-century art. If we think of West's photographs as documents, then they serve as apparently transparent windows into a folk culture. But if we think about them as "works of art," then they are about much more than that.

Implicit in this idea of "photograph as window" (as document) is a cultural, or even a class, difference between two social worlds. The art viewer in New York City looking across the threshold of Rev. Dennis's grocery store does so by visually passing through a prior threshold of the convention of "art photography." Perhaps the viewer even longs for some kind of religious immediacy, a spiritual directness and simplicity that one easily imagines is present in Rev. Dennis's world. What enables the two worlds of the art lover and Rev. Dennis to meet is the artistry of Bruce West. A complex cultural observer, West is a trained artist with an MFA. Through his thematic choices and his skillful use of lens, camera angle, and framing, he takes us into a sacred space and a religious-cultural context that is different from our own.

Not unlike the experience of reading a short story by Flannery O'Connor, we are offered an epiphany of authentic religious feeling through Rev. Dennis. Yet we remain cultural interlopers, for we do not shed our own critical sophistication or distance. And we know that were we transported into the more fundamentalist religious context of the Mississippi Delta, the freshness of emotion we have experienced would run into many conflicts with differing beliefs.

In other words, West's photographs of Rev. Dennis's world lead us toward a double threshold: one is a grocery store *portal* inviting us to enter through faith into a different culture's understanding of divine presence; the other is an art work's *window* — the photograph's physical plane derived through choice of lens and camera angle — that leaves us standing outside as an observer, possibly even as a spiritual voyeur. The *portal*, so easily entered, is the photograph's subject matter. It is what we look *at* within the photograph. The *window*, which cannot be entered, is the photograph's formal convention. It is what we look *through*, enabling us to be moved spiritually by something that, if encountered in reality, might prove to be intellectually problematic. But when we think of the *portal* and the *window* as fused into a single sign, combined as the photograph's whole structure, we encounter West's real content, which is the conundrum of the twenty-first-century viewer's position as both spiritual seeker and detached observer. This is the artist's or viewer's equivalent of Kierkegaard's dilemma over the "leap of faith," or Wittgenstein's searching note to himself in *Culture and Values*: "Go on, believe! It does no harm."[44]

All of this fittingly signifies the situation of twenty-first-century viewers and artists regarding faith and divine presence. One of the questions raised by the exhibition is whether or not art's exploration and celebration of faith can help to make an authentic sense of faith possible. Our culture lacks images and symbols that feel fresh, and yet which are grounded in something larger, such as self-invention or politicized religious ideology. Historically, it is artists who have helped to forge such iconic imagery. As George Steiner has argued, it is often within the direct experience of works of art that we experience something authentic. As Steiner puts it, "There may be in literature, music and the arts lineaments, spoors of a presentness prior to consciousness and to rationality as we know them. . . . We must read *as if*."[45]

The Book

As already noted, the artists considered thus far share a common interest in ideas concerning divine presence, space, intimate objects, and the concrete connections that Flannery O'Connor characterized as insights into the mystery of our position here on earth. But these are not the only broad themes around which artists in *The Next Generation* have clustered. Another central theme that emerges is that of "The Book."

We have already discussed the idea of the Book in its broadest terms as what is written and authoritative, as well as specifically the Bible and the enormous role that it has played in the culture of the West.[46] The theme of the Book inevitably arises in the context of any group of artists asking questions about art and faith. In the themes examined earlier, the role of the artist was about evoking, or visually embodying, a sense of mystery and presence. But in the themes surrounding the issue of the Book, the role of the artist has more to do with a kind of asserting of its claims. In this vein, the role of the artist may become more of an aesthetic analogue to that of the prophet or priest, with the artist seeking to expose society's evils, or to embody the possibilities of healing and grace.

For in the broadest sense — beyond the most central themes of God's existence and the world as a creation related to God — the Bible's essential themes address moral issues. The confrontation of hypocrisy and evil, caring for the poor, the urgency of justice and mercy, the reality of love, forgiveness, redemption, and grace — these themes articulate the meaning of God's existence and the world's relationship to God. Within the biblical text itself, these themes are often best embodied in the twin roles of prophet and priest, signifying as they do the need for moral confrontation and spiritual healing. Several artists in the exhibition can be thought about in terms of a rhythm moving between prophetic and priestly aesthetic postures.

Perhaps the best example to begin with is Michael R. Buesking, because his work implicitly contains the motor force that drives such interests. As we will see, the specific subject matter of Buesking's *Ezekiel Scattering Hair* is one of a series of symbolic acts performed by the biblical prophet Ezekiel (entry 15). But before engaging with that painting, a discussion of the larger theme undergirding its content will be timely.

The inciting incident for Ezekiel's series of symbolic prophetic actions is his encounter with God. Angry at the unfaithfulness of Israel, "a nation of rebels, who have . . . transgressed against me . . . impudent and stubborn," God summons Ezekiel to perform a series of symbolic public acts in order to confront the nation. What is intriguing about the summons, within the context of the exhibition and issues of contemporary art, is the manner of God's initiating Ezekiel for the prophetic task. God addresses Ezekiel saying, "But you, son of man, hear what I say to you . . . open your mouth, and eat what I give you." From a literary standpoint, the text wonderfully appeals to all the senses, as God tells the prophet first to hear, then to eat, and finally to act. What God has to "say" to Ezekiel comes not in the form of words dictated to him, but as a vision in which he sees a scroll bearing "words of lamentation and mourning and woe." In his vision, Ezekiel is told to "eat this scroll, and go, speak to the house of Israel." In response, Ezekiel writes, "Then I ate it; and it was in my mouth as sweet as honey."[47]

The idea of "eating" divine revelation, of Word as food, appears several times in various images within the Bible's text, most notably in Saint John's vision, which he recorded as the book of Revelation. John also has a vision of a scroll that he is told to eat. In his case, the scroll is "bitter" to his stomach, but "sweet as honey" to his mouth.[48] The notion of words written in language and then internalized, becoming a text so powerful that it transforms one's interior being, conveys the biblical attitude toward language. This is not simply the *reading* of language; it is, rather, the *receiving* of language. This goes beyond theories of language in which language is *about* meaning or is a construction of meaning. It posits an understanding that language is *of* meaning. To doubt that language has the capacity to house — or even be — meaning is a view of language as surface. Ezekiel's text offers a more primal, mythic grasp of the mystery by which language becomes deeply psychological, symbolic, and embodied.

What fascinates here, from the standpoint of thinking about art and faith, is that Ezekiel is ultimately instructed by God to go and perform a series of symbolic public acts as a way of conveying God's intentions to Israel. It must be stressed that Ezekiel is not given a sermon, a set of words, or an abstract theological proposition; rather, he is given a set of symbolic acts, which he is to deliver through the vehicle of his body. These are to be accompanied by an interpretation spoken in words after the performances, the point being that there is a deep mind/body unity within the meaning of "The Word," or the Bible. Here, language is understood as something belonging to the whole being, as something heard, eaten, digested, and enacted. "The Word" is portrayed as something physical, not just conceptual. This is the sensibility of the biblical text. It is a sacramental understanding of reality in which knowledge and matter, mind and body are contiguous with an earthy holiness.

Artists have always understood this kind of embodied meaning because they do not separate idea from matter. In the contemporary period, the emergence of Performance art and the use of the artist's own body as a site of expression are latter-day (though often secularized and romantically narcissistic) rememberings of the Bible's prophetic acts. Numerous artists in the exhibition get at the notion of revelation as embodied text. Several, as we will see, follow Buesking's lead, offering works related to prophetic symbol, parable, story, or image. Others literally use the Book as image or source in order to evoke a *logos* — a language as meaning structure — underlying reality.

Buesking's painting is about the scattering of hairs, which is the third symbolic act that Ezekiel performs.[49] The prophet is told to take a sharp sword, pass it as a barber's razor over his head and beard, gather the cut hairs together, and then divide them into thirds. One third he is to burn in a fire in the midst of the city, another third he is to take and strike with the sword round about the city, and the final third he is to scatter to the winds. Each act signifies a dimension of the violent judgment that will befall Israel.

Buesking gives us a painting of an aging man with a naked torso, his left arm upraised as he scatters the last third of the hairs into the wind. Stylistically, the work seems to pay tribute to the great mystical realism of the Baroque era, as exemplified, for example, by Jusepe de Ribera's *Saint Onuphrius* of 1637 (fig. 5). Although he is interested in the historical aspect of the prophet narratives, Buesking eliminates any visual context that would merely historicize the story, thus letting the contemporary viewer witness a public ritual that could be happening at any time or place. Though the viewer need not know it to value the painting, Buesking used himself as his model, thereby identifying the artist as belonging to the tradition of prophetic acts. This also places Buesking within the contemporary tradition in which the artist as shaman, or the artist as cultural critic, uses his or her own body and stylized gestures to make statements about society and the human condition.

It is interesting, however, that Buesking offers a genuine variant within this tradition. As he points out in his artist's statement, he consciously reverses the usual emphasis on the "artist as prophet," so central in avant-garde art, in order to explore what he refers to as the "prophet as artist." Indeed, regarding the question of art and faith, if one were to read the Bible in search of an explicitly Jewish or Christian aesthetic, one would not be found. The Bible says very little about art, as it was written — in Hans Belting's phrase — "before the era of art."[50] But if one reads the text with an eye toward behavior, symbol, and ritual, one finds there an extremely rich "aesthetic" that is part of the fabric of reality and revelation.

It is an evocative idea that the symbolic acts crafted by the ancient Jewish prophets can be seen today as still relevant to contemporary art. It is also a problematic one. Hans Belting has discussed the real complexities of the role of images before the era of art, and how the rise of thinking in terms of "art" as beauty and self-conscious image has changed our perceptions of how images embody meaning. And Herbert N. Schneidau has written about the Old Testament rhythm of "sacred discontent," in which God initially blesses Israel with security and material success, Israel then grows complacent and presumptuous, and finally God judges Israel, all by way of radical prophetic confrontations. Schneidau points out that although such rhythms were specific to ancient Israel's understanding, they are relevant to other religious cultures. And he argues that the same rhythm of blessing, presumption of entitlement, and prophetic critique continues to operate today within the secularized tradition of avant-garde opposition to bourgeois society.[51]

Many viewers are shocked by some of the odd or extreme acts of performance artists. From feminist Carolee Schneemann publicly extracting a scroll poem from her vagina while standing naked on a platform, to Chris Burden lying across a Volkswagen as if crucified while nails were driven through his palms, to Adrian Piper confronting racism by handing out cards at dinner parties challenging people when their conversations turn unconsciously racist, contemporary art is rife with confrontational, transgressive actions.[52] But are these really any less difficult or shocking than the symbolic behavior of the ancient Jewish prophets? One can only imagine how scandalous their acts were when they were performed as metaphors for the spiritual condition of the religious publics of antiquity. Isaiah walking naked and barefoot through Israel for one year; Hosea's public marriage to the prostitute Gomer, followed by her repeated humiliations of him; or Ezekiel burning, slashing, and scattering his own hair in public — these were all transgressive actions offensive to the prophets' societies.[53] In some ways, Jesus continued this "offensive" tradition when he twice drove the money changers from the Temple, and when he healed the sick on the Sabbath, in violation of the religious law.

This is not, of course, to automatically equate any and all modern performance or body artwork with the actions of the ancient Jewish prophets. As in the days of the prophets, all prophecy must be tested within the grounding of its spiritual and moral values. Both then and now, some so-called prophets (and today, some artists) are no more than self-appointed promoters of their own agendas, including romantic self-interest, while others are authentically connected to something larger. But it is crucial to recognize how visceral, even repugnant the "true" prophets' actions were to the daily decorum of religious people, who tend to be self-righteously sure of both their society and its national standing.

The danger for religious people has always been the temptation to domesticate the Bible. But it must be borne in mind that, as Giles Gunn, a scholar of religion and American culture, once put it, "the Bible has [not only] furnished many of the most stable forms of consciousness in the West," it has "at the same time served as a chief source of dissatisfaction with them."[54] Thus, while the Bible seems to underwrite material and emotional comfort as evidence of divine blessing, it is equally true that the same text condemns self-righteous assumptions about entitlement to blessing based on a society's past status or present nationality. At their most profound, transgressive symbolic acts by the prophets (and later by artists) belong to what Herbert N. Schneidau, building upon E.H. Gombrich's term, has established as the tradition of "sacred discontent."

In passing, another dimension of the biblical text's complex structure should be noted. In a poetic sense, the symbolic acts of the prophets and what they express carry great aesthetic beauty, even when the overt content is dark. The enigmatic acts of Ezekiel as signs to repent and receive God's love; the extending of grace to the prostitute Gomer through marriage to a prophet as a sign that God still desires the wayward; and Isaiah walking naked around Israel as a sign that there is still hope if Israel would only repent — all of these acts involve a strange mixture of what is beautiful with what is repellent. And in that mixture is the mystery of art's aesthetic power, wherein the joining of contradictions, the juxtaposing of what attracts with what repulses, stimulates epiphany. It is exactly this juxtaposition, this contradiction within the image, that makes it effective.

This idea sheds light then on Ruth Dunkell's strangely contradictory work *Whose Glorious Beauty is a Fading Flower* (entry 16). In this pen-and-ink drawing, the black silhouette of a lithe, nude woman dances with outstretched arms. Her hands either grasp or morph into long, sinuous stems that culminate in ecstatic, Matissian flowers. The woman's hair bears the same ecstatic shapes and tonality as the flowers. It seems to be an entirely celebratory image. Yet the graphics across the top strike a contradictory tone, as they quote a phrase taken from the prophet Isaiah: "whose glorious beauty is a fading flower." Although at first glance the words might seem to suggest joyous celebration, their actual meaning brings them closer to a lament. For as the woman dances in her beauty, the flowers bloom into wild exaggeration, passing towards death. Visually, it is hard to justify the darker reading of such a svelte, almost art nouveau image. But not only is the phrase latent with impending decay, its original context is downright ominous. For Isaiah, chapter 28, opens with a terrifying oracle of woe directed at the thoroughly corrupt and self-justifying tribes of Judah and Ephraim. It begins this way:

Woe to the crown of pride, to the drunkards of E'phra-im, whose glorious beauty is *a fading flower, which* are *on the head of the fat valleys of them that are overcome with wine!*
Behold, the Lord hath a mighty and strong one, which *as a tempest of hail* and *a destroying storm, as a flood of mighty waters overflowing, shall cast down to the earth with the hand.*
The crown of pride, the drunkards of E'phra-im, shall be trodden under feet: and the glorious beauty . . . shall be a fading flower.[55]

Another artwork in the exhibition, Paul Hebblethwaite's *Forest Communion on Foxridge* (entry 17), was created more directly within the role of the performance artist. The piece was a performance event, documented through five photographs displayed with the phrase, "The Earth Parched in the Thirst of His Wounds Ripped Open." Hebblethwaite's artist statement takes the form of a letter addressed to the master of artist-as-shaman Performance art, Joseph Beuys.[56] The letter is a description of the event, in which Hebblethwaite treated a fallen tree and the barrenness of winter as a metaphor, journeying out into the snow and pouring wine onto three sections of a tree trunk. He has preserved the performance piece with documentation, including a trinity of photographs of the wine-spattered, fallen tree. This Tree as Christ (who was crucified on a tree), with the wine as the blood poured out, serves as a surrogate Mass, with Hebblethwaite the artist as surrogate priest.

Beuys was one of the most important twentieth-century artists to raise questions about the spiritual role of art. His conviction was that in a modern secularized culture, art and artists could still play an authentic role in making humans aware of suffering and the need for healing. In *I Like America and America Likes Me (Coyote)*, for example, he created a situation in which the elements of the piece metaphorically represented the spiritual condition of America (fig. 6). Beuys identified the violent encounter of European culture with that of America's indigenous peoples as one of the traumatic and as

FIGURE 6
Joseph Beuys
I Like America and America
Likes Me (Coyote), 1974
Action at the René Block
Gallery, New York City

yet unhealed points in the history of North America. He believed that the energies and traumas involved had deeply affected the fabric of history, and that indeed they continued to influence contemporary life. In order to reestablish a connection with what had been ruptured, Beuys spent one week in New York City, in 1974, occupying an empty space in the René Block Gallery with a coyote. For American Indians, the coyote represented a range of deities and mythical powers, and the animal's presence brought all of that into the encounter. Beuys, or Man, brought things from his Western world: blankets of felt, a walking stick, gloves, a flashlight, and copies of *The Wall Street Journal.* The week together constituted a "dialogue," during which the coyote pissed on each item that Beuys presented to him, marking it and thereby claiming it as part of his territory. In turn, Beuys performed certain ritualistic acts, such as wrapping himself in the felt and tapping three times on the floor with the walking stick. The idea was to reestablish on some primal level a connection between nature, spiritual animism, and modern culture.[57]

While paying homage to Beuys, Hebblethwaite's *Forest Communion on Foxridge* takes its grounding from the Christian tradition of the Eucharist and its liturgy. The artist symbolically enacts a healing ritual in nature, the winter season, the fallen tree, the pouring out of the wine, and the intermediary of artist-as-priest representing a healing connection between divine and natural elements. The Eucharistic quality of the ritual places the action within the context of the Christian Incarnation, which is the great event that bridged the gap between spirit and matter, eternal and temporal. In a sacramental performance mentality, the symbolic act maintains a sense of that connectedness.

The idea of making a symbolic artwork, one bearing a ritualistic meaning coincident with the form of the artwork as a sign of that meaning, is also investigated by Makoto Fujimura. His installation *Eirenepoios* addresses universal conflict with a spirit of peacemaking (entry 18). For Fujimura, two separate paintings on paper symbolize male and female counterpoints. The male and female principles permeate all of nature's being, as well as signifying humanity's own bearing of the *Imago Dei.* As such, they are symbiotic, collaborating in the wholeness of creation; but they are also opposites, symbolizing the conflict with "otherness" that inhabits all things and actions.

Between these dualities stands *Precious Nard*, a boat that holds in its hull a long, narrow painting. In both Eastern and Western art, the boat can serve as a metaphor for life's journey from birth to death, as well as embodying life's precariousness, as a small boat playing against the vast scale of the ocean. A journey has many layers of meaning. Here, the initial layer of the journey is that of the peacemaker. As the artist has said, "A peacemaker must be willing to travel to both shores of hostility and to act as a bridge between the two."[58]

The painting within the boat formally implies the reconciliation offered between oppositions. Not only does its long, narrow form and imagery suggest a linking, but two different kinds of paper, which respond differently to the wetness of the paint, are joined into one image. Furthermore, the title

Precious Nard suggests both the costliness of making peace and images of anointing. Fujimura notes that the ancient painting technique he employs (called *Nihonga*) uses pure and reflective raw minerals which are themselves very costly. This seems to be an echo of the New Testament story in which Mary, the sister of Martha and Lazarus, pours an entire pound of pure nard onto Jesus to anoint him.[59] Nard was an expensive, fragrant ointment in the ancient world. The full context of Mary's sacrificial act is illuminating, and seems relevant to Fujimura's conviction about the high cost and sacrificial nature of peacemaking.

For in John's Gospel, the author makes the setting clear:

Six days before the Passover, Jesus came to Bethany, where Lazarus was, whom Jesus had raised from the dead. There they made him a supper; Martha served, and Lazarus was one of those at table with him. Mary took a pound of costly ointment of pure nard and anointed the feet of Jesus and wiped his feet with her hair; and the house was filled with the fragrance of the ointment.[60]

John's interweaving of elements is extraordinary here. Mary's action is interpreted by Jesus as an anointment of his body beforehand for his burial (John 12:7; Mark 14:8). John's account stresses that the anointing occurred in the presence of Lazarus, whom Jesus had raised from the dead only days before. John also makes clear that it happened six days before Passover, when Jesus would begin the *Via Dolorosa* toward his own sacrificial death. Thus, the anointing with the precious nard symbolically marks and honors with costly sacrifice Jesus's own travels between the shores of life and death. That is, it marks Jesus's ultimate peacemaking, between humans who die and God the Father who redeems them by pouring out his precious son.

For the viewer, these are some of the meanings to be found in Fujimura's *Eirenepoios*. But for the artist himself, another layer is apparently important, though it is not available to the viewer as a meaning at firsthand. That layer involves the significance of the artistic process. Fujimura notes in his artist statement that he made a video recording of the working process during the painting of *Eirene I*, the malachite green and azurite blue portion of the installation. His purpose was to document the creative process, especially the sheer beauty of how a painting changes as it dries. While drying, colors darken and change, and for Fujimura, it is that process of changing that conveys "the sense of fleeting transcendence I observe in such moments." Although an esoteric point, it is one worth noting, for in the very embodiment of the working process resides a parallel with the gospel narratives. Namely, the specific events recorded there happened within time and space, but are now long past. In Emmanuel Levinas's terms, the moment of epiphany is the "saying," but almost instantly the "saying" recedes into the "said" of the past. Only the recorded text of the Gospels (and only the finished painting of the artist) remains to evoke the original event.

Within the context of a group exhibition, unintended resonances can sometimes occur between works that are otherwise not connected. There is just such a resonance between Fujimura's *Eirenepoios* and Dee VanDyke's *Anointed* (entry 19). Her painting also bridges two kinds of space, running as it does down the wall and onto the floor. Additionally, the sense of the painting as a process of unscrolling, and then descending, nicely connects sky to earth, and spirit to matter. *Anointed* has a luminosity that reinforces this sense of heaven and earth, or of an unfolding of spirit into the material. All of this is secured by the title concept of an anointing.

In VanDyke's case, the imagery itself is relatively abstract. And her intent, as expressed in her artist statement, likewise emphasizes a sense of mystery in how meaning is felt through the act of faith required to make a painting. At the same time, the sense of mystery and process is not ungrounded. Rather, it finds a connection in the senses' experience of meditation in and before nature. As VanDyke says, living on a bay near the Gulf of Mexico, "There is a constant play between stillness and motion, light and shadow, silence and sound, surface and depth. Every morning I sit outside and listen. It is often a time of holy dictation. *Anointed* evolved from those mornings."[61]

VanDyke, Fujimura, and Hebblethwaite all lean strongly toward the priestly pole within the alternating rhythm running between the roles of prophet and priest. Several other artists, however, stress a more prophetic or critical stance toward their societies. Like Buesking, they have taken a narrative with prophetic, that is to say socially critical, qualities from the biblical texts as a way of confronting the twenty-first-century viewer with moral and spiritual issues. For example, to make a commentary on contemporary culture, Helen Zajkowski and G. Carol Bomer both draw from the Genesis story of the Tower of Babel, by way of appropriating Pieter Bruegel's fantastical image of the tower from his painting *The Tower of Babel* (1563, variant 1567–68; fig. 7).

In her own *Tower of Babel*, Zajkowski uses a wonderfully ironic mix of elements, combining a child's pop-up book format, a biblical story, and current ecological problems into a strangely playful yet cataclysmic collage (entry 20). A sense of the Bible's prophetic energy is felt through the opening of the work, as a pop-up version of Bruegel's tower surges upward into the three-dimensional space of the viewer. As the tower rises upward out of the book's gutter, the pages of the book seem to flow downward into a vortex of darkness. The tower stands like an island, while all around its base a brooding storm of inky black acrylic washes over the pages like an apocalyptic flood. Or, more accurately, like a terrible oil spill violating the world. Within the sea of black is a swarming of objects suggestive of the litter and waste produced by our massively consuming culture. Zajkowski points out that her goal is to echo the biblical cycles of creation and destruction ironically, by juxtaposing biblical stories against the arrogant disregard of creation's ecology that is so evident in our wantonly throwaway society. At the core of her work is "the Judeo-Christian philosophy calling for universal stewardship of our natural resources."[62]

In *Global City Babel (Foundation)*, Bomer also uses a tower appropriated from Bruegel to suggest layers of cultural commentary (entry 21). Long before postmodernist thinkers supposedly discovered and deconstructed the idea that language is power, the Genesis story of the Tower of Babel hauntingly laid out the issues of language, human pride, and imperial ambition (and God's opposition to such national-

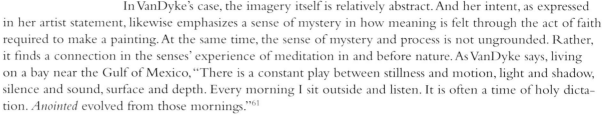

FIGURE 7
Pieter Bruegel the Elder
The Tower of Babel,
ca. 1567–68
Oil on oakwood

istic constructions). As the narrator of Genesis tells us in terse and mythic prose: "Now the whole earth had one language and few words." And within this linguistic condition, men gathered together in their insecurity and decided to establish themselves in a powerful confederation: "Then they said, 'Come, let us build ourselves a city, and a tower with its top in the heavens, and let us make a name for ourselves, lest we be scattered abroad upon the face of the whole earth.'" With the biblical text's usual forthrightness, the narrator suddenly shifts to God's perspective, and tells the reader that, indeed, humans have the power to do such a thing.

And the LORD came down to see the city and the tower, which the sons of men had built. And the LORD said, "Behold, they are one people, and they have all one language; and this is only the beginning of what they will do; and nothing that they propose to do will now be impossible for them. Come, let us go down and there confuse their language, that they may not understand one another's speech." So the LORD scattered them abroad. . . . Therefore its name was called Babel, because there the LORD confused the language of all the earth.[63]

Bomer's work echoes this narrative. At the top, in the wood section, she rubs and thins the black paint in a circle, revealing a knot in the wood, which implies the eye of God that sees all. Beneath the eye is a popularized image of the head of Christ, below which are the musical staff and words of a hymn, overprinted with Hebraic letters. The hymn appears to be Donald Busarow's arrangement of "The Church's One Foundation," that "foundation" being Christ. But the words of the hymn are, in fact, scrambled in their lettering, so that if one tried to sing them, the resulting song would be a confused gibberish. As the few legible words in the collage clearly reveal, "The Church's One Foundation" is an early American tune. Bomer thus subtly suggests a connection, or perhaps an analogy, between the confusion of the language of power in ancient Babel and the religious language of America. Near the center, we see Bruegel's Tower of Babel, which now rises on top of rows of letters from the alphabet, suggesting the deep foundational root of language as crucial to culture, pride, and the power inherent therein.

Although Bomer does not elaborate on any historically specific culture in her artist statement, it seems that her intent is to imply the long history of human cultures in general; for she has also collaged in a set of architectural ground plans in relationship to the tower, suggesting the foundations of ancient Babylon as an archeological site, but also implying the ruins of many cultures whose ambitions ultimately lead to their demise.

These broad cultural dynamics of corruption and downfall are easy for the modern mind to accept because they refer to historical conditions so ancient that they seem remote and therefore safe. But it becomes disconcerting to think of them as literally relevant to our own times. This is why Bomer's linking of ancient corruption and judgment to contemporary times (via a modern arrangement of a nineteenth-century American hymn) injects a startlingly specific challenge. But this is consistent with the tradition of the prophetic voice under discussion here, beginning with Michael R. Buesking and continuing through Zajkowski, Bomer, and others discussed below. What soon becomes apparent is that the artists working in the prophetic mode raise issues about a nation's relationship to its sacred texts, as well as to the concept of God derived from their experience in history and their interpretation of those texts in light of that experience.

What Buesking's *Ezekiel Scattering Hair* so poignantly reminds us of is that even God's chosen people, as in ancient Israel, are not exempt from judgment and destruction. The prophetically symbolic gesture of scattering the hair was one of the oracles of warning performed by Ezekiel before the fall of Jerusalem and the exile of the children of Israel.

There is a haunting irony here, for after Ezekiel's oracles of warning, God allowed the conquest of ancient Israel, letting her inhabitants be carried off to exile in, of all places, Babylon. What the artworks of Zajkowski and Bomer seem to ask, by way of Babel, is: "If God would thus hand over even Israel to her enemies, is it not also possible that America could be handed over if it commits hubris?" In other words, for the modern viewer, prophetic artists raise the issue of the national conversation that America has always had about its relationship with the Bible, a conversation that has been renewed in a highly public manner since the tragedy of 9/11 and the re-election of President George W. Bush in the fall of 2004. Giles Gunn has characterized the "American conversation" with the Bible.

In a manner that finds no exact parallel in any other nation, the Bible has become America's book. . . . Americans like to think that they have read it more assiduously than any other people, but also . . . Americans like to think that the Bible is the book that they, more than any other people, have been assiduously read by. . . . Americans have long felt . . . that the Bible has shaped their historical experience in decisive ways. . . . They have become compulsive readers of scripture in order to make certain that their experience not betray scriptural patterns. . . . Americans have run the risk of hubris, and willingly. They have cleaved to the Bible as though it were a national cultural possession for the sake of reassuring themselves that their own history was unfolding according to biblical prescriptions.

Writing as a scholar, but sounding somewhat prophetic himself, Gunn wonders about the soundness of this kind of hermeneutics.

The dangers inherent in America's special claim upon the Bible have been obvious at least since Cotton Mather first attempted in 1702 to fit our own experience into the Bible's epic structure in his Magnalia Christi Americana. *In the name of a sacred text that purports to define the ultimate design of all history, Mather presumed to find an explanation for the uniqueness of America's own.*

Gunn asks if Mather's interpretation does not run the risk of "turning the coin on its side," in that "the Bible could . . . be seen to belong to America because America, it could be assumed, already belonged to the Bible, because America *was* the Bible, or better, the realization of its promises." What Gunn seems to warn against is the danger of hubris in letting this kind of "interpretive turn" shape our national conversation with the Bible. Specifically, he warns against an interpretation that would "reduce the Old and New Testaments to a kind of National Testament and to convert the biblical *Heilsgeschichte*, or history of salvation, into the American salvation of history."[64]

Ever since post-Enlightenment politics and Romanticism gave rise to a wave of intense nationalisms in the modern era, the appeal of nation worship has remained strong. But in the case of American culture, with its particular manner of appropriating the Bible through its own history, the relationship of the culture to the sacred text, as well as to national understandings of God, can be especially vexing. And certainly one can understand the resentful satisfaction taken by our enemies, fully aware as they are that it was the modern remnants of Babylon who destroyed the World Trade Towers, those skyscrapers with their "tops in the heavens."

The somberness of Bomer's work seems worlds away from the more satirical approach of Houben Tcherkelov and David E. Levine. Their prophetic stance is made even more trenchant by their use of the most banal materials juxtaposed with that which is sacred. They join the traditional iconography of sacred art to the materials and visual strategies of consumer culture, forming a testy imagery in which the viewer is unsure whether prophetic irony has deconstructed consumerism, or consumerism has absorbed all that was once sacred.

In his work *St. Ioan*, Tcherkelov appropriated an image of John the Baptist's head on a platter from one of the many such representations in the history of art (entry 22). He painted the image in glitter paint on a ground of decorative wallpaper. In his artist statement, Tcherkelov says that he takes his images from coins, thereby joining the imagery of art (associated with religious contexts and liturgy) and the imagery of government currency (associated with commerce and the state). John the Baptist, of course, was a New Testament prophet who was executed for criticizing the status quo, as exemplified by the power and wealth of King Herod. John's decapitated head was brought on a platter to Salome, Herodias, Herod, and their guests during a party, for the strange and macabre combination of spiritual proclamation, ascetic saint, erotic dancer, and corrupt political power proved deadly for the prophet. In John the Baptist's day, it was common for coinage to bear an image of power, usually that of the Caesar or a deity. The idea that a coin might bear the image of a martyred prophet like John the Baptist, who openly criticized the reigning political powers, would have seemed ludicrous. That would indeed have been a radical statement had it been authorized by a magistrate.

But in Tcherkelov's work, the image of John the Baptist has been transferred, with a visually gentle but intellectually strident sarcasm, onto a piece of household wallpaper. Here, a kind of macabre interior design sensibility gives us a very different sort of spiritual presence within the domestic sphere, one that suggests how easily the radical voices of biblical heroes can be absorbed into the fabric of our daily culture. Perhaps we are meant to imagine such a motif as a decorative element repeated in the patterns of the wallpapers in our own dining rooms.

David E. Levine also positions New Testament content within the context of consumer culture. In a series of biting works, he bluntly places images of Christ onto Wheaties cereal boxes, appropriating masterworks such as Piero della Francesca's *Resurrection* (after 1458), or a 1637 painting of Christ bearing the Cross by the Spanish Baroque master Alonso Cano (entry 23). Levine thus spoofs the practice of placing athletic heroes on cereal boxes to serve as inspirations or role models while we eat our breakfasts. The rhetoric of advertising promises that the consumption of products will give us a better life and then upholds athletic heroes to guarantee the equation. There is, of course, a Christian industry that seeks to replace banal imagery on daily objects with sacred imagery, as a reminder of Christ's constant presence in our lives. One thinks of the clocks featuring Leonardo's *Last Supper*, which read a Bible verse on the hour, or of the Precious Moments Nativity marketed in Christian bookstores during the holidays.[65]

Objects like these operate by "sweetening" or "dumbing down" the somberness and radicalness of religious imagery. Levine's Wheaties series plays with the dilemmas inherent in imagery, advertising, consumer culture, and meaning. His boxes challenge the notion of "Champions," making us wonder why champions like Christ, Martin Luther King, or Mother Teresa — those champions of the sinful, the oppressed, the poor — might not also be placed on consumer objects as role models. But perhaps that would seem almost as ludicrous as the idea of seeing the head of John the Baptist on a first-century coin.

It is probably impossible for a thinking person not to sympathize with the cultural criticism practiced by Tcherkelov and Levine. For even as American culture remains openly and pervasively religious, its devotion to the Gross National Product is clear: witness the relentless spread of consumer goods; the obsession with self-image, wealth, and comfort; and especially the use of things sacred — sexuality, beauty, and language — to promote sales. Indeed, the blessings of an Infinite God and the infinitely expanding availability of nice things are considered proofs of one another in American culture. The artist-as-prophet cannot help but prophesy. But it does no good. The astonishing ability of capitalism's market strategies to defuse, aestheticize, and then enlist even the most critical extremes of avant-garde or prophetic critiques into the market's ambitions has become clear by now. Both the avant-garde and the prophet are passé.

So, in light of what could be called the post-avant-garde era, James Disney's *Through the Eye of a Needle* fascinates (entry 24). This watercolor plays off of Jesus's teaching regarding the dilemma of being faithfully religious and wealthy at the same time. In the story, a young man who has consistently observed the commandments asks Jesus what he still lacks to inherit eternal life. Jesus, seeing that the young man has a bourgeois understanding of the religious laws and faith, tells him to sell his possessions and give the money to the poor, so that he will have treasure in heaven, and then to follow Christ. When the man cannot do this — "for he had great possessions" — Jesus declares that "It is easier for a camel to go through the eye of a needle than for a rich man to enter the kingdom of God."[66]

Christ's disciples clearly understood this radical teaching, for the gospel account immediately reflects their anxiety as they ask, "Who then can be saved?" What person, or writ large, what culture, could ever give up its great possessions to follow an extremist like Jesus? This kind of blunt moral teaching stands simply, without equivocation, at the center of many biblical passages. Frequently, as in the case of the rich young man, the biblical narrative says nothing about the ultimate outcome of such confrontations. All we know of this wealthy man, for example, is that "he went away sorrowful for he had great possessions." The characters of the Bible's narrative sort themselves out around such unbending demands, just as all of us today sort ourselves out with various degrees of faith, rationalization, and denial.

Disney's painting poses this kind of dilemma with quirky visual humor. An odd array of stylized people pose and perch throughout a landscape, all of them flanking a centralized, elongated camel that floats above a ravine in the terrain. These mannered people range in their clothing and gestures from an old lady seated in the foreground doing her needlework, to a circle of gray-suited businessmen seated around a conference table in the board room of a modern building to the right. Perhaps reflecting Disney's fondness for the painters of the Northern Renaissance, the work reads like a contemporary painting by Brueghel, with a cross-section of humanity, social circles, and eccentric types, each completely self-involved, scattered across the face of the earth, with the camel — an absurd moral sign as obstacle — standing simply in their midst. Disney's prophetic stance dares to rely on humor and poignancy simultaneously. The viewer may be challenged or puzzled, but he or she will have to do his or her own sorting out.

In thinking about the priestly and prophetic roles of the artists examined in this dimension in *The Next Generation*, we have traveled from the healing graciousness of Hebblethwaite, Fujimura, and VanDyke, to the confrontational intensity of Zajkowski and Bomer, to the ironic sarcasm of Tcherkelov, Levine, and Disney. Anyone familiar with the biblical text as a whole knows that its narrative is — to use a biblical phrase — like a double-edged sword. That is, while it speaks of life and grace, it also confronts with judgment and death. To quote Giles Gunn again, "The Bible has simultaneously furnished some of the most stable forms of western culture, even as it has also supplied a discontent with those very forms."[67] Chief among the Bible's destabilizing energies is its confrontation of established social orders with the threat of judgment. This is the theme of Ezekiel and the whole prophetic tradition discussed here. It is the thrust of Jesus's confrontation with the rich young man, who was, really, a typical upstanding citizen — moral, observant of religious codes, and a solid contributor to the economy. Yet, within a spiritual economy involving compassion for the poor and liberation from his own possessions, the rich young man was in fact bankrupt.

This kind of disconcerting epiphany (in which people who are not what they see themselves as being, are confronted with the shock of that fact at the climactic moment of choosing between God and self) occurs repeatedly within the biblical text. Such reversals of identity can take the form of a prophet confronting an individual (King David and Nathan, the rich man and Jesus), a group of people (the politically and economically powerful religious leaders of Jesus's society), or an entire nation (Israel and Ezekiel). Or it can take on an apocalyptic scale, as in Noah's Flood or the warning to the churches in the book of Revelation, in which ultimately the entire earth is destroyed and then renewed.

Perhaps the most disturbing dimension of such biblical "reversals of identity" is that they seem to occur most often to respected people who justify themselves religiously. The reader need only list each aggressive harangue by the ancient prophets or Christ to discover that those who use religion self-righteously to justify their position in the world receive the worst tongue-lashings. Those who know they are doing evil will also face judgment in the Bible, but they do not require an abrupt reversal or contradiction of their respectable self-image to experience the downfall that is necessary for grace.

Given this, one of the most troubling books in the biblical canon is the book of Revelation in the New Testament. It is the book of final things, of judgment and end times. Yet it is not merely an account of wholesale destruction and violence, as its early chapters are a prophetic confrontation with the seven Christian churches of early Christendom. Like the rich young man, each church is told what is good about it, but each is then warned that it has grown cold, false, or self-involved.

Anita Breitenberg Naylor uses the book of Revelation to present the viewer with, in her own words, "fresh, elegant, lavish pictorial poetry that beguiles, captivates, compels, and confounds the viewer by means of visual biblical commentary."[68] The richly patterned elegance of the imagery in her large-scale collages references a diverse host of sources, including quilts, Tibetan mandalas, Indian rangolies (painted prayers), kaleidoscopes, Byzantine mosaics, and medieval Christian and Renaissance art from both the Catholic and Orthodox traditions. But their sumptuous and tactile appeal is interrupted by the harsh language of biblical judgment with which Naylor titles her collages. For example, Naylor's *Revelation 3:5* (entry 25) references a passage in the book of Revelation that reads, "He who conquers shall be clad thus in white garments, and I will not blot his name out of the book of life; I will confess his name before my Father and before his angels." The speaker is the Spirit of the churches, or, depending on one's interpretive theology, Christ. And although the single verse cited is a redemptive image, its context is a severe prophetic warning of damnation, even to those in the church.

The context is the Spirit's confrontation of the early church at Sardis, which has "the name of being alive, [but is] dead," for its works are not perfect in the sight of God. God's complaint against the church is that it has not remained true to what it originally heard and believed. But the text at least holds out hope to a few ("he who conquers") if they avoid compromising their faith and integrity. It is to these few that verse five (quoted above) speaks: "Yet you have still a few names in Sardis, people who have not soiled their garments; and they shall walk with me in white, for they are worthy."[69]

Naylor says that her intention is "to stimulate and evoke a spiritual response from a visual experience and to significantly impact the viewer's perceptions of reality through thought and emotion, inspiring and intriguing the viewer to ponder and engage the infinite embrace of salvation, and to promote worship of the embodiment of love." There is, in a sense, a certain disconnect—or reversal—of expectation experienced between the visual richness of her collage and the strident harshness of the source of the work's title. That jarring sense is felt more specifically when the viewer draws near to examine the collage in detail.

Close examination of *Revelation 3:5* moves the viewer from an overall luxurious patterning to a series of internal details expressing Christ's suffering. The larger kaleidoscopic pattern draws the viewer from the outer edges into the center of the collage; but at the same time, the internal forms (standing figures, raised arms and hands, and linear movements) lift the viewer away from the center, up and out to the perimeter. As the eye follows these movements, the mind encounters a visionary imagery drawn from Revelation, itself a vision experienced by the exiled Saint John on the island of Patmos. Starting from the center, a quadruple-mirrored imagery emanates outward in concentric levels. At the innermost level, eight pairs of figures stand clad in white garments. The figures play against ornate conch shells. Above them, large forearms and hands seem to emerge three-dimensionally from what looks like portals or holes in the surface. As the eye moves upward and outward to the next concentric level, a series of Christs as the Man of Sorrows (here, the naked upper torso, head, and outstretched arms of the dead Jesus) guides the eye toward the four corners, leading to a smaller-scale crucified Jesus with conch shells filling in behind. Spreading out behind the conch shells are pairs of golden wings resembling dragonfly wings, which evoke heavenly visions of seraphim and cherubim. Between the corner passages are four other pairs of Christ heads, larger this time. These pairs of Christ heads, also Man of Sorrows, mirror each other, as they silently grieve against a background of blue stained glass windows in a mysterious architectural space. Within the windows are pairs of gothic-like arches with roundels at their centers, each roundel filled with a more iconic, almost Pantokrator-type of Christ looking out at us.

The result is an ecstatic, but also obsessive, visionary collage. This is somehow fitting with the content of the piece, its source, and the discussion here of the Bible's priestly and prophetic dimensions, for this work by Naylor both frightens and exalts. While priestly in its sumptuous beauty, it disturbs in its prophetic warnings of destruction to the church. And yet at the center of the warnings, and of Naylor's collage, is the promise of redemption, of being clad in white robes, for those who avoid corruption.

Faith and Healing by Grace

Although the difficult theme of prophetic judgment runs as a consistent current throughout the Bible, other themes mediate the darkness of such matters. In fact, the themes of faith and healing by grace exactly offset those of judgment, in direct proportion to the capacity of biblical characters to acknowledge their flaws and to turn towards hope. Among the many themes touched upon in the exhibition, one of the most moving then is that of faith as it relates to healing and grace. Seven artists in particular address different dimensions of healing, and in doing so, they confront pain, violence, sexual abuse, mental illness, crime, and disease with the possibilities of faith, compassion, hope, courage, and, ultimately, redemptive epiphany.

In Erica Grimm-Vance's *Binding Up, Healing Vision I*, we encounter a diptych of seemingly complete opposites (entry 26). On the right is a human head in profile, exquisitely rendered in graphite and encaustic. The upper part of the head is bound in cloth, the layers equal part bandage and blindfold. The head conveys an intense human pathos, partly because its alert tilt suggests attentiveness, as if it were listening expectantly from within the darkness, and partly because there is a cadmium red wound at the base of the throat. As the head listens, waiting, a radiant white-yellow light emanates from beneath the chin, illuminating the expectant but blindfolded face.

Pitched to the left opposite this human head is a panel of equal size, an empty black square of steel. Its impenetrable surface is a staring into the darkness. Against the alert expectancy of the head, it remains resolutely mute and passive. As images, the two sides of the diptych seem like entire opposites. They exist within separate aesthetics, one a non-objective minimalist abstraction, the other a sensitive naturalism. They belong to utterly different orders of being.

And yet, when one stands before *Binding Up, Healing Vision I*, the two halves do not actually feel incompatible. The unyielding black void does not necessarily seem indifferent, just silent. Indeed, though made of steel, its patina is warm, velvety, even inviting. The left panel is as sensuous, in its steely nature, as the head is in its fleshy nature. And for all the alertness and vulnerability of the head, there is a steadfastness about the steel's "otherness" that is almost comforting. Thus, if the head exists and waits within the fragility of a painful moment, the silent dark steel seems safely eternal. The head belongs to the world of time and light and the senses, and so as well to the pain inherent in these. The black square's mode of existence is not sensory in the same way; and though it therefore seems detached, it is this very quality of disinterestedness that gives it its strength. This is also borne out in the materials of being: if the head is rendered in the fragile material of encaustic (wax being as vulnerable as skin), then the steel seems indestructible. The difference in sheer mass and weight between wax and steel suggests a terrible lightness of being versus a profundity of being. If the side with the head is transient, flickering in the light, and pulsing with blood, then the side with the steel is of a different order, free of the terrible flux to which blood, flesh, and need are constantly subject.

If the ineffable black steel offers any solace or answer to the question of suffering implicit in the waiting attentiveness of the head, then its "answer" must be in terms very different from those in which the question is posed. What we always seek when suffering is an answer that corresponds directly to the specifics of our suffering. If blind, then we place a small lead *milagro* depicting eyes on the cross, and pray for sight. But faith is not a one-to-one equation of restitution for our physical losses. In the end, the whole body will fail anyway. So perhaps to be "answered" is to be granted some understanding that there is a different order of being, a companionship with the Other. As Flannery O'Connor said, "Faith tends to heal if we realize it is 'a walking in darkness' and not a theological solution to mystery."[70] There is something reassuring about O'Connor's claim that faith reveals to us that suffering has a purpose even when we do not receive a rational explanation for it, because her own art and life of faith were crafted in the dark face of the Lupus that would kill her at the age of thirty-nine.

Erica Grimm-Vance's work is a powerful example of how art navigates questions of faith. For in it, she has placed the fundamental terms of both faith and art into a finely tuned tension that feels precisely right. What is meant by the fundamental terms of faith is that tension between what is essentially invisible and what is visible, between what is ineffable, abstract, Other, and what is named, concrete, and natural. One way or another, all theological (and much philosophical) inquiry works at the borders between the physically concrete and the spiritually abstract. We think at the edges of experience and the senses, calling out questions couched in the terms of experience and the senses. Then we listen attentively, through our blindfolds and wounds, for some returning echoes, whose contours have been reshaped as they rebound off the "Other," indicating the nature of that Other. But even if what is Other — God — bears a rich resonance towards us, the terms of God's being may still not be the same as the terms in which we seek answers. What we might take to be silence, indifference, or even void may well be an "answer," if we could only grasp the terms. Like the vertical stripe of 23-karat gold that Grimm-Vance uses to divide the head's space from the steel square, the border between the sanctuary of inscrutable depth and the highly specific details and pain of our sensory organs — of ears, skin, eyes — is made of precious, sacred material.

There is here an analogue between the fundamental terms of faith and experience and the terms of art. In the modernist tradition, beginning with Wilhelm Worringer's *Empathy and Abstraction* (1911) and Kandinsky's *Concerning the Spiritual in Art* (1913), purely non-objective or abstract forms have been understood to be one of the primary domains for expressing the ineffable.[71] From Malevich's radical Suprematist icon, *Black Square* of 1915, to Rothko's Abstract Expressionist paintings of the 1950s (brooding, feather-edged rectangular forms suspended in color), to Ad Reinhardt's hard-edged Black Paintings of the early 1960s, the impenetrable black abstract form has served as a visual metaphor for the ineffable.[72] Grimm-Vance's *Binding Up, Healing Vision I* draws powerfully from this long tradition.

These issues are extended in different ways by sculptor Stewart Luckman in his large marble piece *Last Testament of Job* (entry 27). Here, fragments of powerful facial features are merged within a stone monolith and patterns suggesting scarification, creating an image of suffering that is as much internal as it is external. Luckman evokes, rather than depicts, the multiple violent losses that destroyed Job's well-being. Marble, a material associated with the classical beauty of the figure, but one often fragmented by time and accident, lends itself well to capturing Job's ancient, decimated head. After Job suffered the slaying of his servants, the loss of his flocks, and the deaths of his children, followed by the affliction of his body with loathsome sores, "he took a potsherd with which to scrap himself, and sat among the ashes." When his three friends came to comfort him, Job was so disfigured that "when they saw him . . . they did not recognize him; and they raised their voices and wept."[73]

The story of Job is the Bible's extended examination of the problem of suffering. Like a sadistic novelist, its author sets up the terms of Job's sorrow in a terrible dilemma. Although as readers we understand that his suffering results from a spiritual debate between God and Satan, Job seems every bit the unfortunate victim caught unawares in the crossfire. Job himself knows nothing of their cavalier wager over his integrity; he knows only that he was a good man who cared for others, prayed faithfully, and offered the right sacrifices for his children. And yet, with the cruelest of irony, Job is not, in a sense, "innocent." His plight reflects the fears of anyone who strives for goodness. Namely, that a person's goodness is also his vulnerability. Indeed, it may be precisely one's genuine goodness that draws the fire of evil because evil despises anything authentic.

Job can only cry out to God and declare his integrity. When the absurdity of loss strikes him down, Job's wife offers up the mocking human response of despair and nihilism: "Do you still hold fast your integrity? Curse God, and die."[74] After the usual initial commiserations, Job's friends become incensed that he does not believe his suffering is deserved, that he denies some unconfessed sin that brought on the deaths of his children, the loss of his wealth, and the destruction of his health.

The ancient story then takes up the discourse of suffering that religion and society typically embrace, which fails to comfort Job in his pain. In the end, Job's faith is one of defiance against stereotypical answers and religious conventions. He blames God, without knowing the full dynamics, for what has befallen him. And he demands that God be put on trial until He answers Job. And finally, God does answer him. But God's answer is not in the terms of the human question that was posed by Job.

Like Grimm-Vance's black square juxtaposed against a human head, God's silence throughout Job's outcry has seemed impenetrable. But now, when God's answer comes, it is on an entirely different order than the terms of explanation that Job had demanded. Instead of responding to the debate over suffering, God simply draws near to Job, the Divine immensity of Being thereby reframing the question. What Job receives is a sublime sense of the Other which, though never explaining to Job what has happened, absorbs the question into a larger reality.

Job's last testament is his epiphany. Though still lying in the ash heap and covered with sores, his vision of God has reordered his suffering.

Then Job answered the LORD:
"I know that thou canst do all things,
    and that no purpose of thine can be thwarted.
'Who is this that hides counsel without knowledge?'
Therefore I have uttered what I did not understand,
    things too wonderful for me, which I did not know. . . .
I had heard of thee by the hearing of the ear,

but now my eye sees thee;
therefore I despise myself, and repent in dust and ashes."[75]

Luckman's sculpture bears the dignity and pathos of this speech. In an aesthetically smart move, he carved two crossed Band-Aids on Job's face. The odd realism of such contemporary objects within the context of ancient material (marble) and heroic image (Job) gives the work an immediacy that is convincing. Like the great Philip Guston self-portrait (*Untitled*, 1980), in which the artist's greasy pink head looms gigantically (one existential eye staring into a stark, littered landscape and refusing to blink), Luckman keeps an almost cartoon-like grittiness in his piece. He makes Job a common man who would have despised sophisticated theological rationalizations, and who would have had the audacity to insist upon his own integrity even though he does not fully comprehend what has happened to him. Only such a working-class man would be able to accept the terms of God's overwhelming presence as an answer, however humbling, without equivocation or self-pity.

FIGURE 8
Titian
The Entombment,
ca. 1520
Oil on canvas

The muscular, existential spirituality of Luckman's *Last Testament of Job* finds its match in the raw intensity of painter Edward Knippers's aesthetic. His monumental eight-by-twelve-foot painting *Ash Wednesday (Christ and the Demoniac)* asserts the body, the sheer incarnation of Christ, and the madman in a dramatic moment of healing (entry 28). In the gospel narrative, the Demoniac is a man possessed by so many demons that he is called Legion. His mental illness causes him to be so violent that he is chained to protect both himself and others. Here, a bloodied and devastated man cringes unshaven among the rocks and skulls of a graveyard, while a naked Jesus confronts him, casting out the demons into swine.

Knippers, who has said that he intends to reinvigorate the great biblical narratives that the church has domesticated, radically affirms the Christian belief in the Incarnation by painting Christ as a powerfully human figure. In his groundbreaking study, *The Sexuality of Christ in Renaissance Art and in Modern Oblivion*, Leo Steinberg observed that Renaissance artists regularly emphasized the male genitalia of both the Christ Child and the dead Christ.[76] The reason, though shocking to decorum, was theological. If Christ was not gendered, then he was not human and the Incarnation would be a sham, as would the theology of salvation. Knippers has pressed this conviction of the Incarnation to the fullest, using the nude figure as a way of insisting upon the flesh of creation and Incarnation, as well as to argue for universality. And in doing so, he extends the radicality of the Incarnation — of God unclothed of pure divinity and dressed in flesh — by portraying Jesus as nude before a humanity that is naked.

On the theoretical level, the theology of the Incarnation is challenging enough to the modern mind. But on the aesthetic level, the challenge to a painter seeking to visualize these ideas is extreme. In developing his manner of portraying the figure, Knippers acknowledges that it is the artistic traditions of the West that he knows best. And so his figurative style draws from the rich diversity of that heritage, revealing influences ranging from the deep humanism of Renaissance and Baroque painters, as embodied in Titian's *Entombment* (ca. 1520; fig. 8), to the angular intensity of German Expressionism, as exemplified by Max Beckmann's *Christ and the Woman Taken in Adultery* (1917; fig. 9).

FIGURE 9
Max Beckmann
Christ and the Woman Taken in Adultery, **1917**
Oil on canvas

Melanie Weaver takes up other dimensions of suffering and healing as part of faith in her outspokenly therapeutic aesthetic. Her work is partly autobiographical, serving as "a journal of healing from being used in child prostitution and pornography."[77] And her studio is open to other women artists who have suffered from similar violence. But her sculptures also extend beyond autobiography to address larger cultural issues of violence, war, trauma, and spirituality. For her assemblages, Weaver takes objects that reference childhood, domestic activities, play, war, and religion, combining them into monochromatically black totemic figurative forms. These almost fetish-like figures are reminiscent of the folk sculptures of the Saints used in processions in Mexico, as well as of the Madonna della Misericordia, the Madonna of Mercy. In this traditional Renaissance image, the Virgin Mary stands with her full-length robe held open to gather and shelter humanity within its protective folds (for a late-fourteenth-century example, see fig. 10).

In Weaver's *Inhabiting/Flying* (entry 29), a doll's head and body double as the Virgin and a little girl-cum-saint. Surrounding her head like a halo is a round basket. A bird hovering by her head suggests both the Holy Spirit and the soul's freedom or release. A many-tiered dress flows down, recalling a dedication or baptismal dress and childhood innocence, but there is also a macabre element suggesting womanhood imposed prematurely on the child. Long strings of round beads trail down the dress, doubling as jewelry and Rosary; further down there is a strange grouping of a well-dressed woman holding a little bird in her hand next to an open bird cage, a basket in which a toy army man stands, and a chair on which another toy army man hauls back his arm to throw a grenade, all within the folds of the dress. The mixture of lace, feminine elegance, domesticity, and male violence all contained within this little girl/saint/Virgin Mary makes Weaver's work strangely spiritual, innocent, haunted, and disturbing.

The reality that faith is deeply related to suffering—existing as an integral ground for healing and grace for those who have known mental illness, sexual abuse, or terrible loss—has long been expressed in both art and religious practice. What is more difficult is to acknowledge the suffering and faith of those who have perpetuated violence and abuse upon others. In a series of intense black-and-white

FIGURE 10

**Anonymous
(Tuscan School)
Madonna della Misericordia,
late 14th century
Polychromed wood**

photographs, Serge J-F Levy documents the spiritual lives and search for healing of men and women in prison (entry 30). In a manner reminiscent of Mary Ellen Mark's photographs of Mother Teresa's home for the dying in Calcutta, Levy finds a presence of love, compassion, and hope in prisons, those places of darkness. They are, so to speak, ultimate places, where extreme actions have eclipsed life's open possibilities. For prisoners locked away in maximum-security prisons, any sense of freedom and hope must be internal, and Levy's title for the series, *Faith from Inside: Religion in Prison,* carries the right double entendre. His powerful compositions of prisoners within an enclosed geometry of bleak spaces, with a diffused light that feels both natural and spiritual, transform the overtly religious gestures of prayer depicted here into something authentic and credible.

Most of us will never have to face the suffering (and needed healing) incurred from violent abuse, war, or crime. But all of us will face the failure of our bodies, whether in old age or through disease. Kathy Hettinga's photographic work *Chemotherapy Journey: Chemotherapy Patient, Gynecological Oncologist Surgeon,* which deals with cancer, surgery, and chemotherapy (entry 31), directly asks the question, "How do we live with and through suffering?"[78] In a remarkably symbolic coincidence, Hettinga's own stage-three cancer was diagnosed on Good Friday, the day that Christians recognize as the day that Christ took their sufferings and death upon himself. But on that particular Good Friday, Hettinga realized a new level of the Imitation of Christ tradition, as she entered her own Great Saturday of suffering, fear, and sense of abandonment by God. Those who have experienced such things understand why some of the most despairing words in the New Testament are actually the most hopeful, when Christ cries out from the cross, "*Eloi, Eloi, lama sabach-thani?*" (My God, my God, why hast thou forsaken me?).[79]

In a second remarkably symbolic coincidence, Hettinga's surgeon would be a Cuban-American doctor named Misas, which in Spanish means Mass. The Mass is the Eucharist, the partaking of Christ's body and blood, which was shed for the healing of sin and death. And so her surgeon became for Hettinga an embodiment of grace and healing. Or as she has put it, Dr. Misas "has been to me like a healing Eucharist." He was her surgeon, her priest, her Christ. In the Catholic Mass, when the communicant takes the elements of the bread/body and wine/blood of Christ, the priest says, "Just say the Words and I shall be healed."

The works of art that Hettinga made from her experience with cancer echo these symbolic coincidences both in their imagery and their structure. That is, the diptych format, in which large, single figures rise above a shelf or table laden with artifacts, evokes the installation of art in a gallery as well as altarpiece paintings in a church, while the works also literally document the actual hospital setting of her surgery. *Chemotherapy Journey* consists of two very large digital prints, one of Hettinga and one of Dr. Misas. The surgeon is dressed in the familiar blue-green surgical garb, while the patient is dressed in a darker, more somber color. The strange garb, complete with the shroud-like headgear, places doctor and patient within a hospital/medical setting, but it also alludes to the robes and gowns worn by the Madonna and saints in Renaissance altarpieces.

The installation of the photographs further establishes the parallel between medical and church settings. As noted, Hettinga's artwork and the altarpiece both share the structure of a large figural image standing above a horizontal surface with objects on it. Altarpieces bear images of the Madonna and Christ, with the elements of the bread and wine placed on the altar table; *Chemotherapy Journey* bears images of patient and surgeon, along with smaller photographs from Hettinga's earlier series documenting old gravestones in Colorado, which often carry poignant epitaphs expressing love, faith, and hope. Thus, the objects on the artist's shelf are her own artifacts relating to death, while the objects on an altar are the artifacts of the Mass relating to the triumph over death through faith.

Coincidences are accidental. But to coincide is not. The coincidences that Hettinga experienced in real life — and those that she creates in her art — recall the Symbolist concept of "correspondence," not in the sense of occult magic, but rather in the sense of there being parallel structures of experience and understanding that suggest connections between the physical and the metaphysical. Such a correspondence was given voice by T.S. Eliot in his poem "East Coker," in which a surgeon/priest/Christ figure operates on a patient on Good Friday. Like the compassionate Dr. Misas, Eliot's surgeon is himself bleeding as he probes human disease

The wounded surgeon plies the steel
That questions the distempered part;
Beneath the bleeding hands we feel
The sharp compassion of the healer's art.

Hettinga's description of "the terror of cancer; the poisoning, yet healing work of chemotherapy"[80] suggests another correspondence identified in Eliot's poem. But this one is metaphysical; it is the great irony at the center of the Christian faith. That is, as in the practice of medicine, the Healer must increase our sickness in order to cure us. As Eliot puts it

Our only health is the disease
If we obey the dying nurse
Whose constant care is not to please
But to remind of our, and Adam's curse,
And that, to be restored, our sickness must grow worse.[81]

Just as Susan Sontag examined disease as both personal crisis and larger metaphor in *Illness as Metaphor*, so in faith do we understand that a doctor's healing of today's disease is but the prelude to a larger, inevitable confrontation with total bodily failure and death.[82] So, too, was Hettinga's making of *Chemotherapy Journey* an act of confession and faith. It was, and for the viewer is, a kind of pilgrimage made into disease, into the terrible Great Saturday when (as the Orthodox Church believes) Christ was in Hades redeeming us, and into the hope of Easter Resurrection to which faith holds fast. As confession, she has included the perfect touch by photographing herself in her chemotherapy head covering holding the camera. An artist's confession is most true through the language of her medium, and the presence of the camera here beautifully stands as a documenting (bearing witness), a confession (one's own portrait), and an interpretation of meaning (the artwork). This richness of layers is what one would hope for in art exploring faith.

Another photographic work in *The Next Generation*, Michael Mills's *Hosts (Triptych)*, shares in this idea of visually identifying the Mass with the processes of human living (entry 32). In this work, Mills takes up the Renaissance theme of the "Three Ages of Man," in which artists portrayed an individual in the three primary phases of a life—youth, adulthood, and old age. These artworks served as artistic/philosophical contemplations on the passage of time, the process of maturation, and the facing of death. They asked about the meaning of one's life, one's choices, and what one has found on the journey toward death.

In his photographic triptych, Mills places three black-and-white photographs in the chronological sequence of that aging process. Instead of suggesting a single individual, or couching the universality of his theme in male terms, Mills uses three different models and includes both female and male. The first image is of a seventy-eight-year-old man, the second is of a thirty-six-year-old woman, and the third is of a nine-year-old boy. Echoing Flannery O'Connor's conviction that human knowledge begins through the senses, Mills says that his work operates on "the assumption that human beings understand themselves in relationship to their world most fully through their bodies. One's sense of who one is, both as an individual and as a member of a community, grows out of the experience of being physical."[83]

Mills then superimposes the image of the crucified Christ and the letters "INRI" (commonly embossed on the surface of the Eucharist wafer, the Host) over each of the human torsos. This creates an identification of the viewer with Christ, of the communicant with Christ's body in the Eucharist, and of the triptych itself with art and religion. Such an identification of our own bodies, our fundamental source of being and identity, with Christ's body is essentially the response of placing one's self in Christ through faith. What thoughtful religious believers and artists instinctively know is that this identification needs to be secured by being embodied symbolically. Hence, it is required that meaning be expressed physically, that it be enacted, as in participating in the Mass or in making a work of art. The necessity of actual embodiment is, of course, an echo of the Incarnation, through which God identified with human suffering by taking on flesh in the body of Jesus.

At the risk of sounding blasphemous, I would argue that by taking on a body and thereby entering human experience and being, God experienced the particular kind of knowledge that comes only through being flesh, being creatures, whose means of registering reality is through the senses of the body. And as Christian theology maintains vigorously, salvation comes—and can only come—through the reality of the body. As Mills eloquently concludes, "It is my hope that *Hosts* will invite people to consider their own bodies, with their inherent power, frailty, ambiguity and idiosyncrasies, as authentic bearers or *hosts* for Christ."

Here, the complexity of Mills's title word—"host"—is critical. In social terms, when one is a guest invited to a meal, one has a host. The host honors the guest by serving food, but the guest also realizes that he or she is only present through the grace of the host. Indeed, the guest eats at the expense of the host, even as the host is enriched by establishing a loving relationship with the guest. In biological terms, one is a host when something lives off of one's body. The dependent being—the guest—lives only by partaking from the body of the host. And the host gives of its body to the dependent being. In liturgical and theological terms, these meanings are compressed together. Mills places the image of the Host from communion wafers — the body of Christ Crucified — onto the body of the dependent being for whom Christ died, strangely inverting the equation of host and guest. For now the guest, as it were, becomes host to the Host. This is the paradox of the Incarnation. For in Mills's triptych, the human body now actually bears the Host. Yet it is only through the Host's marking of the body that the body lives. The guest's Eucharistic eating of the Host — who has borne the guest's body of flesh in himself, even as the guest now bears the image of the Host on himself — is the realization of salvation. This is what establishes the relationship of love between Christ and his human believers.

The Altarpiece and Book as Idea

The last two works of art considered have ushered us fully into the Christian content of the Incarnation, the Church's sacrament of the Eucharist, and the identification of the self with these meanings. It is worth pausing here to observe that both Hettinga and Mills used the visual/structural device of an altarpiece format as a way of working within this matrix of ideas. Even a casual observer will have noticed the frequent and telling appropriation of the altarpiece form by the artists in the exhibition. Examples range from Joel Sheesley, who appropriated the *Portinari Altarpiece* as an object internal to his painting, to those who have selected the triptych or diptych for their format (Couture, Murphy, Prescott, Feldman, Grimm-Vance, Hettinga, Mills). While not surprising, given that the theme of the exhibition is art about faith, there is something worth lingering over in such multiple borrowings.

Of course the appropriation of the altarpiece form, with which artists can charge their works with powerful spiritual or cultural allusions, is by no means limited only to those who are overtly interested in faith. Twentieth-century art is rich with works using (or implying) the altarpiece form, ranging from Max Beckmann's mythic triptychs and Picasso's *Guernica* to works by Emil Nolde, Georges Rouault, Henri Matisse, Francis Bacon, Graham Sutherland, Barnett Newman, Michael Tracy, Andy Warhol, Renée Cox, and Anselm Kiefer, to name only a few.

Clearly, on a basic level the altarpiece format is simply a frame. But it is a frame whose shape and history bear such rich cultural and religious associations that its form is, essentially, far more "idea" than it is "object." It is an idea operating within the category of "frame" in much the same way that "Bible" is an idea operating within the category of "book." For the same can be said of the Bible. While as "book," the Bible is merely a physical cover holding a multitude of stories and poems (the surprising diversity of which might otherwise disqualify them as a unity), under the "idea" of "Bible" it ceases to be a pluralism and becomes an integrated whole. Indeed, in this sense, "Book" and "Altarpiece" are literary and visual equivalents. They are "canon" and "icon." It is right to speak of both the image and the book together in this context; for the early Church, as Hans Belting has shown, the testimony and authority of both image and text were bound up together.[84]

Generically, both book and frame contain story, narrative, sign, symbol, and metaphor. Anything can be written or pictured within their perimeters. Yet "Bible" and "altarpiece" stand as ideas that, given their cultural status, bring interpretation to whatever is written or pictured within their perimeters.

No matter what an author writes or a painter depicts, if placed within the scope of "Bible" or "altarpiece," what has been created is automatically conjugated against a context of "scripture" or "icon." Whether in harmony or in conflict with the meaning of the sacred "texts" referenced, being placed within such "sacred structures" guarantees a certain tone and a set of interpretive dynamics. In this regard, there is an interesting grouping of artists in the exhibition who use either the altarpiece or the book *as* an idea or structure within which to explore ideas.

An exploration that leverages itself, so to speak, off of the form of the altarpiece or the book possesses an important additional dynamic for contemporary artists who are interested in exploring religious content. Namely, many artists feel the desire to explore faith through the great traditional formats, but they have, in fact, no real social contexts for doing so. The Church has long ceased to be a significant patron of artists. Even more so, American Protestantism has often seen art as the enemy. Furthermore, there is very little sense of a community with an imagery integral to its liturgy or congregational worship. Although today images are certainly present in the Catholic and Orthodox Churches, these are mostly works made in earlier times when the church was still a vigorous patron of the arts, or ones that are merely imitations of older traditions, and so not requiring a creative artist's fullest abilities. Thus, abandoned by their religious culture and working without a liturgical context for their art, artists find themselves free to experiment more personally with traditional forms.

In this light, several artworks in the exhibition not only deepen the themes already discussed, but also become interesting in terms of this type of personal experimentation. Tyrus Clutter takes on the altarpiece form and the dilemma of context directly in his *Altarpiece of St. Francis of L'Abri* (entry 33). Here, it is the polyptych rather than the diptych or triptych that serves the artist's interests. Clutter has done a series of works in which he addresses a long and deep pattern in the history of Christianity. Noting that it was common in the Catholic and Orthodox traditions for artists to create altarpieces devoted to specific saints, venerating them for their faith and miraculous acts through contemplation and imitation, Clutter makes modern-day altarpieces devoted to twentieth-century Christians who have also done significant things, but who will never be sainted. That is, they will never be sainted in the Christian tradition from which Clutter comes, which is Protestantism. As he observes in his artist statement, since the Reformation, that branch of the church has veered toward a piety of *sola scriptura*, which has meant not only favoring the Bible over tradition, but also the word over imagery. Indeed, this part of the church has rejected imagery as a legitimate language for both theology and the liturgy, just as it has rejected saints as spiritual mentors and intercessors.

Nonetheless, Clutter tries to bridge these two worlds by creating a modern hagiography, devoting his altarpieces to, for example, Dietrich Bonhoeffer, T.S. Eliot, Flannery O'Connor, and, in the work featured in *The Next Generation*, Francis Schaeffer, who founded the L'Abri Fellowship in Switzerland. All of these "saints" are known to us through their writings, not their miracles, and so Clutter has created small devotional altarpieces with imagery appropriate to each of them. In the *Altarpiece of St. Francis of L'Abri*, he has lined the individual compartments with written words, for Schaeffer was not only a Reformed Protestant theologian who deeply embraced the principle of *sola scriptura*, but he was also a writer who significantly impacted Evangelicalism in the 1960s and 1970s. Schaeffer is best known for his writings, as well as for his gifts as a teacher and preacher. Thus, in the open state of Clutter's altarpiece we see him seated in the left wing and standing, with arms gesturing, in the right. Surrounding him are his own words, an exegesis of The Word.

A strict Calvinist like Schaeffer sees humans as totally depraved, or naked before God. In the center panel of the altarpiece (as well as twice in its closed state), we see the saint standing in naked supplication. Above him are two mysterious chambers. One holds a pair of stoppered vials containing what appears to be the bread and wine. While the uppermost chamber is empty, its background, one without words, is a richly abstract flowing of deep red and gold, an ecstatic passage signifying the ineffable. Thus, two chambers, one "empty" and one with the bread and wine, hover above a naked Schaeffer, whose right arm is raised up, creating a central hierarchical axis that rises to transcendence and mystery.

FIGURE 11
Duccio
Maestà **altarpiece (detail),
1308–11**
Tempera on wood

Clutter's work makes for a fascinating project. For although Protestants think that they do not hold to a theology of Saints, Intercession, and Veneration, anyone raised in a Protestant church knows full well that there are modern, desacralized versions of such traditions, which function psychologically very much like the originals. One need only read David Morgan's study of Warner Sallman's *Head of Christ* to discover the unacknowledged surrogates of the Catholic and Orthodox traditions.[85] The interesting challenge for an artist like Clutter is to discover an iconography that suits the non-sacramental nature of Protestant spiritual genealogy, while at the same time celebrating it with an aesthetic of spiritual beauty that Protestantism itself often suppresses.

Several other artists in the exhibition also employ the altarpiece form as a way to bridge the distance between personal expression and traditional, community-based imagery. In *The Madonna and Child Enthroned with Angels and Saints*, Rosemary Scott-Fishburn has translated Duccio's monumental *Maestà* altarpiece (1308–11; fig. 11) into an impressive four-by-seven-foot copper relief drawing (entry 34). In Duccio's masterpiece, which was commissioned for the high altar of the Cathedral of Siena, the centrality of the Virgin and Christ Child enthroned is asserted. But also crucial to the composition is the gathering of prophets, saints, and martyrs that surrounds the holy pair — in short, a kind of spiritual genealogy that serves as a host of witnesses to the Incarnation of God in Christ through the person of the Virgin Mary. This trans-historical assembly was made credible by Duccio's innovative composition. The use of low-relief architectural framing sections, gold gilt, and Italianate late-Byzantine-style figuration work together to express an ancient holiness within what was at the time an innovative form of the altarpiece.

Although with Scott-Fishburn we are speaking of another modern appropriation — one suited to the twenty-first century — it is worth dwelling for a moment on the ideas embedded in Duccio's early-fourteenth-century altarpiece. For only with some understanding of those visual ideas can we fully appreciate what is happening in Scott-Fishburn's work. As Hans Belting has pointed out, "It has long been known that Duccio conflated two important traditions of the image for the high altar of Siena cathedral: the Marian panel and the altarpiece as polyptych."[86] The Marian image, of course, has a long history dating back to the earliest icons and, indeed, to the Church's belief that St. Luke himself painted the first and only truly authoritative portrait of Mary during her lifetime. Luke's image is, then, the original and authoritative source for all subsequent portraits of Mary, all of them understood as venerations of the archetype made by Luke. According to Belting, it is this Marian image that Duccio has for the first time successfully integrated within a polyptych. In the *Maestà*, Duccio unites a single Marian image and the Christ Child with a host of witnesses surrounding the pair. The composition includes architectural framing devices in the upper register, which allow Duccio to bring in a lineup of Old Testament prophets, while the cunning use of Mary's throne separates her and the Christ Child from the others, and yet unifies everything within a setting of adoration.

Out of this emerges the visual idea of *memoria*, which is crucial to an understanding of Scott-Fishburn's work. As Belting has observed, although Duccio's *Maestà* "was the first successful application of the full-length Marian panel to a high altar . . . the figure of Mary appears much like a picture within a picture, since the very different structure of the altarpiece did not allow an easy integration of her image."[87] Within this sense of a "picture within a picture," this slight visual slippage, resides the stylistic evidence of how holy images are transmitted down through time. That is, we feel here the memory of the image as something copied (venerated) from one generation to another, always being passed down from an ancient archetypal original. Belting makes clear the deep significance of this by reminding us that what is involved here is *memoria* (memory). *Memoria* is partly about the veracity of the image, because it can be traced all the way back to an archetypal original. But *memoria* is also about the fact that the image is an aid to our memory. It causes the viewer in meditation to recall the original spiritual events, both as portrait (*imago*), which carries the divine *presence* of the holy persons depicted, and as historical narrative (*historia*), which recalls the real events in time and space that make salvation possible.[88]

All of this fullness of meaning within the image was carried forward by Duccio, even as he invented a new form to house it. And all of this is what was embraced by Duccio's community as a living tradition relevant to its liturgical practices in worship. Whether or not one agrees with Protestant theology and liturgy, the point here is that the Reformation sharply truncated the tradition of the image for Protestant believers. And so for an artist working in the context of twenty-first-century Protestant America, and laboring as well under the desacralizing force of modern scientific positivism and the Church's cessation of patronage, what happens to the instinct of veneration through *memoria*? While we should hesitate to pile all of these issues onto Rosemary Scott-Fishburn as part of her conscious intention, it seems that at least instinctively she is continuing the ancient practice of copying (venerating) from the original. Recent developments within Protestantism have made it increasingly clear that there still exists a deep longing for a meditative practice to enrich the usual explanatory exegesis of The Word. Once again, something approaching the sacramental is wanted. But no context outside of "Art" exists for such a practice.

What fascinates about Scott-Fishburn's work is her use of copper (a material with its own iconic traditions) to translate Duccio's painting into a different medium. Copper relief drawing is itself rich in meditative qualities. It is a painstaking process, which the viewer can feel on an almost tactile level. But more subtly, at least for this writer, there is a sense of a kind of mold or shell, rather like a three-dimensional rubbing lifted from a tomb or a gravestone at a pilgrimage site, bearing witness by its very formation to the idea of an earlier original. Though the overt subject of the work is the Madonna and Child Enthroned with Angels and Saints, and the covert content Duccio's great *Maestà,* Scott-Fishburn's artwork is also a kind of postmodern reliquary. The sacred relic that it houses in its copper-clad body is not so much a fragment of a saint's bone as it is a medieval altarpiece that was once a living presence within the Eucharist. Thus, Scott-Fishburn's copper relief drawings, beautiful in and of themselves, are deepened—given their own *memoria* and *historia*—by way of their medium. The real poignancy here it that her work is offered up in the context of "Art" because there is no contemporary context of a worshipping community to receive it as witness.

This kind of "altarpiece"—highly personal, and yet also grounded in the orthodox traditions of Christian spirituality (one, so to speak, in search of a congregation beyond that of the aestheticians of the art world)—is also explored by other artists in the exhibition. The painter Bruce Herman, for example, uses a diptych altarpiece to celebrate the Incarnation through the theme of the Annunciation (entry 35). His large *Annunciation* belongs to a series of works that he calls *Elegy for Witness*. The work bears a spiritual energy and intensity suited to the theme of God breaking silence and entering human experience, but it has not been conceived in a sweet, decorative, or idealized classical mode. Instead, Herman prefers the notion of what he calls "broken beauty." Hence, his Virgin is painted in a fashion that partly references the classical tradition. That is, she is a nude whose powerful dignity comes from her three-dimensional presence. And yet, she is also a fragment, with one arm broken off, suggesting that the classical, rational conception of beauty does not redeem.

There is, in fact, a somberness to this Virgin that speaks of other visual influences on Herman's notion of "broken beauty." Partly, he has been influenced by the more somber, sculptural, and slightly stiff figurative styles of Giotto and Piero della Francesca. But he also looks to the more gritty and existentialist figures of Leon Golub, Francis Bacon, and his own former teacher, Philip Guston. These artists mediate "beauty" with raw experience and intensity. Herman has little interest in a beauty or a transcendence that is not felt through pain, tragedy, or grief. His art is a visual calling for a transcendence of grit that acknowledges what is shattered and bruised. Herman's *Annunciation* is not solely an embrace of the flesh by God; it is also an elegy, a visual "poem" expressing sorrow and lamentation.

Using the diptych format, Herman juxtaposes the Virgin (in the right panel) against a panel that is essentially an abstract, geometric painting. In his diptych (like Erica Grimm-Vance's diptych), the human side is more naturalistic and figural, while the divine side is abstract and ineffable. Herman's geometric grid (the left panel) flashes with gold and silver leaf, luminous blues, deep terracotta orange-reds, and blacks. Although eschewing any gentle or decorative sense of beauty, Herman does acknowledge Fra Angelico as an influence. That reference illuminates Herman's visual strategy. For what he likes in Fra Angelico is that painter's surprising mixture of naturalism and highly abstract forms. As Georges Didi-Huberman argues powerfully in his *Fra Angelico: Dissemblance & Figuration*, a deep reality is conveyed through the surprisingly radical juxtaposition of figuration and abstraction (or dissemblance) in Fra Angelico's works.[89] This point has been reinforced more recently by Stephen James Newton in his *Painting, Psychoanalysis, and Spirituality*.[90] Both authors examine the kinds of radically, almost ecstatically abstract passages that one sees in such works as the *Annunciation* of ca.1440 (fig. 12). Here, the swirling and brilliantly colored inset marble panels in the wall behind the Annunciate Angel and the Virgin, as well as the patterns in the floor, are wildly ecstatic. These colorful abstractions are juxtaposed with the naturalistic figures, calmly gesturing in their traditional iconographic poses. As such, they provide a more spiritual "ground" against which the otherworldly being of an angel can convincingly enter the natural world of Mary.

Herman's contrasting panels beautifully employ the idea that such different manners of handling paint, image, and form can be the best means of evoking the encounter between the spiritual and the flesh. But he increases the complexity of his abstract passages by condensing fragments taken from a range of architectural sources, iconic surfaces, and abstract art into what he calls the "pentimenti of the Christian tradition."[91] Herman sees this as a kind of reference to the many martyrs throughout history who bore witness to faith, giving their lives in love out of their belief in the Incarnation that is the theme of his painting. If the altarpiece as "sacred structure" subliminally carries forward a rich theological, spiritual, and hagiographic history merely within the idea of its form, then Herman engorges the spaces *within* it, dramatically and sumptuously celebrating the form.

Herman seems especially sensitive to the dynamics of image and word here, as he calls his series *Elegy for Witness*. An elegy is a song or poem expressing sorrow and lamentation for the dead, and it is also a specific poetic form. Technically, an elegy is written in couplets consisting of two dactylic hexameter lines. But while it may be too literal-minded to look for specific visual structures imitating the feet and rhythm of such couplets, there is certainly a cluster of pairings, of dialogues, in Herman's diptych — the Annunciation as the meeting of heaven and earth, spirit and flesh; martyrdom as both life and death; and the now-living honoring those of the past. These pairings beautifully suit the two-part structure of the altarpiece.

The artist in the exhibition who manipulates the altarpiece form most radically is Robert P. Eustace. He describes his mixed-media works as "altarpiece constructions."[92] Eustace says that in addition to the altarpiece form, he is inspired by several important medieval formats, including the illuminated manuscript and the icon. To this list must be added medieval reliquaries, ornate containers designed for housing precious *mementos*, relics of the saints and martyrs.

His mixed-media altarpiece construction *Image: Seed of Divine Life* daringly takes on the theme of the Annunciation by morphing the ornate framework of the altarpiece into a biomorphic form suggesting a cross-section of a womb and birth canal (entry 36). Like the bejeweled case of a reliquary, the work's shape echoes an actual physical relic of the Virgin. It houses the Annunciation at the moment of conception, the seed of life swirling within the Virgin's womb, when the deity becomes *Imago Dei* as the Son of Man.

Like a medieval alchemist, Eustace beautifully, and yet graphically, mediates between spirit and flesh. The eddying contours of his piece are adorned with metals and the heads of nails, recalling the ornate covers of medieval manuscripts replete with filigree, silver, gold, and gems. Yet these contours are also the folds of a womb's interior, rich with the blood-engorged lining of ripe fertility. Swarming within the borders is a field of blue-green and yellow movement, like fluids and sperm, surrounding a fully human image (transported from Italian Renaissance painting) of the Virgin holding the Christ Child in an aureole of divine light with two angels above. As an evocation of divine spirit and light incarnating itself into human flesh and blood, Eustace's work is quite extraordinary, daring, and devout.

FIGURE 13
Margaritone d'Arezzo
Madonna and Child Enthroned, ca. 1270
Tempera on panel

If it were not for the sumptuous beauty of Eustace's piece, the viewer might well find it distasteful because of its direct implications of uterus, birth canal, and body fluids. Yet in a remarkable way, Eustace manages to draw quite close to the corporeal reality of the Christian Incarnation, only to direct the eye toward the spiritual through the near-Byzantine quality of his colors and ornate materials. This pressing of the relationship between spirit and body is part of his understanding of the "*mysterium tremendum*, or a visual approximation of the experience of awe, divine mystery, and terrible beauty." Fittingly, Eustace calls the series to which *Image: Seed of Divine Life* belongs *Aenigmate*. This Latinate word for a series of works embodying "enigma" nicely houses the sensations that the viewer experiences through his art.

While Eustace's art is strikingly unique, it is not without a grounding in the traditions of Christian theology and art. As Patricia Leighten has explored in her essay on Leonardo's *Burlington House Cartoon*, there was an important Byzantine, medieval, and Renaissance iconography that emphasized the actual pregnancy of the Madonna, which was known as the *platytera* tradition.[93] To combat the Gnostic heresy, which taught that Christ "only appeared as a man, but had not taken a real human body," the early church emphasized the bodily motherhood of Mary. Ignatius, Bishop of Antioch, declared around 100 AD that he believed in "Jesus Christ . . . who was 'out of' Mary, who was truly born."[94] In the Byzantine tradition, as Leighten puts it, "the fact that Christ issued from Mary's womb was sometimes portrayed by showing Mary standing in an *orans* position while Christ floats in a mandorla or disc in front of her body."[95] The *platytera* motif is also related to the iconography of the *Theotokos*, or Mary as the earthly Mother of God. In medieval art, Mary sometimes holds the Christ Child on her lap, or even lower, with her thighs slightly parted and her drapery arranged so that the hem or folds tactfully imply a womb shape surrounding him. A tastefully restrained example is Margaritone d'Arezzo's *Madonna and Child Enthroned* (ca. 1270; fig. 13). Whether Eustace has been directly inspired by the medieval *platytera*, or has just intuitively discovered a contemporary way to evoke it through his own visual explorations of the mystery of the Incarnation, his work provides another example of the deep continuities that observance of the biblical text can inspire.

James Larson is another artist who explores the altarpiece form. His *Stations of the Cross* comprises fourteen small paintings devoted to the Stations (entry 37). The sequence of images is well suited to the altarpiece form, while each individual painting can serve the liturgical practice of observing a specific Station during the Lenten season. Larson's work echoes both formats. Referencing the architectural framing device of the church window, Larson has painted each scene within a pointed arch so that it reads like a scene viewed through a portal or the arch of a window. The small size of the panels (eight by six inches) pulls the viewer in close for intimate contemplation. What he or she finds, however, is not the typical preciousness of the miniature. The figures and the spaces around them seem, in fact, monumental in scale and shocking in sensibility. Previously, Larson has created works inspired by the stories of Flannery O'Connor; in *Stations of the Cross*, O'Connor's sense of the grotesque as the best vehicle for revealing grace seems to be at work. Larson avoids the characteristic iconography of the Stations, offering instead "a narrative a little less predictable than those that might be suggested by some of the worn old stories from Sunday school."[96]

The results can be shocking. In Station I, for example, a somewhat scrawny Christ, with a large head and prominent facial features, stands passively against a background of water, wearing only the robe that his tormentors placed upon him in mockery. This is the *ecco homo*, "Behold the Man," when Christ is condemned to death. His robe is opened in the front to reveal his humanity, which must be gendered to be human. More importantly, his nakedness is his vulnerability. On his head he wears the "crown" of a jester's hat because here he plays the role of the Fool. It was Saint Paul who declared that Christians must be willing to be fools for Christ; but as with every Pauline theme, this is premised on our imitation of Christ, who first taught us that God's wisdom involves giving up our power, wealth, and status. It is the very foolishness of Christianity to believe that in Christ God gave up these very things out of love, for if history proves anything it is that such weakness in love never triumphs in the world. As Larson explains, "It is a story about God giving up power and I am interested in what that looks like."

In all of the Stations, the figures are grotesque and oddly distorted, and yet in their volumetric weightiness they maintain a heroic, monumentalized dignity. In each case, they play out the Passion against a backdrop that is either a watery realm or a radically stark and dry landscape. The settings are minimal enough to seem universal, and yet some are uncannily familiar, such as that of Station III, which seems to be a beach scene. Larson sees water as a symbol for the source of life, but also as an ominous force of chaos and destruction, with overtones of both the Creation and Noah's Flood. And water as symbol recalls the story of Jonah, who, as the scapegoat representing rebellion against God, was sacrificed by being thrown overboard during a storm at sea. His three days in the belly of the whale signified, according to Jesus's teaching, what the Messiah would experience during his three days in Hades after the Passion.

In *Stations of the Cross*, Larson reminds us "of the bizarreness of the story and how it connects with basic human experience. A god/man who meets his mother implies such vulnerability [IV]. He is, after all, a child. A woman from a very different cultural context wipes his face with her covering veil [VI]; it is both scandalous and vulnerable. This god falls down three times [III, VII, IX]. And he dies [XII]." In Larson's paintings, the flesh, fragility, organic eroticism, violence, and horror of the story are brought home. Although working on a miniature scale, Larson echoes Edward Knippers's giant scale in his ambition to make us see the Bible again as something visceral, fleshy, real, and glorious in its very absurdity.

The small size of Larson's panels was dictated by a commission of sorts. And in this, among the works we have examined so far which explore the idea of "altarpiece," Larson's *Stations of the Cross* is unique. In his case, the *Stations* were actually created out of a church that has revived a unique form of patronage and liturgical community through imagery. That church is the House of Mercy in Saint Paul, Minnesota. Lead by three innovative pastors, the Reverends Debbie Blue, Russell Rathbun, and Mark Stenberg, the House of Mercy numbers many working artists among its congregation. Each year, a selection of artists is invited to create artworks devoted to the Stations of the Cross, and during the Lenten season they are installed around the sanctuary between the stained glass windows. On the appointed Sunday, the congregation proceeds around the Stations, pausing by each work for the liturgical reading and prayers befitting it. For the Lenten season of 2004, the House of Mercy provided fourteen artists with fourteen eight-by-six inch canvases, the idea being that each artist would paint all fourteen Stations. These were then installed in groupings of the fourteen Stations, with one of Larson's paintings at the center of each configuration. The artists involved in the project ranged from a seven-year-old girl to several MFA-trained painters, as well as several self-taught artists. Styles ranged from minimalist abstraction to expressionistic figurative narratives, and from expressive abstraction to Larson's own exotic naturalism. Nevertheless, a rare unity of artists, patronage, sensibilities, worshipping community, and liturgical practice was re-invented (figure 14).

FIGURE 14
**Station X: Jesus is Stripped of His Garments, 2004
House of Mercy Church, St. Paul, Minnesota
Artists: Kjellgren Alkire, Maria Bianchi, Jane Cameron, Maria DiMeglio,**

      Los Angeles-based Lynn Aldrich is another artist who fits well within the context of this discussion. Her work has varied widely throughout her career, but the piece chosen for *The Next Generation* connects with our discussion of both "altarpiece" as idea and "Bible" as idea. Aldrich works exclusively with objects and materials that already exist in the world as something other than "Art." This is her artistic beginning point, a premise based on what she sees as the "incarnational possibilities" of the world's mundane objects.[97] Aldrich always seems to find a subtle point of resonance between the mind's recognition of an object's role in the world and the imagination's discovery of how that object's formal properties, once inflected by the artist, point to something transcendent. Her *Baptistery*, for example, consists of 128 pages of swimming pool designs assembled onto the wall in a grid (entry 38). Aldrich covered each page with gold leaf, leaving untouched only the blue shapes of the pools, which now read like moments of abstract blue form scattered almost randomly across a golden tiled wall. *Baptistery* does not so much reference the altarpiece form as it does the mosaic-work in Byzantine ecclesiastical architecture. Though she is not referencing any specific sacred architectural space, the sixth-century mosaics in the Baptistery of the Arians in Ravenna come readily to mind. *The Baptism of Christ*, for example, its gold ground playing against the blue water, resonates uncannily with Aldrich's work (fig. 15).

Lisa Erickson, Michelle Haunsperberg, Emily Hoisington, James Larson, Cherith Lidfords-Lundin, Sonja Olson, Mike Rathbun, Jon Reischl, Jeremy Szopinski, Dawn Wenck.

      Byzantine mosaics lifted the stories and holiness of the Bible out of the book and onto the wall, creating a kind of "visual Bible." Aldrich's mural-sized "mosaic" similarly transforms pages collected from glossy coffee table books, taking them from the mundane world of suburban California by dematerializing them on the wall, and thereby evoking the sacred space of a Baptistery. In Aldrich's words, "I have attempted to re-present a 'text' describing . . . an architecture for the sacrament of Baptism."

FIGURE 15
The Baptism of Christ,
6th century
Mosaic
**Baptistery of the Arians,
Ravenna, Italy**

Although radically different from the paintings exploring divine Presence within the domestic interior that we began with, Aldrich's *Baptistery* in fact comes nicely full circle in the way that the artist has poetically transformed domestic images of people swimming recreationally in their backyards into a shimmering "icon" of people immersed in the baptismal waters of rebirth. What makes the piece so successful is the way that it causes the eye and mind to shift constantly between what is ordinary and what is spiritual. This happens partly because of the way the patterning operates, and partly because of the way the blue shapes read simultaneously as recognizable objects and as abstract forms—the familiar becomes uncanny, but not utterly foreign.

In terms of the patterning, the eye and mind naturally try to make sense out of the arrangement of the blue forms. The eye seeks a pattern, a repeating order. As when looking at the constellation of stars in the night sky, there is a feeling of a spontaneous and random scattering of points across the larger field, and yet there is also a feeling of a rhythm created. Caught between a sense of accidental chaos and a sense of ordered arrangement, the eye and mind become engaged in trying to understanding the visual field. But there is no discernable pattern beyond a sense of overall distribution of highly varied shapes. Coherence is achieved because a limited number of geometric shapes are referenced, but there is also a seemingly infinite number of variations upon those shapes, scattered into dozens of permutations of placement. In addition, the shapes play with the mind's perception, since some of the pools read more easily as planes receding in perspective while others read as purely flat. This causes the spatial sense of the work to move back and forth between flatness and depth, between pure abstraction (otherworldliness) and the natural spaces of known objects. The fluctuating blue forms dance within the equally fluctuating field of gold, because each page is slightly different in intensity and the subtle curvature of the pages causes the light to reflect at different angles (much like Byzantine mosaics, whose individual tesserae are set into the mortar at varying angles). All of this keeps the eye extremely active.

Although modern Christianity's amputation of image and meditation from the practice of communion and worship brings a sense of loss, perhaps there is also an offsetting gain. For once turned loose from the restrictions of patronage and liturgy, contemporary artists who are interested in faith have found remarkable ways of gathering up the components of traditional practices and weaving them together into new forms. Donald J. Forsythe, for example, gathers up many ingredients from past practices into an extended series of "contemporary manuscript paintings" that he began in 1988, including *Turf Painting/ Ireland* (entry 39). He draws from the idea of "Book" on three levels in the series, referencing illuminated manuscripts, pages from the Bible, and pages from hymnals. The grounds of the works begin with pages cut out of one or more of these books, and the pages are then glued down on a surface. Over these Forsythe adds layers of paint and imagery.

The Book, however, is not Forsythe's only reference. For by taking the format of a book, with its twin pages divided by the binder's gutter, and placing the pages on the wall, Forsythe creates a diptych, thereby linking book to altarpiece. Furthermore, inspired as much by Giotto's great fresco paintings of the Bible's narratives as by illuminated manuscripts, Forsythe covers the ground of his collaged pages with both paint and plaster. In this, he conflates book and altarpiece with the frescoed murals of church walls.

At the same time, Forsythe sees another dimension of meaning inherent in the structural format of the diptych as altarpiece-cum-book. Namely, he sees in the bipartite format a mirror of fundamental human tensions. That is, although the twin images suggest a whole, they also suggest a division. Within the diptych format, Forsythe often contrasts subjects that play against each other in conflict. Thus, works in the series bear titles like *Plenty/Want*. Forsythe is interested in "the viewer's need to compare or contrast the ideas on either side of the overall composition."[98]

Here, Forsythe touches upon foundational matters. All human knowing depends upon a process of comparing and contrasting. We discover the distinctions between things this way, and thereby establish identity. The polarities of I/Thou, subject/object, nature/spirit, mind/body — all of these we know to be artificial schisms. And yet, without setting up such polarities to compare and contrast, we could not establish knowing. And these binary constructions echo deeper, human moral conditions. Forsythe's *Plenty/Want* exemplifies such moral pairings. Morally and psychologically we humans are, as it were, diptychs, torn constantly between vice/virtue, justice/mercy, law/grace, taking/giving. These are the tensions that Forsythe's "overall composition" acknowledges and seeks to balance.

Forsythe does not treat these matters only within abstract generalizations. His work in the exhibition links these broad conceptions to the specificities of human history and politics. In *Turf Painting/Ireland*, the left panel is a rich, loamy darkness. Its color, material, and name (Turf) derive literally from the earth of Ireland. As Forsythe points out in his artist statement, "Turf is an important material in rural Ireland. It is a five-thousand-year accumulation of compacted vegetable material, which is excavated, dried, and burnt as fuel for heat. It is literally 'the stuff of life' in that part of the world. I mixed the turf with acrylic medium to make a crude paint." In *Turf Painting/Ireland*, Forsythe pits real Irish turf on the left against a map of Ireland on the right. Here, "turf" takes on other meanings, those of territory, nationalism, ownership, politics, and possession. Against the left-side turf, seen up close, as if the viewer belonged to the actual earth, stands the right-side "turf," seen from above, as if in a map or an aerial view. Now the human lines of power, ownership, politics, religion, and economics have been drawn. The map of Ireland is demarcated along the lines of human schism, the lines dividing vice/virtue, law/grace, and war/peace. The schisms are both underwritten and lamented in the pages of the books on which the painting is grounded. And so, too, are they referenced in the imagery of the altarpieces from which Forsythe draws his inspiration.

Like Lynn Aldrich and Donald J. Forsythe, Christine A. Forsythe also explores the rich fluidity connecting book, word, illuminated manuscript, image, icon, altarpiece, mosaic, and ecclesiastical architecture. In her case, the artwork is literally a book. In Forsythe's *Lenten Book: Book of Forty Number Three*, pages of abstract patterns evoke deeper spiritual structures (entry 40). One opens a book expecting to find patterns of words that convey some kind of narrative or meaning. In *Lenten Book*, however, the viewer finds a series — or better — a "liturgy" of grids composed of five squares up by eight squares across, creating blocks of forty squares each. The columns of squares are reminiscent enough of columns of characters to imply a text that is, after all, well known to the viewer. However, in lieu of actual text, we find instead a variety of grids expressing, not so much linguistic terms, but rather a more meditative content of form, pattern, and color.

If we mostly associate language with naming, describing, and the telling of narratives, we associate form and geometry with a deeper, underlying structure and order. Strings of words and sentences propel the mind forward in a chronological telling of content, but patterns of geometric shapes suspend the mind's forward motion; stepping outside of a chronological unfolding, they hold the eye more in Being. Thus, with only a whisper of language's nominal activity implied here, the viewer is invited to contemplate something closer to a structure of forms held in suspension. Yet, this is a book, and there is a sort of progression, or change, that unfolds as the pages are turned. Given its Lenten orientation, a viewer of the work is conscious of a set of forms related to the season, and the meanings associated with that season. The eye may linger on each page, but it is equally allowed to look at the whole together.

This creates an interesting visual equivalent of meditation. Like the forty days of the season of Lent, the pages of *Lenten Book* ask for a pattern of repeated meditations on the same basic idea, but in variations that convey richness and depth. Forty is an important symbolic number in the Bible. As Forsythe points out, it is often associated with a substantial passage of time during which a penitent person experiences a spiritual or character lesson.[99] Moses spent forty years in the desert, where he learned that anger and murder are not the right means for liberating his fellow Jews from oppression. Jesus spent forty days fasting in the wilderness, where he resisted the temptation to believe that material sustenance, political power, or elite status would enable him to liberate humans from sin and death. And for the church, the forty days of Advent and the forty days of Lent are times of sustained remembrance, abstinence, and meditation; these are times for acknowledging the deeper spiritual structures or forms of being that exist within the normal chronological flow of life that language describes.

Forsythe says that she associates her Lenten books with the idea of penitence, or seasons of penitence, which the number forty reflects in sacred history. She gives the viewer a different grid for each meditation. One page might feel more brooding, with a very pronounced grid in which each square, filled in with black and indigo, feels "closed." On another page the same grid now feels "open," its squares made simply of stitched lines on the white page, the threads trailing off freely at the ends of each axis.

In addition, the materials used for *Lenten Book* convey related meanings. Most poignantly, the covers of the book are made with bark cloth. This is the same material that is used in Uganda to wrap the dead. Forsythe became aware of the material through a student who had visited Uganda during the period of political purge and mass slaughter, and who saw thousands of the dead wrapped in bark cloth. Thus, the cover of Forsythe's *Lenten Book* becomes an equivalent of the death that is contained in all human meditations, but it also echoes the shroud that wrapped Christ in death. It is through faith that Christian believers identify with Christ, and it is through meditation that they make faith their own internalized reality. In this way, Forsythe's meditative piece becomes a "place," a "text" through which one's being comprehends redemption.

As we have seen, the idea of turning the book into an object fits with the complex meanings associated with "The Book," the Bible. Since the Bible is grasped within Western culture as both a series of narrative/symbolic texts and a sacred object, and since its theology involves a rich fluidity between Word as inspired language, Word as Book, and Word as the second person of the Trinity, then the Bible as a sacred object — housing all of this as if it were its own reliquary — becomes a highly appealing form to the visual artist.

Sandra Bowden has created a significant body of work using these possibilities. Her *Book of Nails* is a good case in point (entry 41). It is both Book and container. In its open position it recalls an altarpiece, but also a reliquary holding mementos of a martyr's death. In this case, it is both the Word (Bible) and the Word (Christ Crucified). The textured cover, as well as the linear quality of the nails in the interior, implicitly evoke the qualities of text and typography, but now the lines are incarnated into physical objects from the narrative of Christ's Passion. Bowden's ability to navigate between book, symbolic object, and narrative makes *Book of Nails* an intense occasion for contemplation.

Having followed art about faith as they relate to both the biblical text and the history of art this far, it seems fitting to end with several works whose themes, like the Bible's own narrative, refer to "Last Things." It is impossible to fully gauge the shaping power of the idea of "Last Things" or "End Times" in the history of the Western mind. The notion — operating as both conscious subject matter and deep imaginative structure — that human existence is best grasped through the paradigm of narrative has been one of the central means by which we have "thought" ourselves. The very shape of narrative structure (with its beginning, development, moral choices, overcoming of evil, and concluding resolutions, followed by some form of coda allowing characters to continue their existence in an after-world in which conflict does not exist) has been a primal frame of reference. It inhabits our foundational shaping stories and treatises, from Homer's *Odyssey* to the Bible's book of Revelation, and from Plato's *Republic* and Saint Augustine's *City of God* to John Winthrop's "City upon a Hill" and Tolkien's *Lord of the Rings*. The structure of the heroic narrative and the dream of achieving the utopian city have permeated our mental fabric.

There have been, of course, notable postmodernist attempts to deconstruct any notion of meta-narrative. For example, Roland Barthes argues that, for us, Odysseus's ship, the *Argo*, cannot really be conceived of as "journey" and "arrival" in any metaphysical sense. And so he replaces the narrative paradigm of "journey" with an image of the *Argo* as a metaphor of structure, which the Argonauts (humanity) maintain, replacing plank after plank throughout time. The art critic and historian Rosalind Krauss adopts Barthes's Argo model to argue against the idea that art can be "profound," that is, that it can reflect spiritual depths that are real and connected to something transcendent.[100] These thinkers, operating from a consistently materialist viewpoint, seek to dissolve the narrative energy that is driven by the concept of a transcendent purpose or direction. They are the theoretical counterparts to Freud's claim that we cannot truly imagine our own deaths. And it might well also be the case that we cannot truly imagine the history of our own cultures transpiring as meaningless surface, with zero transcendent depth of purpose or direction.

In contrast, any sensibility based on faith involves some conviction of transcendent purpose and some form of accountability or measurement, followed by "judgment," whether as punishment or ecstatic consummation. It is not surprising then that several artists here would investigate these themes. What is a bit surprising is the diversity of attitudes with which they explore them. Perhaps the most traditional approach is that of sculptor Aaron Lee Benson. In his monumental clay sculpture *Two Witnesses*, he employs imagery taken directly from the book of Revelation, drawing his theme and figural elements from its eleventh chapter (entry 42). The setting is visionary. In the previous chapters, the Seven Seals have been opened, unleashing war, economic chaos, sword, famine, pestilence, natural disasters, wanton murder, and violence upon the earth. In the tenth chapter, a kind of brief hiatus occurs, as an angel approaches Saint John, who is witness to all of this. John, the book's author, is given a small scroll from the hand of an angel. As in Ezekiel, we see the motif of the eating of the book. A voice from heaven instructs John, "Take it and eat; it will be bitter to your stomach, but sweet as honey in your mouth." The reader cannot help but wonder about the insight revealed in this command. For there is, surely, a sweet pleasure to be had in receiving a clarifying understanding of the world's terrible confusion, as well as in being the one chosen to pronounce the terrible news. But then, once that rush of power passes, the psyche digests the terrible reality and is nauseated.

What John eats and is told to prophesy is "about many peoples and nations and tongues and kings." He is told to "Rise and measure the temple of God and the altar and those who worship there." These are the things that have remained full of integrity amidst the world's violent corruption. But he is told not to measure the court outside, for this is where the nations will trample everything. Against this violent desecration, God places two witnesses, the witnesses of Benson's sculpture. These unnamed figures will prophesy in sackcloth, signifying the possibility of repentance and therefore redemption, for, John is told, "one thousand two hundred and sixty days." When they have finished, "the beast that ascends from the bottomless pit will make war upon them and conquer them and kill them, and their dead bodies will lie in the street of the great city which is allegorically called Sodom and Egypt, where their Lord was crucified." With macabre detail, John's text explains that "those who dwell on the earth" delight over the dead bodies for "three days and a half," refusing "to let them be placed in a tomb."[101] But then the two are raised up by God and taken into heaven, and this is followed by a violent judgment on those who had rejoiced over the dead bodies.

Benson, following the lead of biblical commentators, sees this episode as the "last opening to God's grace and mercy" offered to the corrupt inhabitants that trample the earth. He sees the great arch of his sculpture as a metaphor for "a portal or window unto salvation for one of the last times."[102] The structure is crude, and it reads like an ancient ruin or a Tolkienian vault at a heroic site, such as the ancient Jerusalem described in Revelation. The figures of the Two Witnesses are placed, almost like architectural sculptures, on one leg of the arch. They stand in the act of prophesying, but also like lifeless fragments embedded in a courtyard wall. The arch itself changes color from a natural red-brown earth tone to a blackish blue-green. For Benson, the color change signifies the battle between good and evil. Although no such arch is described in chapter eleven of Revelation, the book's highly pictorial language is saturated with images of figures, violence, and visions, all set within the architecture of the ancient city.

In stark contrast to Benson's high drama is Peter Sheesley's *Four Laws: I, II, III, IV,* four small paintings that are intimate in scale (entry 43). They do not involve large historical movements or a powerful epic narrative. It may seem odd to discuss them in the context of Last Things, but in the end, they are indeed concerned with the ultimate confrontation between God and humans. But rather than engaging with the monumental sweep of history, Sheesley engages with individual humans on a private scale. In these works, four beautifully painted hands—strong but not intimidating—make gestures toward the viewer. The hands emerge out of an inky black darkness with only fingers and wrist visible. Because the forearm seems to have been absorbed into the darkness, the viewer reads it as a deep space that cannot be penetrated by the eye. Thus, the hands float and gesture within a kind of mysterious space.

It is enigmatic whose hands these are. One thinks of the Early Christian and Byzantine prohibition against portraying God the Father, and of the artistic device of symbolically indicating God's actions (without breaking the second commandment) through the image of a stylized hand of God poking through the firmament. If these are, then, God's hands, Sheesley has complicated the issue theologically by painting them with a convincing naturalism, thus linking the abstraction required when portraying God the Father with the naturalness of flesh within the world. But a consultation with Sheesley's artist statement will reveal a different reading of the hands. In it, the artist explains that the hands and the four laws of the title were inspired by an evangelistic tract used by Campus Crusade, *The Four Spiritual Laws*.[103] In the tract, which was authored by Bill Bright, the core initiating beliefs of Christianity are simplified into what Bright calls the "Four Spiritual Laws." Despite the fact that many thoughtful Christians might flinch at such reductionism, throughout its history Christianity (not to mention the Gospels and Epistles themselves) has confronted every human being with the naked facts of life, pride, death, and love. Indeed, there is an interesting point at which, for the sake of showing how radically important moral and spiritual choices are, the subtleties of aesthetics must diminish, lest they soften the force of the confrontation.

Thus, while Benson's work operates on an apocalyptic scale, Sheesley's is intensely personal. Benson addresses the culmination of history, Sheesley the fine point of each individual's interior life. But what they share is that both of their works address ultimate things. There is something else they share. Namely, both artists seem to be utterly in earnest. No irony shades or tempers their visual claims. No doubt appears to haunt their convictions. For many persons of faith, these are qualities that recommend their art. But for many others, including persons of faith as well as those who doubt faith, this earnestness is problematic. It should be pointed out here that thus far, irony and doubt have hardly been noticeable themes in *The Next Generation*. But with the theme of Last Judgments, there may be wisdom in acknowledging irony. From the standpoint of biblical faith, the question is not whether one's life has any ultimate significance or whether one is finally accountable. These are givens. Rather, the question is whether embracing these as givens means that we actually know much about the reality of Last Things. Historically, there has been an astonishing amount of foolishness and presumption committed by Christians claiming hard knowledge of apocalyptic events. But one can believe that our internal and external choices lead either to some ultimate joyous consumption or to tragic loss without having to believe in surrealistic scenarios.

Instead, complexity, mystery, and ambiguity in relation to Last Things, coupled with humility, may be more in order. In this regard, Guy Chase, the final artist under consideration here, brings a significant voice to the matter. Chase's *(Untitled): Ledger for Multiple Adjustments* is also concerned with accountability and bottom lines, but his work operates within a kind of irony that is in search of a deeper wisdom (entry 44). A first look at the painting reveals a work of highly precise, nearly *trompe l'oeil* realism.

Chase has painstakingly painted the page of an accountant's ledger book, even to the point of reproducing every single brown and dark green numeral and line. The squares within the grid of lines are painted more thickly in pale green, so that the viewer's eyes senses texture, and therefore recognizes the work as a handmade, albeit extremely precise, object. The precision of this way of painting recalls the ideal of complete precision in the practice of accounting. Furthermore, the obsessive nature of making such a precise object invokes the kind of meditative discipline that echoes with the idea of complete accuracy in one's own accounts and methods.

And yet a closer examination of Chase's painting reveals strange discrepancies. The columns are not even, and there are unexplained "breakout" boxes inserted into them, which would, in fact, disrupt any clear recording of information or numbers. Furthermore, if one follows the numbering of the columns from left to right, the first four proceed as expected, but then several columns of varying widths interrupt the sequence, until one gets to the far right of the page, at which point column numbers five through seven once again proceed as normal. Despite the rational appearance of the ledger sheet, then, it is clear that if it is to be useful in accounting, it must be in some other, more erratic, or even unknown system that the accounts will be tabulated.

How Chase became interested in ledger pages is worth knowing. His wife is an accountant and so such materials are obviously present in his life. But clearly, the metaphor of accounting is also referenced frequently in the Bible. The image, for example, of the saved having their names written in the Book of Life, while the names of the damned are erased, is a powerful one.[104] However, something more specific and immediate inspired Chase's pursuit of the metaphor. In recent years, and all across the country, there has been an intense emphasis on employee productivity initiatives, including at the college where Chase teaches. The idea that all things of value — especially in the fields of art and teaching — can be quantified by placing numbers in the correct columns and adding them up struck Chase as not only misguided but misleading, for meaningful work is only partly measurable through quantification. In addition, Chase soon observed that some people knew cleverer ways of entering the numbers than others, so that the mission of uniformly evaluating the effectiveness of an institution through spreadsheets began to seem dubious.

It was also at this time that corporate accounting scandals, like the Enron debacle, were in the news. Once again, it became obvious just how deceptive the quantification of numbers on a ledger sheet can be. Indeed, as Chase puts it, "The idea of making numbers say whatever you want them to say allowed even bogus things to pass, and the culture then has this pseudo-science of quantification with which to justify things that do not really add up."[105] These issues were driven home for Chase because he happened to be in Charlotte, North Carolina on an artist's residency when the Enron scandal broke. Charlotte is a major banking center, and in fact the grant supporting Chase during his residency was tied to the banking industry.

What Chase concluded was that the *reality* behind the numbers, which determines the numbers, does not fit in the ledger columns. What is needed are extra notes in the margins. Or better yet, extra columns and breakout boxes distributed here and there, so that explanations of what the numbers mean can be added in. Such "multiple adjustments," of course, would create an accounting and auditing nightmare, and yet only with them is the truth knowable.

For Chase, it was an easy stretch from these issues to the metaphor of the Book of Life in the Bible. In fact, Chase's first ledger paintings were slightly distorted, so that the pages took on the form of a triptych altarpiece. The question now becomes, if tracking money — a relatively objective procedure — becomes radically subjective given human motives and qualifications, what about tracking the human heart? What does the ledger account for that operation look like? Is God a rigid accountant, or does he allow multiple adjustments in the margins? Is it all strictly the law, or does grace mediate the hard numbers? Or indeed, is our notion of how God keeps records even relevant?

It is interesting to trace the use of the image of "accounting" in the biblical text. One of its first uses is in Job. There, however, it is quite startling, because Job uses it to try to call God to account. Job knows that his suffering is not the direct result of his sins. But when he complains to God, literally asking God for an account, his highly pious friends take him to task for hubris. The speech of Elihu is particularly poignant. Elihu begins by actually declaring his own uprightness before God, as a validation of his right to criticize Job. He then blames Job for daring to say, "I am clean, without transgression; I am pure, and there is no iniquity in me. Behold, he [God] finds occasions against me, he counts me as his enemy." To this, Elihu responds, "Why do you contend against him, saying, 'He will answer none of my words'?"[106]

Elihu's speech actually seems to be quite full of wisdom. And certainly, his warning to Job that God does not need to give account to humans is theologically sound. And more so, the likelihood that God is wrong and Job right seems even more unlikely than a banking error being in the customer's favor. The full text of the speech establishes it as wise and theologically solid from a human point of view. At least it would be if Elihu were speaking to a man whose sufferings really were the result of his sin. But concerning Job, Elihu is simply wrong. Elihu does not know the larger picture, and so his pious words actually wound Job, falsify the truth, and anger God.

The point is that the depths of a person's heart and motives, the complete reality of his or her inner life, as well as the larger reality of the spiritual world, are complex and mysterious. To account for them, or to judge them, calls for caution, if not outright uncertainty. And with surprising frequency in subsequent Bible passages, images of "taking account" can prove to be problematic for temperaments favoring neat ledger books of judgment based on quantification. In Matthew 12:36, Jesus speaks to no less than the religious leaders of his culture. Having found them hypocritical, even though they carefully observe the laws (keeping good account), he warns them against speaking falsely: "I tell you, on the day of judgment men will render account for every careless word they utter." Here, too, at first appearance it seems that God uses a direct accounting column when passing judgment. But these religious leaders, while highly observant of religious practices, are in fact hard-hearted and are merely self-righteous. So, what initially looks correct from a religious standpoint turns out to be false from a spiritual standpoint. Such ironies are not lost on Chase.

It is not that no final accounting is required, and certainly no one can afford to be smug. It is just that the divine calculus may not jibe with human figuring or social appearances. Thus, Chase's wonderfully ironic treatment of the ledger (the Book of Life) warns us against a theology of Last Things that is too neat and orderly. One must always consider the frequent biblical ironies regarding spiritual economy. For example, Jesus says, "Not every one who says to me, 'Lord, Lord,' shall enter the kingdom of heaven" (Matthew 7:21); "If anyone would be first, he must be last of all and servant of all" (Mark 9:35);

"Whoever would save his life will lose it, and whoever loses his life for my sake will find it" (Matthew 16:25); "But many that are first will be last, and the last first," (Matthew 19:30); "Blessed are you that weep now, for you shall laugh" (Luke 6:21); "Woe to you that are rich, for you have received your consolation" (Luke 6:24); and, finally, "Unless you turn and become like children, you will never enter the kingdom of heaven" (Matthew 18:3). The Bible's frequent reversals of what is expected argue for the wisdom of Chase's *(Untitled): Ledger for Multiple Adjustments*. The ironies merely echo the supreme irony that is the Bible's central theme. Namely, that all of the aggression, violence, hatred, and power grabbing of the human will, and all that operates by way of the Machiavellian and Darwinian principles of "might makes right" and "survival of the fittest" — all of this is only the outward illusion of power. The deeper reality lies in the repenting of human pride's desire to "be like God, knowing good and evil."[107] And the deeper power that gives life exists in the "weakness" of love and grace. Indeed, the Bible's entire meta-narrative can be read as a divine irony. For in the end, the biblical narrative dares to claim that those who are sinners, and who are weak, but who acknowledge their poverty of spirit, will be blessed and saved; and that those who believe they are saved, thinking they need nothing but themselves, are lost.

This returns us to Job's seemingly outrageous demand that God give an account of God's self to a human. Taking this as a metaphor for the larger human condition, in which humans do bear responsibility, what is truly outrageous is that in Christ, God actually did step into history, not to give an account of God's self, but more radically, to pay up, with Christ's blood, the accounts owing to human sin. Hence, when Job cries out in his agony, "I know that my Redeemer lives, and at last he will stand upon the earth," he prefigured this deepest of mysteries.[108] And just as God never answered Job with an explanation, but only made his Presence known as answer, so, too, the mystery of divine grace and love resolves matters with God's presence in Christ.

Chase's *(Untitled): Ledger for Multiple Adjustments* accommodates these mysteries. And it does so with an artistic grace that embodies a greater mystery; namely, that in the end, a profound humor may illuminate more fully than a deadly serious earnestness. This is an argument for judgment as grace given through faith. Again, as Flannery O'Connor said, "Faith tends to heal if we realize it is a 'walking in darkness' and not a theological solution to mystery."

Epilogue

In *The Next Generation*, we have seen forty-four contemporary artists engage with a set of very ancient stories. Or, more accurately, we have seen them engage with a complex history consisting not only of the Bible's originating stories but also of many centuries of culture, art, and interpretation that have evolved in the light of and in resistance to those stories. From the dialogues of the Jewish Midrash relating to the primary texts of the Hebrew scriptures, to the variegated discourses of Orthodox, Catholic, and Protestant Christianity relating to the texts of the Old and New Testaments, an extraordinary matrix of religious thought, art, and tradition now exists.

It goes without saying that the Bible's narratives have been some of the most formative stories to shape our civilization. And to a remarkable degree, they have long been "read" through a dialogue between visual images and verbal exegesis. From the extensive murals in the third-century synagogue at Dura Europos to the doors and walls of medieval baptisteries and churches, to the giant achievements of Renaissance and Baroque artists, the Bible's stories have maintained a vital energy for artists. In the modern and postmodern periods, the institutions of both art and the church have changed. For art, patronage has shifted from church and state to private collector, gallery, and academia. For the church, Protestantism has rejected imagery, and Catholicism has embraced its treasures from the eras of creative culture formation of the past, while ceasing to be a source for new expression.

And yet, with their deep psychic and spiritual power, their offering of meaning, and their prophetic bite, these ancient stories remain vigorously alive for those who read them, or who at least see how ingrained they still are in the culture's psyche. Even a "bad boy" artist like Mike Kelley, for example, uses Christian imagery, and with intentionally contradictory meanings (anti-religious, positive symbol, and metaphor). In an interview with Robert Storr, Kelley said, "I use Christian imagery because that's the kind of imagery that we still speak through. . . . It's a part of our culture whether you like it or not. You speak through these metaphors and you're going to speak through them no matter what. Forget simple yes/no dichotomies.[109] Or perhaps more probing is Leo Steinberg's observation at the end of *The Sexuality of Christ in Renaissance Art and Modern Oblivion*. There (and surprisingly, within the pages of *October*, a journal unsympathetic to faith, which first published his study), Steinberg recaptures the primal power of the Christian icon by looking again at the dialogue between Christian art and Christian text. Although his field is Renaissance art, Steinberg concludes his study with a challenge to modernity on the basis of what he has discovered: "The field I have tried to enter is unmapped, and unsafe, and more far-reaching than appears from my present vantage. . . . But I have risked hypothetical interpretations chiefly to show that, whether one looks with the eye of faith or with a mythographer's cool, the full content of the icons discussed bears looking at without shying."

And in so daring to look, Steinberg chides our modern/postmodern culture, which no longer looks at or reads these "texts." On such matters, he argues, "our era has educated [itself] into incomprehension. But this incomprehension—the 'oblivion' to which the title of this essay refers—is profound, willed, and sophisticated. It is the price paid by the modern world for its massive historic retreat from the mythical grounds of Christianity."[110]

In saying this, Steinberg points to the key question. Given that crucial aspects of our cultural and psychological ecologies are encoded by the biblical texts (not only in the larger and visible patterns, but also in the subtle and connective tissues whose role in our deeper ecologies remains unknown), the question is: is it risky, desirable, or even possible to expunge the seminal points of our psychological and spiritual origins? It is precisely on this point that the energy of the Bible is most confrontational. For unlike the mythologies of, say, ancient Greek culture (also fundamentally formative stories), the Bible's narrative is not so easily assimilated as metaphor. Although indisputably rich in metaphor, the biblical text itself keeps insisting upon "belief."

But "belief" is problematic for thoughtful people today. We now see that throughout the course of religious history, purity of spiritual motivation is hardly a sure thing. The question for many is whether human fallibility can be deconstructed, leaving "belief" intact and healthy, or whether the entire enterprise is misguided. Martin Buber once offered an insightful analysis of this question. No one, he wrote, doubts the historical significance of the Bible to our culture. But asking how those stories matter today — in asking what we do or can believe today — he points out that "the thoughtful reader" may be able to do little more than "believe that people once did believe as this book reports."[111] But the problem is that this book still confronts us in terms of good and evil, faith and responsibility. And so the question is, are these ancient religious stories, even though still so "present" today, anything more than history, myth, or aesthetics? Is their relevance primarily as usable metaphors, which the artist can appropriate as tools for exploring essentially secular perspectives?

To this question of "belief," Buber says that although a person today may feel "no access to sure and solid faith, nor can it be made accessible to him, . . . he is not denied the possibility of holding himself open to faith." And to this end, "he must read the . . . Bible as though it were something entirely unfamiliar, as though it had not been set before him ready-made, as though he has not been confronted all his life with sham concepts and sham statements that cited the Bible as their authority."[112] Instead, Buber urges the reader to allow these stories to be "strange" and "uncanny" once again, for in reality they are strange and uncanny; or, as Harold Bloom has paraphrased Buber, we must "read and feel at once estranged and yet at home."[113]

Perhaps this is the most central of the artistic tasks taken on by the forty-four artists in *The Next Generation*. As artists working in the early twenty-first century, they have probed the ancient stories from the vantage points of their contemporary experience, holding themselves open to see if the narratives are indeed still "unmapped and unsafe." And if so, to then see if the Bible's ancient stories still yield life.

Unless otherwise indicated, all quotations by the artists are taken from their respective artist statements.

1 Hebrews 11:1. Unless otherwise noted, all biblical quotations are taken from the Revised Standard Version (Old Testament Section, Copyright 1952, New Testament Section, Copyright 1946, by the Division of Christian Education of the National Council of the Churches of Christ in the United States of America).

2 Abba Bessarion, quoted in Kathleen Norris, *Amazing Grace: A Vocabulary of Faith* (New York: Riverhead Books, 1998): 169–70. In fairness, it should be noted that Redon added, "But what an eye!" For Redon's views on naturalism, which he rejected it in favor of ideistic art, see Odilon Redon, *A soi-même: Journal (1867–1915)* (Paris: Corti, 1961; first published 1922).

3 Martin Buber, *The Way of Man: According to the Teaching of Hasidism* (New York: Citadel Press, 1964, 1994): 5.

4 Flannery O'Connor, "The Church and the Fiction Writer," *Mystery and Manners, Occasional Prose*, selected and edited by Sally and Robert Fitzgerald (New York: Farrar, Straus & Giroux, 1957, 1969): 144.

5 Ibid., "The Nature and Aim of Fiction," 67.

6 Ibid., 68.

7 See Sheesley's artist statement, p. 86.

8 Jane Kenyon, *Otherwise: New and Selected Poems* (Saint Paul, MN: Graywolf Press, 1996): 21.

9 Telephone interview with the artist, July 30, 2004.

10 "Distance and Relation," *The Martin Buber Reader: Essential Writings*, edited by Asher D. Biemann (New York: Palgrave Macmillan, 2002): 207.

11 Ibid.

12 Bruce Marshall, *The World, the Flesh, and Father Smith* (Boston: Houghton Mifflin, 1945).

13 The URL for this link is: www.chesterton.org/qmeister2/questions.htm.

14 "Dancing in the Dark" was originally written for a Broadway revue and was later used in the 1953 MGM Fred Astaire musical, *The Band Wagon*. See *Reading Lyrics*, edited and with an introduction by Robert Gottlieb and Robert Kimball (New York: Pantheon Books, 2000): 275. I want to thank Mary McCleary for providing information about this source.

15 II Corinthians 4:18. McCleary takes her text from the King James Version.

16 I John 1:1. McCleary takes her text from the New International Version (NIV).

17 See King's artist statement, p. 90.

18 Telephone interview with the artist, September 20, 2004.

19 See Huck's artist statement, p. 92.

20 See Wingate's artist statement, p. 94. For an overview of Wingate's career, see Bruce Herman, "Looking Again: The Art of George Wingate," *Image: A Journal of the Arts & Religion*, Issue # 43 (Fall 2004): 103–9.

21 T.S. Eliot, *The Varieties of Metaphysical Poetry*, edited and introduced by Ronald Schuchard (New York: Harcourt Brace, 1994): 50. The italics are Eliot's.

22 Ibid.

23 Published as *El arte de la pintura* (Seville, 1649). For excerpts, see Robert Enggass and Jonathan Brown, *Italy and Spain, 1600–1750: Sources and Documents* (Englewood Cliffs, NJ: Prentice-Hall, 1970).

24 *Theories of Modern Art: A Source Book by Artists and Critics*, edited by Herschel B. Chipp (Berkeley: University of California Press, 1968): 18.

25 Archie Rand, "Judaism and the Visual Arts," lecture delivered on March 8, 2001 at the conference *Divine Perversities: Religion and Contemporary Art in the Public Sphere*. The conference was presented jointly by the Department of Art and The Humanities Institute, College of Liberal Arts, University of Minnesota, February 7–April 20, 2001.

26 See Auxier's artist statement, p. 96.

27 Personal conversations with the artist at Trinity Western University, October 10–12, 2003.

28 Genesis 1: 2; John 1:1.

29 See Couture's artist statement, p. 100.

30 Norman Maclean, *A River Runs Through It, and Other Stories* (Chicago: University of Chicago Press, 1976): 95.

31 John 1:1, 3, 14.

32 Jacques Derrida, *Writing and Difference* (Chicago: University of Chicago Press, 1978): 64ff.

33 See Prescott's artist statement, p. 104.

34 For a good layman's explanation of the rules that govern the two-dimensional cellular automaton "Game of Life," see Eric W. Weisstein, "Life." From *MathWorld*—A Wolfram Web Resource, http://mathworld.wolfram.com/Life.html.

35 Genesis 1: 1–3, 27.

36 See Perkins-Buzo's artist statement, p. 106.

37 See Feldman's artist statement, p. 108.

38 Gaston Bachelard, *The Poetics of Space*, translated from the French by Maria Jolas (Boston: Beacon Press, 1994). For example, Bachelard sets up such categories as House and Universe, Intimate Immensity, and Dialectics of Outside and Inside.

39 See Wohl's artist statement, p. 110.

40 See Blow's artist statement, p. 112.

41 See West's artist statement, p. 114.

42 Quoted by West in his artist statement, p. 114. Mockbee includes Margaret's Grocery in his list of the ten most significant architectural sites in the South; see Raad Cawthon, "Samuel Mockbee's Vision in an Invisible World," *The Oxford American*, Issue 41 (Fall 2001): 56–61.

43 For helpful discussions of the issue of mainstream culture "naming" folk, outsider, or isolate aesthetics, as well as reproductions (some color) of works out of those traditions, see the essays by Lucy R. Lippard, "Crossing Into Uncommon Grounds," and Russell Bowman, "A Synthetic Approach to Folk Art," both in *Common Ground/Uncommon Vision: The Michael and Julie Hall Collection of American Folk Art in the Milwaukee Art Museum* (Milwaukee, WI: The Museum, 1993).

44 Ludwig Wittgenstein, *Culture and Value*, translated by Peter Winch (Chicago: University of Chicago Press, 1980): 45e.

45 George Steiner, *Real Presences* (Chicago: University of Chicago Press, 1989): 229. The italics are Steiner's.

46 See p. 30 and note 32, above.

47 Ezekiel 2:3–4, 2:8–3:3.

48 Revelation 10:8–11. Also see Jeremiah 15:16, where eating the scroll is a joy to the prophet.

49 All three acts are described in Ezekiel, chapters 4–5; each symbolizes the spiritual and moral state of the nation of Israel through a different material and gesture. The distinct gestures signify how Israel will be judged for its rejection of God.

50 Hans Belting, *Likeness and Presence: A History of the Image before the Era of Art*, translated by Edmund Jephcott (Chicago: University of Chicago Press, 1994).

51 Herbert N. Schneidau, *Sacred Discontent: The Bible and Western Tradition* (Berkeley: University of California Press, 1976).

52 For Carolee Schneemann, see *More Than Meat Joy: Performance Works and Selected Writings*, edited by Bruce R. McPherson (Kingston, NY: Documentext/McPherson & Co., 1997): 234–39; for Chris Burden's TRANS-FIXED, see Jonathan Fineberg, *Art Since 1940: Strategies of Being* (Englewood Cliffs, NJ: Prentice Hall, 1995): 342; for Adrian Piper, see *Art and Feminism*, edited by Helena Reckitt; survey by Peggy Phalen (New York: Phaidon, 2001): 138.

53 See: Isaiah, chapter 20; Hosea; and Ezekiel, chapters 4–5.

54 Gunn, Giles, "Introduction," *The Bible and American Arts and Letters*, edited by Giles Gunn (Philadelphia, PA: Fortress Press; Chico, CA: Scholars Press, 1983): 2.

55 Isaiah 28:1–4. Dunkell takes her text from the King James Version.

56 See Hebblethwaite's artist statement, p. 122.

57 Caroline Tisdall, *Joseph Beuys* (New York: Thames and Hudson, 1979): 228–35.

58 See Fujimura's artist statement, p. 124.

59 John 12:3; Mark 14:3.

60 John 12:1–3.

61 See Van Dyke's artist statement, p. 126.

62 See Zajkowski's artist statement, p. 128.

63 Genesis 11:1, 4, 5–9.

64 Gunn, *The Bible and American Arts and Letters*, 1–2.

65 See Colleen McDannell, *Material Christianity: Religion and Popular Culture in America* (New Haven: Yale University Press, 1995). See also, *The Visual Culture of American Religions*, edited by David Morgan and Sally Promey (Berkeley: University of California Press, 2001); and David Morgan, *Visual Piety: A History and Theory of Popular Religious Images* (Berkeley: University of California Press, 1998).

66 Matthew 19:16–30.

67 Gunn, *The Bible and American Arts and Letters*, 1.

68 See Naylor artist's statement, p. 138.

69 Revelation 3:4.

70 O'Connor, "Catholic Novelists," *Mystery and Manners*, 184.

71 Wilhelm Worringer, *Abstraction and Empathy: A Contribution to the Psychology of Style*, translated by Michael Bullock (Chicago: Ivan R. Dee, 1997; first published in German in 1908); Wassily Kandinsky, *Concerning the Spiritual in Art*, translated by M.T.H. Sadler (New York: Dover Publications, 1977; first published in German in 1913); Kazimir Malevich, *Essays on Art* (Copenhagen: Borgen, 1968).

72 The history of "black icons" and spirituality is discussed in the broadest terms in key essays by Maurice Tuchman, Charlotte Douglas, W. Jackson Rushing, and Donald Kuspit in *The Spiritual in Art: Abstract Painting 1890–1985* (New York: Abbeville Press, 1986). For a study connecting spirituality, Ad Reinhardt's Black Paintings, and the Christian tradition, see Naomi Vine's discussion of Thomas Merton's relationship with Reinhardt in "Mandala and Cross," *Art in America*, Vol. 79 (November 1991): 124–33.

73 Job 2:8, 2:12.

74 Job 2:9.

75 Job 42:1–6.

76 Leo Steinberg, *The Sexuality of Christ in Renaissance Art and in Modern Oblivion*, second edition, revised and expanded (Chicago: University of Chicago Press, 1996; first published in the summer 1983 issue of *October*).

77 See Weaver's artist statement, p. 148.

78 See Hettinga's artist statement, p. 152.

79 Mark 15:34.

80 See Hettinga's artist statement, p. 152.

81 T.S. Eliot, *The Complete Poems and Plays, 1909–1950* (Harcourt, Brace and World, Inc., 1971): 127.

82 Susan Sontag, *Illness as Metaphor* (New York: Farrar, Straus, and Giroux, 1978).

83 See Mills's artist statement, p. 154.

84 Belting, *Likeness and Presence*, pp. 8–10. It is actually not accurate to refer to the altarpiece as if it were a single, monolithic phenomenon. Again, Belting's work is helpful here, for he demonstrates how the form developed slowly and with various permutations, tracing its multiple sources in the Byzantine iconostasis, the Romanesque casket shrine, medieval icons, and the emergence of the liturgy, as well as, more banally, in the competitive nature of local parishes wishing to out-do each other in creating the latest innovations contributing to civic pride. See, for example, p. 377ff.

85 See *Icons of American Protestantism: The Art of Warner Sallman*, edited by David Morgan (New Haven: Yale University Press, 1996). Also see, *The Visual Culture of American Religions* (see note 65 above).

86 Belting, *Likeness and Presence*, 404.

87 Ibid., 398.

88 Ibid., 3–11.

89 Georges Didi-Huberman, *Fra Angelico: Dissemblance & Figuration*, translated by Jane Marie Todd (Chicago: University of Chicago Press, 1995).

90 Stephen James Newton, *Painting, Psychoanalysis, and Spirituality* (New York: Cambridge University Press, 2001).

91 See Herman's artist statement, p. 162. Additional information from a telephone interview with the artist, October, 15, 2004.

92 See Eustace's artist statement, p. 164.

93 Patricia Leighten, "Leonardo's *Burlington House Cartoon*," *Rutgers Art Review*, Vol. 2 (January 1981): 31–42.

94 Hilda Graef, *Mary: A History of Doctrine and Devotion*, Vol. 1 (New York: Sheed and Ward, 1964): 33–34.

95 Leighten, "Leonardo's *Burlington House Cartoon*," 32. Leighten reproduces several Italian examples of the Virgin Platytera.

96 See Larson's artist statement, p. 166.

97 See Aldrich's artist statement, p. 168.

98 See D. Forsythe's artist statement, p. 170.

99 See C. Forsythe's artist statement, p. 172.

100 For Rosalind Krauss's embrace of Barthes's Argo model and her importation of it into art criticism, see Krauss, "Poststructuralism and the Paraliterary," *The Originality of the Avant-Garde and Other Modernist Myths* (Cambridge, MA: MIT Press, 1985): 291–96. For Donald B. Kuspit's critique of the Barthes/Krauss model, in which he reasserts the depth of "person" and creativity, see Kuspit, "Conflicting Logics: Twentieth-Century Studies at the Crossroads," *The Art Bulletin*, Vol. 69, No. 1 (March 1987): 126.

101 Revelation 10:9, 11; 11:1, 7–10.

102 See Benson's artist statement, p. 178.

103 See Sheesley's artist statement, p. 180.

104 See, for example, Revelation 3:5; 20:12–15; and 21:27.

105 Personal interview with the artist, November 18, 2004. Also see Chase's artist statement, p. 182.

106 Job 33: 9–10, 13.

107 Genesis 3:5.

108 Job 19:25.

109 Robert Storr, "An Interview with Mike Kelley," *Art in America*, Vol. 82 (June 1994): 90–93.

110 Steinberg, *The Sexuality of Christ in Renaissance Art and Modern Oblivion*, 106.

111 Martin Buber, "The Man of Today and the Jewish Bible," *On the Bible: Eighteen Studies*, edited by Nahum N. Glatzer; introduction by Harold Bloom (New York: Schocken Books, 1982): 1–13.

112 Ibid., 5.

113 Ibid., ix.

God in the Details

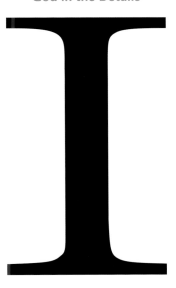

Joel Sheesley

Education **1974** MFA, Denver University, Denver, CO **1972** BFA, Syracuse University School of Art, Syracuse, NY
Position Professor of Art, Wheaton College, Wheaton, IL

Winter Conversation is a view of a print of the *Portinari Altarpiece* that hangs in the hall of my house. Over time I have watched the print interact with a wide range of family activities and artifacts. In 1999, I began using my house as a context in which to set a variety of subjects for visual/poetic exploration. The presence of Christian subject matter sometimes becomes a feature guiding the interpretation of these paintings.

Winter Conversation presents a complex view of the *Portinari Altarpiece* print. As seen from this angle, a window reflection on the glass covering the print fills up the central panel of the altarpiece. Thus, a snowy Midwestern morning invades the print. The silhouettes of two women sitting on a couch in front of the reflected window block out the sun and allow part of the print to be visible. The figures and shapes in the print now interact with these reflected figures. The world of the Incarnation is seen to be co-existent with this suburban-life reflection. *Winter Conversation* records a simple phenomenon and at the same time invites the viewer to consider the collision of worlds this optical phenomenon suggests.

2 *Allegory of the Senses,* 2002.
Mixed media collage on paper.
48 x 72⅞ inches.

Mary Fielding McCleary

Education 1975 MFA, University of Oklahoma, Norman, OK **1972** BFA, *cum laude*, Texas Christian University, Fort Worth, TX
Position Regent's Professor of Art, Stephen F. Austin State University, Nacogdoches, TX

I made my first three-dimensional collage twenty-six years ago. Since then, my work has grown in size, complexity, and meaning. The collages are made by attaching layer upon layer of materials such as paint, paper, rag board, foil, glitter, sticks, wire, mirrors, pencils, nails, glass, painted toothpicks, string, leather, lint, small plastic toys, and other found objects on heavy paper, much in the way that a painter builds layer upon layer of paint on canvas. Often these materials are used symbolically. My aim is that the obsessive images that result from this method of working convey an intensity, which the viewer finds compelling. I am interested in the spatial complexity and visual tensions that come from the fact that the collages are illusionistic, while at the same time they are composed of three-dimensional objects that often retain their own identities. Drawing my subject matter from history and literature, I like the irony of using materials that are often trivial, foolish, and temporal to express ideas of what is significant, timeless, and transcendent.

3 *4 or 5 Trees,* 2002.
Video.

Gregory King

Education **2003** MFA, Hunter College, New York, NY **1993** BFA, Kansas City Art Institute, Kansas City, MO
Position Artist and Graphic Designer

At the core of my work is the desire to engage perception, to visually interpret the fundamental material and spiritual dimensions of the world, to navigate the possibilities of how they are distinct and yet intertwined, and to recognize art as a potent means through which to experience and connect the two. I am compelled to create paintings, drawings, films, videos, photographs, and combinations of such media to produce visual experiences of poignant content and immanent meaning, which also focus one's ability to observe and respond to the environment as a physical and metaphysical entity.

Much of my work involves the act of poetically transforming the infinitely complex interactions between humanity and the environment. This is intriguing to me in terms of the "constructed" and the "unintentional," such as how architecture, the urban grid, and the systematic or indiscriminate "marks" made by society interact with and compose transitory landscapes and physically profound spaces. It is not a matter of factually reiterating what already physically exists, but rather exploring how these forms and networks allow for a visual dimension that engages the imagination in time, embodying the terrain of the mind within the broader "environments."

Christine Huck

Education 2003 BFA, *cum laude*, University of Illinois at Urbana-Champaign, Urbana, IL
Position Custom Framer

Common, man–made objects that reveal histories of use, wear, and tear are a consistent theme in my work. I am interested in painting these objects as portraits and see them as metaphors representing humanity in its broken, downtrodden, but also beautiful reality. By painting these objects as personified, I try to shine a light on truth and raw experience through the hinted histories that are marked on the surface of each object. I try to reveal the beauty in these histories, no matter how sad and ugly, neglected and abused. There is beauty in the places where people do not tend to look. What beauty is apart from God? Any delight, any good thing, any sweet spilling of pleasures comes from him. Out of nothing. Out of dirt. Take the cracks and burns of life, he will draw beauty out of even that.

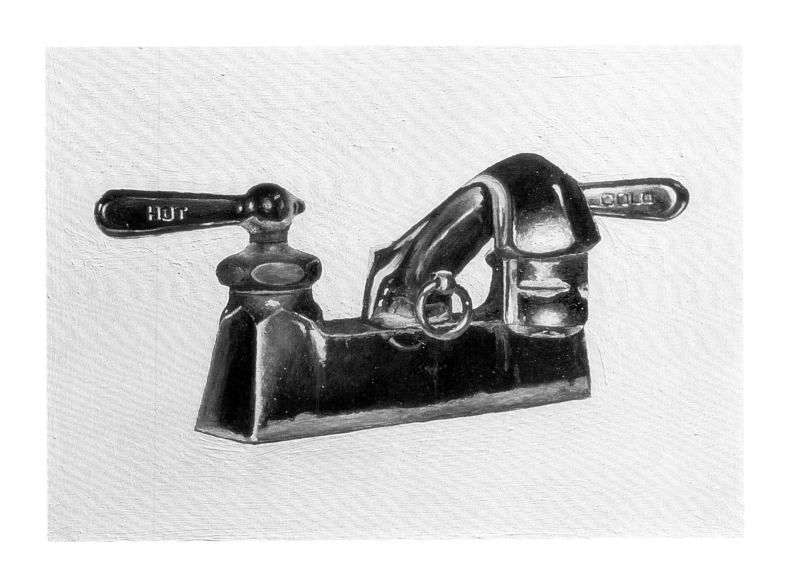

George Wingate

Education **1992** MFA, Vermont College of Norwich University, Montpelier, VT **1963** BA, University of Rochester, Rochester, NY
Position Artist

My paintings are my celebration of the beauty and the mystery of the commonplace. We strive so often for the significant that we devalue the most dear.

Doris Hutton Auxier

Education 2001 MFA, Vermont College, Montpelier, VT **1992** MA, University of Arizona, Tucson, AZ **1974** BA, University of North Dakota, Grand Forks, ND
Position Coordinator of Art Department, Trinity Western University, Langley, BC, Canada

Several decades ago, postmodern cultural theory hit North America like a giant storm, toppling many secure ways of knowing and reassuring meanings. Navigation in a dizzying, shifting, and newly burned cultural landscape is difficult. Slashing and burning is noisy, busy, intense; it drafts art into its purposes, leaving little room for quiet reflective painting. The works from the *Solitude Series*, of which *First Temptation* is a part, represent a transition period, from immersion in a culture where the deafening noise of the cultural demolition project of postmodernism was at times horrifying, to a time of intense crying out to God and of longing to hear his solid, sure voice. It marks a year of my soul's withdrawal to a still, silent place where even that which has been discarded becomes sacred and refueled with God's presence and breath.

The image sources for the pieces in the *Solitude Series* come from nature's detritus that has been sheared from its original organic source. The flayed bits of nature act as a metaphor for a discarding of the responsive longing for God that according to Romans 1 has been encoded into nature. Even the bits of nature that have been stripped and isolated from their sources resonate with God's presence and send up a cry for longing and meaning. In my studio, I hold bits of flayed and dying nature while working and reflecting on each piece. Through drawing and re-drawing, painting and re-painting, I parallel and mark the passage of my own changing set of questions, doubts, and comforts. The subtitles of the paintings reflect these concurrent cognitive searches. Through multiple surfaces of graphite and paint on each board, I build up the layers of specificity that originally attracted me to each piece of nature's detritus. The layers, as they become obscured and changed or sanded off, mirror the changing cultural and personal narratives that I bring to each piece as I reflect upon God's general revelation in nature. Each piece ends up becoming a silent death mask or icon that holds within it the ancient, current, and future voice of its creator.

God in the Mystery

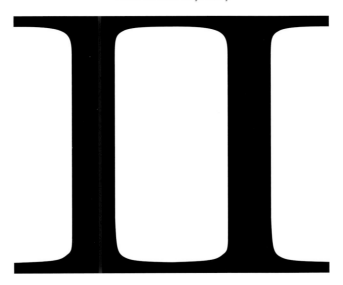

7 *Reflections on a Poet God: Between the Space and the Echo (l); Kenosis (c); Between the Word and the Entry (r),* 2004.
Integrated digital media on fine paper. 11½ x 29 inches (left); 15 x 11 inches (center); 11½ x 29 inches (right).

Theresa Couture

Education **1995** DMin, Graduate Theological Foundation, South Bend, IN **1981** MFA, Rhode Island School of Design, Providence, RI
1972 MA, Rivier College, Nashua, NH **1964** BA, *cum laude*, Rivier College, Nashua, NH
Position Professor of Art, Rivier College, Nashua, NH

What is most captivating to me about the arts is that they give substance to an intensely engaging perception that everything of consequence in life is hidden. Everything that really matters is a mystery: the cycles of nature, the rhythms of our bodies, the capacity to have ideas and to make things, the expanses of the human heart, the convergences of all things true, good, and beautiful. Life's major challenge is to welcome mystery. The way of art is to approach mystery through indirection and metaphor, acknowledging that even the humblest of things is more than it is, and that God, too, is hidden in a world of appearances. So, as all artists must, and as the artist in all of us is inclined to do, I spend time wondering about hiddenness and wholeness, about oneness and uncompromising individuality, about silence and revelation, about what is fragile and what is solid, what is dark and what is radiant, what is close and yet distant, how things appear to be and what their fuller reality might prove to be, and what there is within our deepest selves, both individually and communally, that waits for our art to discover and rediscover it.

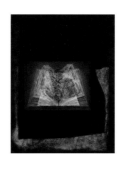

8 *"In the beginning was the Word. . ."*
(Binary Triptych), 2001.
Clay, metal, wood, and cement.
1⅓ x 6 feet; 1⅓ x 7 feet; 1⅓ x 8 feet.

Ellie Murphy

Education 1992 MFA, Yale University School of Art, New Haven, CT **1987** BFA, Washington University School of Fine Art, St. Louis, MO
Position Artist

This work is from a series I call *Digital Sculpture*, in which I was contemplating the idea of creation vis–à–vis individual existence. *Digitus* is the Latin root for both digit, the word meaning finger (implying making by hand and the actual or the physical), and digital, the unseen electronic language of the binary system in which all computers are programmed, the ones indicating that the electronic circuit is on, the zeros that it is off (implying that which is unseen, or the sublime and the spiritual).

By hand, I formed 8-bit binary code out of clay and then strung it on wire to spell out the phrase that is the first verse in the Gospel of John. The three sections literally spell out John 1:1: "In the beginning was the Word" (panel 1), "and the Word was with God" (panel 2), "and the Word was God" (panel 3). I wanted to show how the most recent technological developments continue to relate to man's search for meaning through our own human experience, to show a commonality between art, science, and religion, and to quite literally show the primacy of language and symbol in forming and passing on our basic principles of what is true, beautiful, and divine.

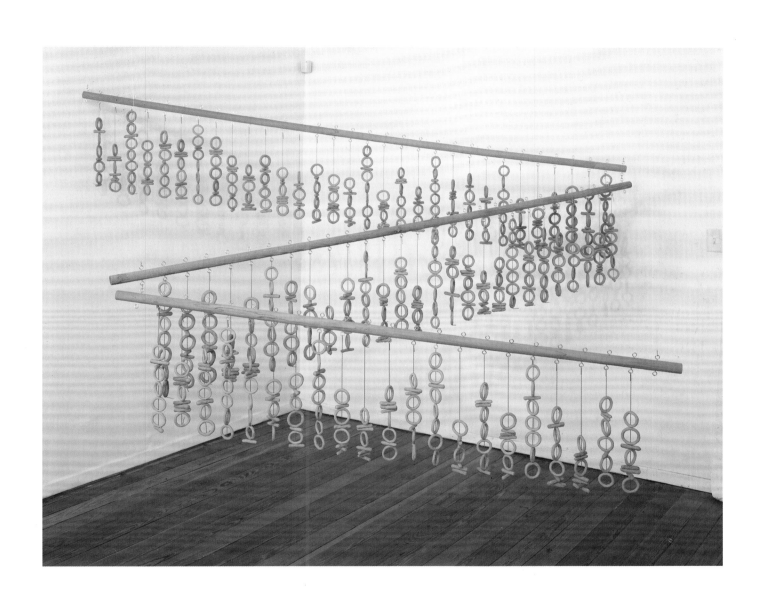

9 *Tabula Rasa II, 2003–4.*
Corten steel and Aflon marble.
84 x 19¾ x 4 inches.

Theodore L. Prescott

Education 1970 MFA, Rinehart School of Sculpture, The Maryland Institute College of Art, Baltimore, MD **1967** BA, Colorado College, Colorado Springs, CO
Position Professor of Art, Messiah College, Grantham, PA

I am drawn to the physicality of our world. Its intricacy, vastness, variety, and coherence are extraordinary to behold. The Scriptures describe creation as a kind of unending speech, and I am struck by the fact that even as we relish creation's glory, we are drawn by it toward the Creator. Similarly, sense and substance, so delightful in themselves, have the capacity to testify to an intangible spiritual reality.

Tabula Rasa II has the form of a book or tablet, and a substance (marble) with a long history of being used in public address. Here, the text is the material of the stone itself, whose normal opacity is contrasted with its potential translucency. The sculpture was designed for exterior installation, so that the passage of time and light will reveal the variable character of form and materials.

John Reid Perkins-Buzo

Education **2003** MFA, Northwestern University, Evanston, IL **2002** Graduate Certificate in Art and Technology, Northwestern University, Evanston, IL
1995 MA, MDiv, Aquinas Institute of Theology, St. Louis, MO **1986** MS, Oakland University, Rochester, MI **1982** BS, Michigan State University, East Lansing, MI
Position Executive Director, Lumen Multimedia Association (lumenmedia@earthlink.net) and Part-time Instructor in Film Studies, Dominican University, River Forest, IL

I create multimedia installations, videos, and films. I am also a member of the Order of Preachers, commonly known as the Dominicans after our founder St. Dominic. In my work I combine scriptural, theological, and philosophical themes with advanced electronic media work involving video, interactivity, virtual reality, and audio. Our relationships with God — as Creator, as Christ both divine and human, as divine Guarantor of Justice and Peace, as ineffably Triune, as revealed and concealed by Scripture, as Spirit-Ruah descended on the Ecclesia, as somehow sought in every spiritual endeavor of humanity, as both highest Infinity and the deepest Nothingness — these are the sources for my work. To be constantly in life-giving relationship with God more or less sums up my goal as an artist and as a Christian.

The Portal, an interactive multimedia installation, concerns the emergence of life from the *tohu bohu* of non-existence under God's constant creative impulse. On one large wall a single channel video stream is projected. The video stream is created by taking video input from a small camera concealed just below the image area, then manipulating its pixels using the population algorithms of mathematician John H. Conway's widely known "Game of Life." A parallel audio component continuously modulates the background audio to the video using granular audio synthesis algorithms also based on the "Game of Life."

As people walk, dance, hug, or play in front of the screen, it bursts with colors and patterns, some of which they recognize as drawn from themselves, and others that are entirely abstract. In response to the installation, many people feel the urge to move and dance, delighting in its playfulness. To me, this is their way of celebrating God's continued creative presence in their lives. It is a presence often elusive, sometimes difficult to recognize, yet always responsive as we come to deepen our relationships with God.

11 *Current,* 2003.
Pastel and mortar on wood.
47¾ x 137¼ inches.

Roger Feldman

Education **1977** MFA, Claremont Graduate University, Claremont, CA **1972** BA, University of Washington, Seattle, WA
Position Professor of Design and Sculpture, Seattle Pacific University, Seattle, WA

Since 1976, my three-dimensional installations have explored the fundamental relationship between visual and kinesthetic perception. I create works to be walked on, moved through, and sat upon in order to elicit participatory responses. Auditory aspects emerged, and I have included them in the work from the beginning. All of these perceptual processes have been orchestrated to lead to experiential metaphor, which places emphasis on a viewer's actions as contemplative and symbolic aesthetic experiences. The role of form and the various uses of materials, color, and space are directed toward causing psychological responses. These responses help to reinforce the symbolic value of the sequence of movements.

In *Current*, the drawing of an architectural structure in the context of a large wood substrate gives emphasis to the delicate nature of our lives. Caught between two powerful and high-contrast panels, the small drawing takes on a fragile quality due to its context. The grain in the wood surface suggests a larger flow with nature, while the mortar panels continue the repetition of linear elements that resonate with the wood context. The contrast between the temporal and the apparently permanent is especially important in establishing a spiritual connection to the forces beyond our control.

The drawing of the architectural structure implies a passage or transition between states. While the structure is imagined, it works to connect one reality with another. While the imagined structure is an illusion, it is very much influenced by its surroundings.

12 *Veil of Light: The Protecting Veil,*
2001.
Unweaving® mixed media: gauze
fabric, acrylic paint, collage paper,
modeling paste, and beads. 79 x 19
(diameter) inches.

Laurie Wohl

Education **1968** LLB, Columbia Law School, New York, NY **1965** BA, Sarah Lawrence College, Bronxville, NY
Position Artist

I try to awaken a sense of ceremony and ritual, mystery, celebration, and community with my work. I believe that through art we can encourage and express a faithful life; celebrate the possibilities for the sacred in human life; and elevate the perception of the sacred in our day-to-day faith journeys.

I have developed an unweaving process, a unique method of working with canvas, to evoke a spirit of mystery and celebration drawn from the oldest traditions of narrative textiles. Narratives are conveyed by form, color, and texture. In my textiles, the unwoven spaces form symbolic shapes referring to wings, trees, prayer shawls, veils, ladders, falling waters, and sacred architecture such as domes, chapels, and windows. The process evokes an emptying of the self for meditation and contemplation.

The visual narrative is enhanced by my own iconographic language, indicating guardians, messengers, journeying and praying figures, processional figures, and more. The form and iconography of each piece often serve to illuminate a biblical or mystical text. This combination of image and text constitutes a "visual midrash," a textual interpretation through a contemporary visual idiom.

The beads used constitute prayers and memories, marking points, catching lights, evocative of sparkling waters, and alluding to rosaries, worry beads, and the beaded doorway curtains of Mediterranean countries. A gold wash, signifying sacredness, adds a distinctive glow.

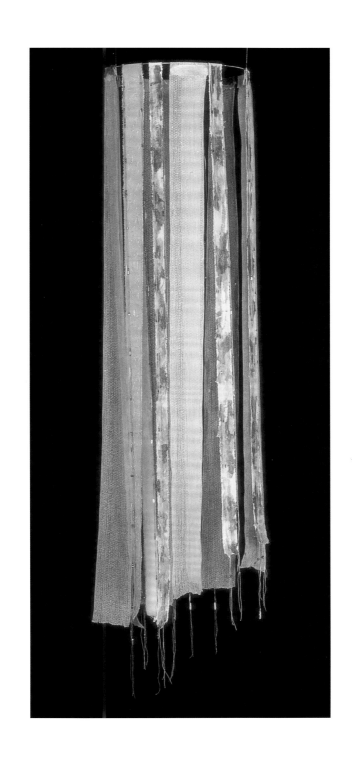

David Blow

Education **1975** MFA, Syracuse University, Syracuse, NY **1972** BFA, Michigan State University, East Lansing, MI
Position Associate Professor of Art, University of North Denton, Denton, TX

Creatively, I am interested in the spiritual emotions of peace, solitude, comfort, and joy, as well as color, rhythm, shape, and pattern. Whether it is the rhythmic circling of the birds overhead or when the air is filled with the aroma of cherry blossom and the song of the robin, you have the feeling of God's guidance and order in the world. I embrace the technological changes that are taking place in our culture while maintaining my love for the beauty of our natural environment. I use multiple images to show the magic of a time found in nature. Using the computer, I can bring the viewer into my vision of universal harmony between nature, man, and technology. Aesthetically, I am seeking to show the harmony between the natural environment and the electronic one.

14 *Reverend Dennis's Golden Chair, MS,*
2002.
C-print. 14 x 17 inches.
Entrance to Margaret's Grocery, MS,
2002.
C-print. 14 x 17 inches.

Bruce West

Education **1978** MFA, The Pennsylvania State University, University Park, PA **1975** BA, The Pennsylvania State University, University Park, PA
Position Professor, Department of Art and Design, Southwest Missouri State University, Springfield, MO

I have been documenting the landscape and culture of the Mississippi Delta and surrounding areas since 1994. I make simple and direct color photographs of people, places, and architecture that hopefully touch upon the diverse aspects of history, religion, politics, etc., which have served to shape and inform the region of the Delta. In my travels, I have befriended and photographed many wonderful and exceptional people, including the Reverend H.D. Dennis, a self-proclaimed preacher, architect, and artist, who has been converting his wife's grocery store into his own very unique church for the past twenty years. The conversion of Margaret's Grocery is an inspired labor of love involving the construction of several towers (some over two stories tall), the creation of an Ark of the Covenant containing tablets inscribed with the Ten Commandments, the invention of new religious iconography, and very elaborate painting and decoration. The towers and exterior of the former store are covered with bands of high gloss red, white, blue, green, yellow, and pink paint. The interior walls and ceilings of the store as well as an old school bus are encrusted with old religious artifacts, Mardi Gras beads, plastic flowers, hubcaps, Christmas lights and decorations, stuffed toy animals, and various discarded items. A sign at the entrance of Rev. Dennis's church announces: "Welcome Jews and Gentiles — This Church Open 24 Hours a Day." These creations are in a constant state of evolution and change. As noted architect and MacArthur Fellow Samuel Mockbee has written of Margaret's Grocery in his list of the ten most significant architectural sites in the South, "Its crude materials and methods of construction place it in an ethereal state of being and perpetual state of beauty."

The two photographs featured in *The Next Generation* come from an extended collective portrait of Rev. Dennis, Margaret, and Rev. Dennis's creative work. Over the past ten years, I have come to realize that one of my primary motivations for pursuing my photographic work in Mississippi as well as other projects (including a survey of the current social and political situation in Northern Ireland) grows out of a personal desire to reconnect with a greater sense of spirituality and religiosity in my own life. My photographs affirm the possibility of a more spiritual and enlightened sensibility.

The Book

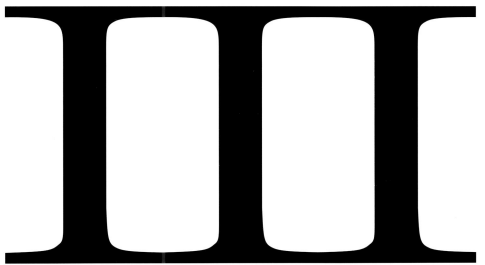

Michael R. Buesking

Education 2002 MFA, University of Missouri, Columbia, MO **1987** MS, College of Education, Southern Illinois University, Carbondale, IL **1985** BFA, *summa cum laude*, Southern Illinois University, Carbondale, IL
Position Assistant Professor of Art, Evangel University, Springfield, MO

Ezekiel Scattering Hair is from a recent series based on the symbolic actions of Old Testament prophets entitled *Prophet as Artist.* As the title of the series indicates, I have reversed the order of the often-quoted phrase "artist as prophet." The trend in contemporary art movements toward action and performance is partially responsible for a revision in the way I view the ancient prophets. Many contemporary art actions seem laden with ceremony and ritual (just peruse Jonathan Fineberg's 1995 study, *Art Since 1940: Strategies of Being,* for a few obvious examples). The strangeness of some of these contemporary art actions reminded me of some of the physical tasks performed by prophets like Ezekiel.

The whole idea of the prophet acting as a voice to the people by *artistic* means was exciting to me. In addition, though the stories of prophetic actions are found in the Bible, one of the West's most traditional sources of subject matter, I was not aware of any iconographical tradition associated with them. This gave me the freedom to develop my own imagery. I reduce the images to include only the prophet involved and the action, so that the viewer becomes witness to the event. This treatment of the image also moves the image further from the illustration of a Bible story and closer to archetypal or metaphorical imagery: man scattering hair. I have also limited or conflated references to a specific time period so as to make the paintings less illustrative and more symbolic.

Soon after beginning this series of images celebrating the symbolic actions of the prophets, I decided to use the self-portrait as a basis for the prophet. This decision had the advantage of making the prophet figure less of a generalized, non-specific personality, certainly less idealized, and placed the prophet more in the realm of real people. It enhanced the physical nature of the action as having been an actual event. It also enabled me to identify myself strongly with the monotheistic ideology of the Old Testament—in stark contrast to the resurgence of polytheism evident in much contemporary ("ritual") action art. The prophets of the Old Testament, laboring in a time of spiritual declension, sought ways to communicate effectively with the people of their day. So now, by quoting or re-imaging their symbolic actions, I align myself with their ideology and restate their messages.

16 *Whose Glorious Beauty is a Fading Flower,* ca. 2001.
Pen-and-ink drawing.
18⅛ x 24 inches.

Ruth Dunkell

Education 1945 BFA, Brooklyn College, NY
Position Artist

Whose Glorious Beauty is a Fading Flower is part of a group of six hundred densely cross-hatched drawings executed with india ink on Arches paper. Drawn over the course of the past twenty years, they range widely in size, from quite small to more than seven feet across. Once primarily abstract, but with strong figurative elements, the drawings are now largely figural. In some, there are six or more figures moving, dancing, interacting. They feature landscapes, animals, birds, and even words. My technique — which employs dense and less dense cross-hatching to define the forms, depth, and space — results in blacks and grays that have subtle perceptual shifts.

17 *Forest Communion on Foxridge, 2004.*
Photographs on inkjet prints. 6 prints, 11 x 14 inches each.

Paul Hebblethwaite

Education 1998 BA, Purdue University, West Lafayette, IN
Position Director of Programs, Project ACHIEVE, Glendale, CA

Dear Joseph Beuys,

This February it snowed on Foxridge. The leafless trees stood stark against the white field of ground spread at their base. The creek flowed slowly with cold deliberation between ice and stone. My wife and dog joined me as I meandered down the hill to the creek with bottle in hand. For days I had been eyeing a fallen tree across the creek as a suitable cross for communion. Hands gloved against the cold, I poured the wine across the log; the splatter melted holes in the snow revealing the dead tree beneath. The wine stained the snow, leaving countless wounds behind, pockets of violence against this once proud specimen. I focused my lens on each section of the tree, documenting the forest communion, preserving the action, and hoping to retain some of the moment's power.

The snow has melted and the trunk lies bare under the protection of the other trees. I brought the prints home and can meditate on the moment some more. Unlike the singular repetition of the crucifixion scene in our old paintings, the images both simplify and expand upon the violence of Jesus's redemptive action. I am repetitively printing the negatives, raising the blood to the surface, reaching for the moment again and again. I am not a creator of objects, but a shaman seeking out symbols of transformational power. As I work, I stare out the window at Foxridge, still alienated from humanity, in need of stewardship, love, our repentance. Before I leave Springville, I hope to act one more time, to bury myself in its leaves, to walk with God through its paths, to listen to the Spirit move across the creek.

Sincerely,
Paul Hebblethwaite

THE EARTH
PARCHED IN
THE THIRST
OF HIS WOUNDS
RIPPED OPEN

Ranier Maria Rilke

18 *Eirenepoios, 2003.* Installation with video.
Eirene I, 2003. Azurite and malachite mixed with Hyde glue on Kumohada paper. 60 x 83 inches.
Eirene II, 2003. Japanese vermilion mixed with Hyde glue on Kumohada paper. 60 x 83 inches.
Precious Nard, 2003. Birch wood, Kumohada paper, Gampi paper, and azurite wash. 48 x 90 x 19 inches.

Makoto Fujimura

Education **1992** Post-MFA Program in Nihonga, National Cultural Affairs Scholar, Tokyo National University of Fine Arts and Music, Tokyo, Japan
1989 MFA, Tokyo National University of Fine Arts and Music, Tokyo, Japan **1983** BA, *cum laude*, Bucknell University, Lewisburg, PA
Position Artist and Member, National Council on the Arts, 2002–2008

Eirenepoios is the Greek word for peacemaker. This word suggests that peace is something that can be crafted, like a piece of poetry or art. I videotaped the working process during the painting of *Eirene I.* My intent was to capture a physical document of the creative process. I often find myself marveling at a painting as it dries and wanted to capture the sense of fleeting transcendence I observe in such moments. *Eirene I* and *Eirene II* are paintings symbolizing male and female counterparts.

    Two kinds of paper — laid gently inside the boat — were used in the piece entitled *Precious Nard.* The heavier paper is called *Kumohada* (cloudskin) in Japanese; it buckles and stretches, creating stain marks. The lighter paper is called *Gampi*; it is delicately made from mulberry fibers. Both papers are handcrafted in Japan. The boat symbolizes the creative process, as I feel I am journeying from one shore to another. A peacemaker must be willing to travel to both shores of hostility and to act as a bridge between the two. The pure and reflective raw minerals used in the ancient *Nihonga* painting technique are exuberant and costly. The paper is both delicate and durable. In *Precious Nard*, the marks made by pouring minerals onto the paper reflect both the sacrifice and the devotion needed to create lasting peace.

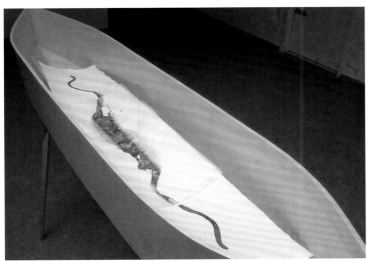

Dee VanDyke

Education 1974 BFA, University of Georgia, Athens, GA
Position Artist

Sometimes I think that I know what my art is about during the actual creative process, but after making drawings, paintings, and sculpture for thirty years, I have concluded that I rarely do. Like faith, action precedes understanding, and making art confirms that the ways of the Lord are both mysterious and paradoxical. I believe that my role is to pay attention and let the art come through me instead of from me. There is a lot to pay attention to.

I live on a bay that feeds from the Gulf of Mexico. There is a constant play between stillness and motion, light and shadow, silence and sound, surface and depth. Every morning I sit outside and listen. It is often a time of holy dictation. *Anointed* evolved from those mornings.

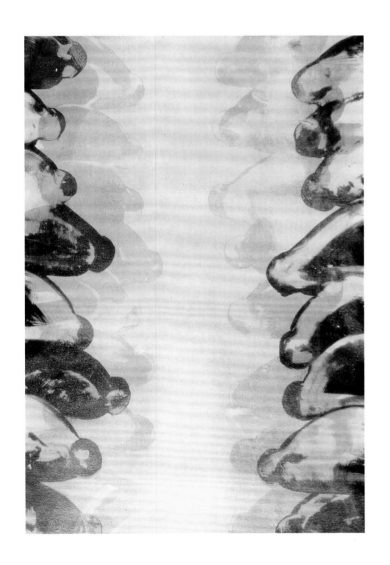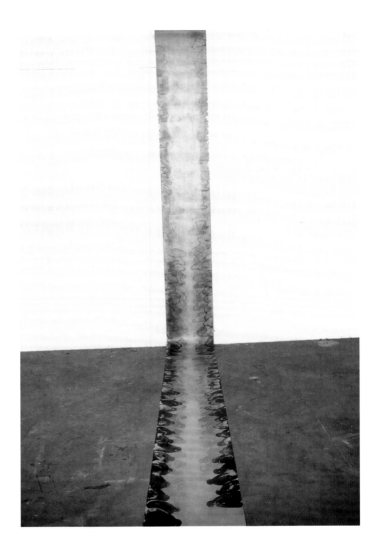

20 *Tower of Babel,* 2002.
Acrylic collage pop–up book.
20 x 36 inches (open).

Helen Zajkowski

Education **1994** MFA, Mason Gross School of the Arts, Rutgers University, New Brunswick, NJ **1990** BFA, Mason Gross School of the Arts, Rutgers University, New Brunswick, NJ **1978** BA, Alvernia College, Reading, PA
Position Artist and Teacher

The core of my work is the Judeo–Christian philosophy calling for universal stewardship of our natural resources. My art deals with the biblical cycle of creation and destruction in ironic terms. By taking a well–known image from the Scriptures and juxtaposing it with a current ecological issue, I aim to awaken the viewer to the new dimensions of the Old and New Testaments, as well as to our current understanding of our environment.

21 *Global City Babel (Foundation),* 2002.
Mixed media on wood.
30 x 30 inches (framed).

G. Carol Bomer

Education **1970** BA, Dordt College, Sioux Center, IA
Position Artist

"We see through a glass darkly" only the dimmest shadows of what truly is and will be. I hope my work conveys something of the visual experience of mystery and metaphor that is sometimes experienced when reading the Word of God. I want my work to bring glory to the God who has revealed himself in the face of Christ.

To reclaim the holism of imagination and intellect, spirit and flesh, I believe that artists must find direction and truth in the richness of the Holy Scriptures. My work often comes out of meditating on God's Word. Christ, the God/man, both Spirit and flesh, as well as Word and image of God, resolves the many dichotomies of artistic imaginative work. Through Him, I attempt to join the tangible world, and the spiritual world, apprehended through the eyes of faith.

My artwork is an ongoing series of media explorations combining collages of various papers, low relief, impasto, gold leaf, graphite, acrylics, waxes, oils, and varnishes. It focuses on changing the conceptual and spatial contexts of recognizable figurative forms, sometimes taken from past Christian imagery, and then placing them on non-objective grounds of text and image or manipulating them in other ways. In my *Global City Babel* series, word and the confusion of words since the fall of Babel are layered together with an image appropriated from Pieter Bruegel's *Tower of Babel* (ca. 1567–68).

Houben Tcherkelov

Education 1998 MFA, National Academy of Fine Arts, Sofia, Bulgaria
Position Artist

The current atmosphere of super–patriotism and fear of terrorists has loaded traditional American symbols with an extraordinary excess of meaning. In my recent work, I paint images, all borrowed from coins, on various household surfaces, such as wallpaper, vinyl, insulation materials, and cotton tablecloths. Although they are technically figurative, I consider these works to be abstract in the sense in which the NASDAQ, credit cards, and sacred objects are abstract. The question then becomes: what is the value of the material as such (wallpaper, tablecloth, paint, glitter, etc.) and at what point does value become a matter of faith? Or in other words: wherein lies the value of the material world and when does that value become a matter of faith?

David E. Levine

Education **1978** MEd, Boston University, Boston, MA **1978** Summer Institute in Media Arts, Tufts University, Medford, MA **1978** BA, University of Massachusetts, Amherst, MA
Position Artist

It seems to me that in the twenty-first century, the largest religion in America, the one that unifies much of an entire nation of diverse peoples, is consumerism. The holy words, in the form of slogans and jingles, are a constant reminder of whom we should be loyal to. Advertisements are modern-day fables created by corporate America that "inspire" us to use certain products in order to "enrich our lives." Some corporations have a messenger, a spokesperson to add personality and credibility to their products. We find such images comforting and familiar and thus we embrace them. In my artwork, I appropriate imagery found along the aisles of the modern-day supermarket. I combine this facet of popular culture with art historical references, creating the appearance of an artifact that comments on the new American religion.

Supermarkets are temples of our consumer culture. Each product is carefully crafted with a look to attract new buyers and to instill loyalty in current customers. The creators of these products are mostly interested in profits and will stretch the boundaries of truth and morality to achieve their objective. One product claims to make you more popular and another product insists it will give you a better life. Here, I focus on the breakfast cereal Wheaties, also known as "The Breakfast of Champions." This is a powerful subtitle. If Wheaties is truly the Breakfast of Champions, then why are only sports figures depicted on the boxes? Did JFK or Martin Luther King Jr. eat them? How about Einstein or Sophie Germain? And what about Mother Teresa, "Champion" of the poor? This rhetorical context sets the stage for my artwork.

James Disney

Education **1985** MDiv, Concordia Seminary, St. Louis, MO **1981** BA, Johns Hopkins University, Baltimore, MD
Position Senior Pastor, St. John's Lutheran Church, Buffalo, MN

Perhaps I am more a pastor than a painter. I have no pair of shoes with paint splattered all over them. I spend most of my time at church with other Christians. What this means for me as an artist is that when I make a picture, what's going on in my church often becomes the subject matter. Jesus said something satiric about us: "It would be easier to get a camel through the eye of a needle than to get a rich man into the kingdom of God." My picture is about all the ways that we try to but do not succeed in getting that camel through the eye of the needle. Whether it be anger, gluttony, melancholy, or vanity, there is something theatrical about the roles we play out. Though our sin can feel like a mask, we can be reluctant to set it down for fear, perhaps, that it is the sum total of our identity. My picture pays tribute to the bliss of letting go that has come to the woman who is knitting in an orange grove. She has made peace with the loss of life and is getting "the camel" through the eye of the needle. Forgive me if this is a bit preachy. Mostly, I offer this picture to celebrate with you the glorious absurdity of our human predicament.

Anita Breitenberg Naylor

Education 1977 BA, George Mason University, Fairfax, VA
Position Telecommunications Specialist with the United States Federal Government

My mission is to create fresh, elegant, lavish pictorial poetry that beguiles, captivates, compels, and confounds the viewer by means of visual biblical commentary. I aim to stimulate and evoke a spiritual response from a visual experience and to significantly impact the viewer's perceptions of reality through thought and emotion, inspiring and intriguing the viewer to ponder and engage the infinite embrace of salvation, and to promote worship of the embodiment of love.

My current body of works, *Exhibiting the Spirit*, consists of large-scale hyper-collages in the visionary style. They incorporate various shapes reminiscent of Tibetan mandalas, Indian rangolies (painted prayers), kaleidoscopes, and architectural domes. The pictorial content combines elements taken from medieval Christian and Renaissance art, from both Catholic and Orthodox perspectives and expressions. These elements merge metaphorically to form a consistently captivating universal topic, that of redemption. Paradoxical themes and contrasting images depict a psychological portrait of my own spiritual journey and inner revelations. Artistically, the timelessness of the works attempts to bring order, harmony, and beauty out of fragmented chaos, thus emphasizing the nature and destiny of mankind.

Each of my works uses a specific biblical reference as a starting point. I combine elements of various styles to suggest the drama of the cosmos. Vivid references to earthly forms reflect the eternal heavenly dimension. My works' narrative purpose does not confine itself to only the historical circumstances; indeed, it lends itself to current manifestations and leadings of the Spirit within an individual, culminating in their transformation.

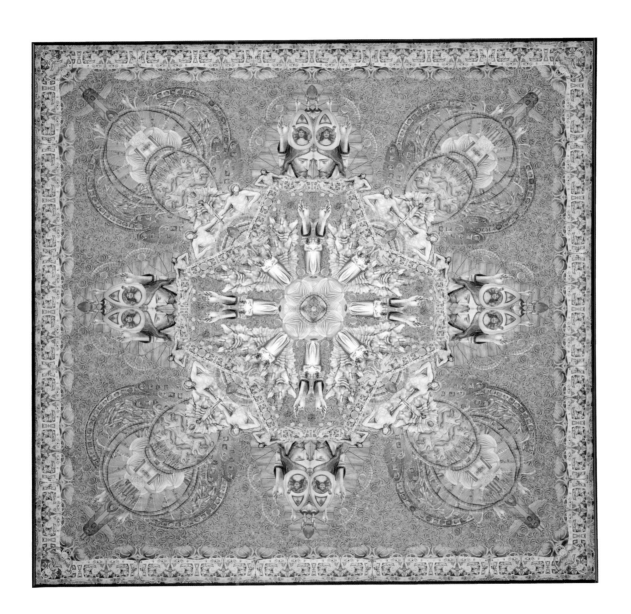

Faith and Healing by Grace

26 *Binding Up, Healing Vision I, 2004.*
Graphite, encaustic, steel, and 23-karat
gold. 12 x 24 inches.

Erica Grimm-Vance

Education 1982 BFA, University of Regina, Regina, SK, Canada
Position Sessional Assistant Professor and Visual Arts External Coordinator, Trinity Western University, Langley, BC, Canada

Embodiment has been the theme of my work for almost twenty years. All we know is mediated through the body, and as such, it is the central site of meaning. Simone Weil used the Platonic word *metaxu* to describe anything that could be a bridge or mediation between us and God. The created order, including the human body, is a barrier, and at the same time it is a way through. "Two prisoners whose cells adjoin communicate with each other by knocking on the wall. The wall is the thing that separates them but it is also their means of communication. It is the same with us and God. Every separation is a link." The figures in most of my work echo Weil's insistence on our bodily fragility. "Our flesh is fragile . . . our soul is vulnerable. . . . Our social personality is exposed to every hazard." But it is precisely this intimate fragility that connects us at the core of our being to the cross of Christ.

The figures in most of my images are contrasted with silent planes of steel and gold, which heighten the corporeal, fragile reading of the figure. In recent years, the discovery of materials has been exhilarating. Materials carry meaning. Gold, steel, wax, ash, and lead are all ripe with metaphoric meanings, ranging from precious to toxic. Weil would see both the human body and these materials as *metaxu*, bridges between us and God. Hence, both the body and materials are potential sites of transcendence.

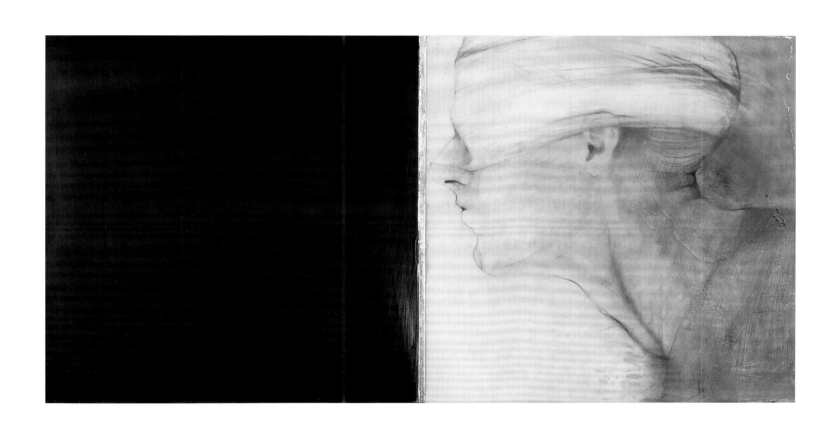

Stewart Luckman

Education **1973** MFA, University of Minnesota, Minneapolis, MN **1970** MA, University of Minnesota, Minneapolis, MN **1961** BFA, Macalester College, St. Paul, MN
1961 BA, Bethel College, St. Paul, MN
Position Professor of Art, Bethel College, St. Paul, MN

For me, Job's word and testament have been a daily reminder of the challenges I face in living and making, of peeling and bruising, of carving and polishing. The stone becomes an invitation to the eyes and hands of others through the metaphor of sculpture.

28 *Ash Wednesday*
(Christ and the Demoniac), 2001.
Oil on canvas. 96 x 144 inches.

Edward Knippers

Education **1980** Fellow, Atelier 17 (Stanley William Hayter), Paris, France **1973** MFA, University of Tennessee, Knoxville, TN **1969** BA, Asbury College, Wilmore, KY
Position Artist

Ash Wednesday (Christ and the Demoniac) speaks of the condition of us all and of Christ's redeeming power. The title comes from the imposition of ashes on that Wednesday of the Church Year that makes us painfully aware of our mortality and our desperate position in the world. We are all like the demoniac as he wandered among the putridity of the tombs in need of a Savior.

29 *Inhabiting/Flying,* 2003.
Mixed media sculpture.
40 x 14 x 13 inches.

Melanie Weaver

Education **1998** MFA, University of North Texas, Denton, TX **1993** BS, Biola University, La Mirada, CA
Position Director/Owner, Art Haus, San Bernardino, CA

My art deals with healing issues and I use art as a form of therapy. My artwork is my journal of healing from being used in child prostitution and pornography. I have recently begun to speak honestly about my past, and about how I use my art to heal. My studio time allows me to deal with the negative aspects of my past so that I can focus on the positive aspects of the present.

The objects I use in my assemblage work reference my childhood domestic life. I use objects such as plastic toy army men, dolls, dollhouse furniture, plastic flowers, kitchen utensils, jewelry boxes, and platters. The juxtaposition of various objects creates narratives that encompass childhood, war, domestic violence, trauma, healing, and spirituality.

I find resolution and acceptance throughout the artistic process and that peace is evident in the Madonna figure at the top of each work. The Madonna reaches out one hand in blessing, a covering over any chaos in the objects below her. The halo surrounding the Madonna's face is created with toys or domestic objects such as curlers, clothespins, beads, etc. The implication is that there is a spiritual resolution that can be found within the domestic arena, after domestic violence has been vanquished. There is an exalting of form found in the mundane, a healing of the soul and an empowerment in the process of depicting the wounding and the healing.

30 *Faith from Inside — Religion in Prison: Oak Park Heights Super Maximum Security Facility for Men, Stillwater, MN, 2002.*
Silver gelatin print. 15 x 20 inches.
Faith from Inside — Religion in Prison: Women's State Correctional Institution, Muncy, PA, 2002.
Silver gelatin print. 11 x 14 inches.

Serge J-F Levy

Education **1995** BA, Vassar College, Poughkeepsie, NY
Position Instructor, International Center for Photography, New York, NY

Religion is often viewed as a privilege afforded to and practiced by peaceful and law-abiding citizens. Rarely does it occur to one that religion and spiritual enlightenment are practiced and sought by prison inmates convicted of felony offenses, including rape and murder. In fact, many American prisons are thriving pluralistic environments offering inmates the opportunity to pursue their chosen spiritual identities.

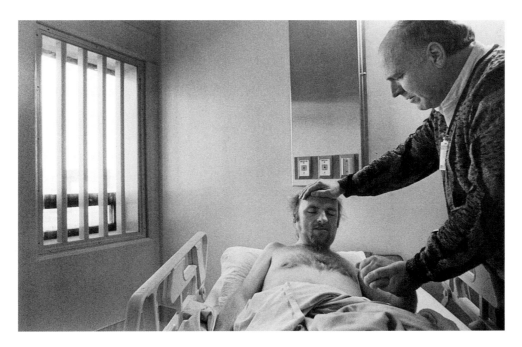

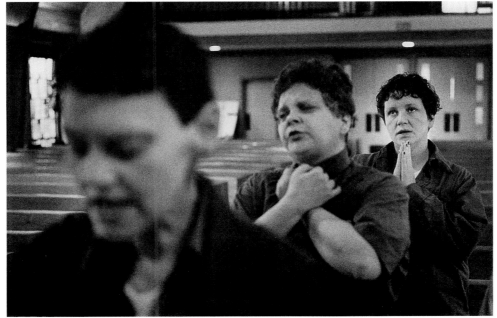

Kathy Hettinga

Education **1985** MFA, Colorado State University, Fort Collins, CO **1978** BFA, Calvin College, Grand Rapids, MI
Position Distinguished Professor of Art, Department of Visual Arts, School of the Arts, Messiah College, Grantham, PA

After my Good Friday announcement/pronouncement of cancer, my doctor referred me to Dr. Misas, a Cuban-American gynecologic oncologist, whose name means Mass in Spanish. Dr. Misas has been to me like a healing Eucharist. He has healing hands as a surgeon; he heals your body and does not forget to comfort your spirit. He acts for me and for the hundreds of others who are his patients.

In the Protestant church, the emphasis is briefly on Good Friday, the day Christ is crucified, and then mainly on Easter Sunday, the day of the Resurrection. Protestants do little or nothing with Holy and Great Saturday. The Greek and Russian Orthodox churches celebrate that Saturday, the day in which Christ descends into Hell; yet, He is resurrected, working to pull Adam and Eve (representing all of humanity) out of Hell. So, it is a conflicted time of both great lamentations (Russian Orthodox) and of great praises (Greek Orthodox). The Protestant church has forgotten Holy and Great Saturday, a time of intense pain and great accomplishment, the conflicted day of paradoxical opposites.

This explains the process I am now in: the terror of cancer; the poisoning, yet healing work of chemotherapy; the loss of my beautiful head of hair, including eyebrows and eyelashes (and yet, the bald female head is an incredible thing of unseen beauty); the loss of identity as a successful workaholic artist/designer; to the new work documenting the fascinating and new-to-me world of healthcare givers, modern medical imaging, and men who heal in a world of blue and green outfits complete with head gear and shoe nets. I go from being depressed and pathetically mired down, to being in a state in which I hear a completely different/distant calling that frees me.

How, then, do we live with and through suffering? I have started a new series that looks at the many faces of healthcare givers, from the parade of nurses, aides, and technicians, to the larger-than-life healer/savior figure of the surgeon. Many of the people in this parade are seen from the perspective of the patient (often lying down), their portraits taken with a Kodak disposable camera. The disposable camera lent itself to the needs of the weakened patient in many different settings.

Michael Mills

Education **1991** MDiv, Wilfrid Lurier University, Waterloo, ON, Canada **1989** CPE, Riverview Psychiatric Hospital, Vancouver, BC, Canada
1986 BS, The University of British Columbia, Vancouver, BC, Canada
Position Artist and President, Ontario Society of Artists

In my work, I begin with the assumption that human beings understand themselves in relationship to their world most fully through their bodies. One's sense of who one is, both as an individual and as a member of a community, grows out of the experience of being physical.

    In this series of digital photographs, I explore the intimate relationship between the Eucharist as the body of Christ and the unique bodies of faithful individuals. I have photographed, at close range, members of my family: a seventy-eight-year-old man, a thirty-six-year-old woman, and a nine-year-old boy. Over the top of their torsos I have superimposed the image of the crucified Jesus that is commonly found stamped on the surface of the Eucharistic wafer or host. It is my hope that *Hosts* will invite people to consider their own bodies, with their inherent power, frailty, ambiguity, and idiosyncrasies, as authentic bearers or *hosts* for Christ.

V

33 *Altarpiece of St. Francis of L'Abri,*
2001.
Mixed media with oil and book
pages. 27¼ x 36¾ x 3 inches (open);
20 x 18¼ x 5 inches (closed).

Tyrus Clutter

Education **1997** MFA, Bowling Green State University, Bowling Green, OH **1994** BA, Spring Arbor University, Spring Arbor, MI
Position Director, Christians in the Visual Arts (CIVA)

This work explores the continuities and disparities within the traditions of the Christian faith. The Catholic and Orthodox branches of the church have a rich tradition of visual imagery, including altarpieces devoted to specific saints, who are venerated for their holy and miraculous acts (which are worthy of contemplation and imitation). Conversely, since the iconoclasm of the Reformation, most Protestant denominations have tended to champion the primacy of the Word (*sole scriptura*). The result has been a lack of visual imagery within Protestant circles.

Altarpiece of St. Francis of L'Abri attempts to bridge this gap. The Christian faith is founded in both the physical, material image (going all the way back to the incarnation of Christ himself) and in the Word (which can mean both Scripture and Christ, who is The Word or Logos). It is both of these things that come together to create the history and tradition of the church. This work fully blends word and image in an exploration of their essential coexistence for faith to occur. The semi-transparent quality of the paint laid over the book pages blends them together seamlessly. Neither the text nor the image is more important than its counterpart; each can be "read," yet the other is still present for equal inspection. This balance seems vital to our understanding of contemporary Western culture, which has its roots in the written word, but which is moving more and more towards establishing the visual image as the common means of communication.

My altarpieces are based on my "personal saints"—those persons who have had some profound and shaping influence on my thoughts and artwork.

Rosemary Scott-Fishburn

Education 2000 BA, Gordon College, Wenham, MA
Position Artist and Program Coordinator, Off-Campus Art Program, Gordon College

This piece is part of *Christ and His Saints,* my most recent body of work, which has been directly influenced by my travels and studies in Europe and the American West. Probably the greatest influence on my work is my continuing love of early Italian Renaissance painting, including the icons and altarpieces of Duccio di Buoninsegna of the Sienese school of painters, which I first encountered in depth while studying with Gordon College's Orvieto Semester in 1999. In Italy, I discovered the tradition of creating original artwork *after* another artist, a practice which was and remains integral to conventional iconography, a sort of passing down of visual language. One learns to *read* a painting or other image, recognizing symbols and thus gaining the understanding and depth that these creations bear — and for myself, it took a humbling experience with Duccio's *Maestà* altarpiece in Siena to find that I was somewhat illiterate visually.

Executed in copper foil, *The Madonna and Child Enthroned with Angels and Saints* is after Duccio's great altarpiece. The medium, which is rather unusual, reminds me of Mexican and Native American folk art. I have been creating copper and aluminum pieces for the past two years, and am currently in the process of creating an exhibition, *All Saints,* depicting a saint for every day of the year, a project that will be completed by September 2005.

35 *Annunciation,* from the series
Elegy for Witness, 2002.
Oil, alkyd resin, and gold and silver
leaf on wood. 76 x 96 inches.

Bruce Herman

Education 1979 MFA, Boston University School for the Arts, Boston, MA
1977 BFA, Boston University School for the Arts, Boston, MA
Position Artist

The paintings from the *Elegy for Witness* series are Eucharistic images, meant as meditations on the lives of the martyrs as living sacrifices. Each of the images features the human form surrounded by fragments of architecture or abstracted surfaces and the pentimenti of the Christian tradition. The willing deaths of the martyrs mirror that of Christ, real food and drink poured out as a witness to the love of God. My hope in making these images is that they evoke the real presence of all the thousands who have laid down their lives for their friends in obedience to the highest law — love.

36 *Image: Seed of Divine Life,* 2003.
Altarpiece construction/combined
process on wood and metal.
25 x 19 x 3 inches.

Robert P. Eustace

Education **1987** MFA, School of Visual Arts, New York, NY **1981** BA, Montclair State College, Montclair, NJ
Position Artist

My current work is an ongoing extended series called *Aenigmate*: mixed-media works/altarpiece constructions. These images, which are likened to illuminated manuscript pages and icons, stem from my interest in
medieval, conceptual, and narrative modes. They pertain largely to biblical themes centered around the life
of Mary (the Annunciation, the Mother and Child theme), the Passion of Christ, and the Apocalypse (with
the construction of the Heavenly City). My images in the series also focus upon "maps and diagrams" and
can be divided into two subsets: (1) architectural: ancient church plans, ornate windows, and the Paradise
Garden (or outward terrain); and (2) freeform abstractions, which serve to navigate the unknown (internal)
territories of the soul. The series title *Aenigmate* means at this present time (being earthbound and limited
in finitude) to see and ascertain only the dimmest of shadows of what truly is and will be, like looking
through a dark glass. I seek to convey something of the *mysterium tremendum*, or a visual approximation of
the experience of awe, divine mystery, and terrible beauty.

37 *Stations of the Cross,* 2004.
Oil on paper. 14 works,
8 x 6 inches each.

James Larson

Education **1987** MFA, Brooklyn College, City University of New York, Brooklyn, NY **1982** BA, Bethel College, Arden Hills, MN
Position Artist and Woodworker

In *Stations of the Cross,* I am trying to create a visual narrative a little less predictable than those that might be suggested by some of the worn old stories from Sunday school. I like that there is a specific text and number of stations that set the parameters, but beyond that I hope to bring out some of the bizarreness of the story and how it connects with basic human experience. It is a story about God giving up power and I am interested in what that looks like. A god/man who meets his mother implies such vulnerability. He is, after all, a child. A woman from a very different cultural context wipes his face with her covering veil; it is both scandalous and vulnerable. This god falls down three times. And he dies. I deal with water in much of my work. Here, I was thinking about the sea as the source of life, and as a symbol of chaos and death. It is waiting to engulf Jesus, and for that matter, everyone else. I was thinking a lot about the book of Jonah when I was working on this and I tried to bring in elements from that story. Jonah somehow sings from the belly of death. And in the end the people are spared because, as the story puts it, they do not know what they are doing and, oddly and beautifully, there were "also much cattle."

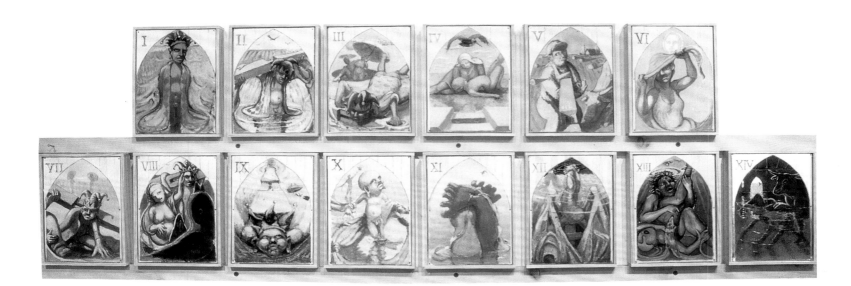

Lynn Aldrich

Education **1986** MFA, Art Center College of Design, Pasadena, CA **1984** BFA, California State University, Northridge, CA
1966 BA, University of North Carolina, Chapel Hill, NC
Position Artist

In my work, I begin with material that already exists in the world, with a respect for its incarnational possibilities. I collect, arrange, and minimally alter it, intending for the completed work to reveal attributes and metaphors that transcend ordinary functionality. The work is designed to perceptually challenge the viewer's expectations, as well as to raise philosophical questions regarding physicality and meaning. For *Baptistery*, I collected pages of pool design images from glossy coffee table books. Then, with gold leaf paint, I obscured each page except for the architectural shapes of pools or windows. Thus, I have attempted to represent a "text" describing, among other tendencies, an architecture for the sacrament of baptism.

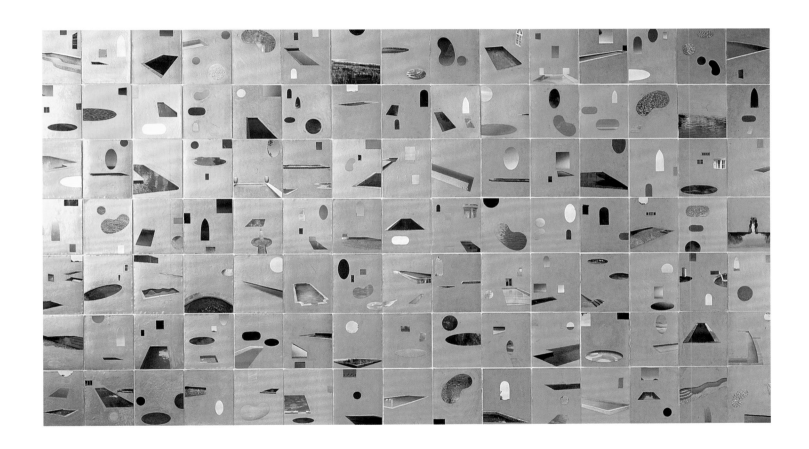

39 *Turf Painting / Ireland, 2002.*
Gouache, acrylic mediums, gold
leaf, plaster, gesso, and County
Mayo turf and turf ash over Bible
pages on Arches watercolor paper.
18 x 24 inches.

Donald J. Forsythe

Education **1979** MFA, Rochester Institute of Technology, Rochester, NY **1977** BS, Indiana University of Pennsylvania, Indiana, PA
Position Distinguished Professor of Art, Messiah College, Grantham, PA

Turf Painting / Ireland continues a series of "contemporary manuscript paintings" that I have been working on since 1988. In them, I reflect on aspects of contemporary faith, while utilizing labor–intensive techniques to promote the idea of painting as a means of personal meditation. I often contrast subjects in a diptych format because it suggests the right and left pages of a bound codex manuscript. Earlier pieces with titles like *Plenty / Want* or *A Fruitful Vine / An Unfruitful Vine* exemplify the viewer's need to compare or contrast the ideas on either side of the overall composition.

I use the materials of historic manuscript illumination (gold leaf, Italian burnish clay, and fine French varnishes) as well as rather unorthodox additives to paint, such as sand, earth, ash, and charcoal. I painted my earliest manuscripts on a ground made of pages from Bibles, devotional books, or hymnbooks glued to watercolor paper; I then partially obscured the texts with layers of color and texture. After viewing Giotto's magnificent chapel in Padua in 1989, I began to consider the stars and the heavens, and I started painting manuscripts over layers of plaster, combining the processes of fresco and manuscript illumination. For me, this combined process is a vehicle for the visual transmission of many ideas about Christianity.

I painted *Turf Painting / Ireland* while on a fellowship in Ireland in 2002. Isolated for a month in a small cottage overlooking the sea in remote northwest Ireland, I was surrounded by ancient standing stones, passage tombs, and ritual circles — a long connection to others looking to the heavens and seeking answers. Turf is an important material in rural Ireland. It is a 5,000-year accumulation of compacted vegetable material, which is excavated, dried, and burnt as fuel for heat. It is literally "the stuff of life" in that part of the world. I mixed the turf with acrylic medium to make a crude paint.

In *Turf Painting / Ireland*, I compare the actual Irish turf with a map of Ireland, as if the country were being viewed from the heavens. Clearly visible is the divide that separates Northern Ireland from the rest of the Republic of Ireland (a line drawn by humans representing a different kind of "turf") and also a fairly accurate road map of the country (many more lines drawn by humans.) One type of line shows us the way, and the other represents a history of political and religious schism. Both types of lines on the map cannot be seen completely from the perspective of a person standing on the ground, but we know they are there nonetheless.

40 *Lenten Book: Book of Forty Number Three,* 2004.
Pages: handmade paper, painted with gouache and metallic pigments, sewn with cotton and metallic threads; endpapers: Chiri paper and Thai soft Unryu; cover: bark cloth; binding: hemp and waxed linen. 9 x 17 x 4¼ inches (closed).

Christine A. Forsythe

Education 1982 MFA, School for American Crafts, Rochester Institute of Technology, Rochester, NY **1977** BFA, Indiana University of Pennsylvania, Indiana, PA
Position Professor of Art, Messiah College, Grantham, PA

Lenten Book: Book of Forty Number Three is the third in a series on the theme of penitence. In biblical and devotional terms, the number 40 is linked to several different events that are tied to a season of penitence: Moses's 40 years in the desert, Jesus's 40 days in the desert before he begins his public ministry, the 40 days of Advent, the 40 days of Lent, etc. The number 40 represents something quite profound, a significant elapse of time but not an eternity. I am interested in expressing complex ideas about faith in a more symbolic manner. Being penitent and the idea of counting time and crossing it off go hand in hand for me. Even while being penitent you start to notice and perhaps become distracted by little things, the cobwebs in the corner, the way the words line up on the page, the feel of the rosary beads in your hand. Sometimes the distraction becomes the focus, and the sin is replaced by a small gift, a reprieve while still fulfilling the act of penitence.

The form of *Lenten Book* is related directly to three encounters I had over the past few years. The first two occurred at a bookmaking workshop, during which two different students gave me crucial elements for *Lenten Book*. One student gave me bark cloth, which became the book's cover. This is the material that is used to wrap the dead in Uganda. The student had visited Uganda during the time of the horrific massacres that took place there, and was overwhelmed by the sight of bodies being wrapped for burial in the cloth. This representation of the shroud of Christ seemed perfect for my purposes. A second student gave me a small piece of material comprised of little triangles of bark cloth that had been stitched together. I do not know its origin, but it must have once been part of a larger cloth intended for a more elaborate use. I found the third element in a Bible from Ethiopia, from the collections of the Library of the American Bible Society. This Bible has an open binding and wooden covers and fits neatly into a leather case. I loved its handmade quality, the notes on the pages, the surfaces worn from use. I had the sense that this Bible was both well loved and very important. I wanted to capture that same spirit with my *Lenten Book*. Though mine is a new book made in the twenty-first century, *Lenten Book* relies on very old ideas and forms that will continue to link the centuries together. In a way, regardless of the form the volume might take, we will always have the need to repent, to reflect, and to prepare for what is to come.

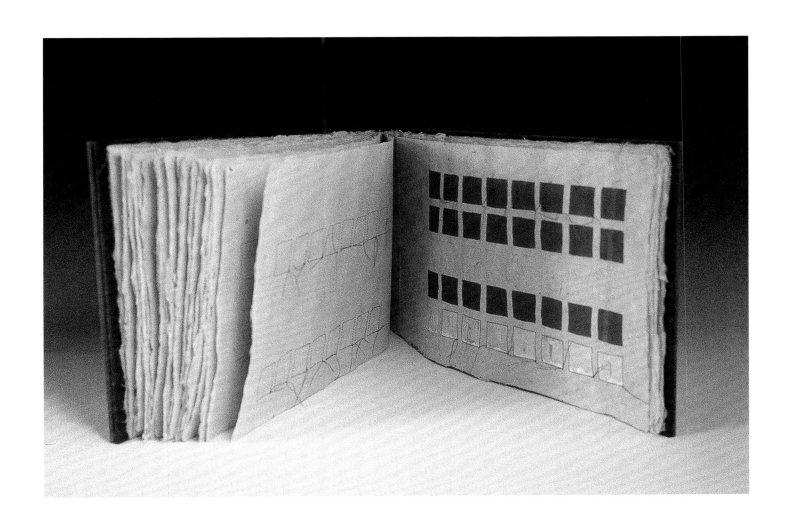

41 *Book of Nails,* 2003.
Mixed media with gold leaf.
9 x 6 x 1 ¼ inches (closed);
9 x 12 x 1 ¼ inches (open).

Sandra Bowden

Education 1977 BA, State University of New York, Empire College, Albany, NY
Position Artist and President, Christians in the Visual Arts (CIVA)

The book itself is the logical progression in the exploration of the word. I look to the tradition of medieval manuscript illumination in which artists lavishly embellished their parchments with gold, demonstrating the preciousness of the words they were preserving for future generations. This dimensional artist's book applies the techniques used in manuscript illumination to the book surface. In *Book of Nails*, a mound of old rusted nails is set in a container lined with precious gold. This unlikely combination calls up vivid contrasts: good and evil; pure and tarnished; eternal and that which decays. Another obvious reference is to the container holding the spikes with which the soldiers nailed Jesus to the cross. The outside of the container is mounted with one large old floor nail and four smaller ones, which refer to the Crucifixion.

Aaron Lee Benson

Peter Lee Scheesley

Guy Chase

Last Things

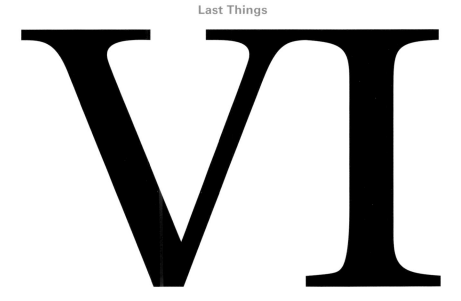

Aaron Lee Benson

Education 1990 MFA, University of Tennessee, Knoxville, TN
Position Associate Professor of Fine Arts, Union University, Jackson, TN

The Two Witnesses is about the two witnesses who are found in the eleventh chapter of Revelation. They will stand in Jerusalem and testify for 1,260 days before they are killed, their bodies lying in the street for three days while everyone looks on. After three days, God brings them back to life and they are taken up into heaven. The work was conceived as a portal or window unto salvation for one of the last times. The piece, a catenary arch, is a metaphor for that last opening to God's grace and mercy. The piece changes from deep black/blue/green on the far left, to a natural red/brown/white earth tone on the far right, where the images of the two witnesses appear. The colors signify the battle between good and evil. The arch form appears often in nature as well as in my work, where it has come to signify the call of love and grace that God continues to issue to mankind. He never tires of His longing for us or of His persistence in letting us know of His longing. This is the true "good news."

43 *Four Laws: I, II, III, IV,* 2004
Oil on board.
4 panels, 9 x 12 inches each.

Peter Sheesley

Education 2004 MFA, *cum laude*, Graduate School of Figurative Art, New York Academy of Art, New York, NY **2000** BA, Wheaton College, Wheaton, IL
Position Illustrator, Pivar Research, New York, NY

Four Laws is based on Campus Crusade's Four Spiritual Laws, which were popularized in tracts written by Bill Bright. Each panel provides an interpretation of a basic tenet of Christianity. A meditation on each tenet is created by combining a hand gesture with a specific light strength and direction. The first panel shows that "God loves you and created you to know Him personally," with a finger pointing strikingly toward the viewer. The second shows how "Man is sinful and separated from God, so we cannot know Him personally or experience His love," with judgmental lighting and knotted fist. The third shows how "Jesus Christ is God's only provision for man's sin. Through Him alone we can know God personally and experience God's love," as a warm light seems to carry a relaxed, open hand. In the fourth, "We must individually receive Jesus Christ as Savior and Lord; then we can know God personally and experience his love," and an open hand holds the light, divinity resting in a hand.

Guy Chase

Education **1981** MFA, The School of the Art Institute of Chicago, Chicago, IL **1977** BA, Bethel College, St. Paul, MN
Position Associate Professor of Art, Bethel College, St. Paul, MN

Untitled (Ledger for Multiple Adjustments) was made in a rather labor-intensive fashion that required meticulous care and concentration. The lines were drawn out to create the grid structure. Then, the light ledger green was applied to the rectangles over and around the lines. The process becomes meditative, the content guiding the "listening" prayer.

I first became interested in ledger paper as a context for meditative painting after I had completed a series of works based on legal pad paper. At least four connections to the light green grid paper synchronized for me to cement my interest: 1) My wife is an accountant and had tablets of columnar ruled paper in her brief case. The small grid was initially off-putting. 2) Then, in the mid-nineties, it seemed that everyone was pushing productivity initiatives, requiring us to justify our existence in terms of numbers. I found myself quantifying mundane activities. It seemed to me that describing anything in terms of numbers allowed for passage into a more secure position. 3) Accounting errors became the news of the day with various financial institutions being held to the fire for "cooking the books." 4) Finally, I spent three months in Charlotte, North Carolina, a center for banking. I thought it was the right place to begin the series *Light Green Paintings*. Blank spreadsheets remind me of grace at the Day of Judgment, any day of judgment.

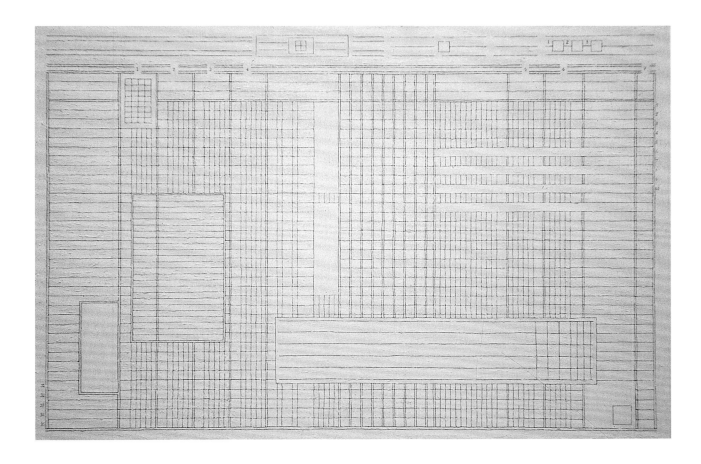

About the Artists

I God in the Details

1 Joel Sheesley

Awards

2002 Artist's Fellowship, Illinois Arts Council

2000/2002 Senior Scholarship Achievement Award, Wheaton College, Wheaton, IL

1996 R. Love Prize, *Sacred Arts XVI*, Billy Graham Center Museum, Wheaton, IL

1991 First Prize, *Sacred Arts XII*, Billy Graham Center Museum, Wheaton, IL

1987 Juror's Award, *Sioux City Biennial*, Sioux City, IA

Exhibitions

2005 *A Broken Beauty*, Laguna Art Museum, Laguna Beach, CA (traveling)

2004 *Paintings*, Trinity Christian College, Palos Heights, IL (solo)

2003 *Intimate Geography*, St. Peter's Church, New York, NY (solo)

2002 *The Painted Journey*, Safety-Kleen Gallery One, Elgin Community College, Elgin, IL (solo)

2001 *Sheesley/Witkin: Fortitude and Forbearance*, Center Art Gallery, Calvin College, Grand Rapids, MI

2000 *175th Annual Exhibition*, National Academy of Design, New York, NY

2000 *Interiors*, Barrington Center for the Arts, Gordon College, Wenham, MA (solo)

2000 *Eve in Suburbia: Paintings by Joel Sheesley*, The Olson Gallery, Bethel College, St. Paul, MN (solo)

2000 *Shake the Coat: A Midwestern Tribute to Gregory Gillespie*, Carlson Tower Gallery, North Park University, Chicago, IL

1998 *The Interior Journey to the Contemporary Landscape*, Northern Illinois University Museum, DeKalb, IL

1996 *Sacred Arts XVI*, Billy Graham Center Museum, Wheaton, IL

1994 *A Summer Sampler*, The Lookout Gallery, Regent College, Vancouver, BC, Canada

1993 *Absence of Paradise*, Adams Gallery, Wheaton College, Wheaton, IL (solo)

1993 *Genesis to Revelation: The Old and New Testament in Contemporary Art*, Richard H. Love Contemporary Gallery, Chicago, IL

1992 *Organized Play*, Sloan Gallery, Valparaiso University, Valparaiso, IN (solo)

1991 *Sacred Arts XII*, Billy Graham Center Museum, Wheaton, IL

1990 *The Chicago Show*, Chicago Public Library Cultural Center, Chicago, IL

1986 *The Sacred Image*, Messiah College, Grantham, PA (traveling)

1983 *Art on Paper: Sixteenth Weatherspoon Annual Exhibition*, Weatherspoon Art Gallery, University of North Carolina, Greensboro, NC

References

Prescott, Theodore, editor, *A Broken Beauty*, Grand Rapids: William B. Eerdmans Publishing Company, 2005.

Romaine, James, "A Conversation with Joel Sheesley," in *Objects of Grace: Conversations on Creativity and Faith*, Baltimore, MD: Square Halo Books, 2002: 137–49.

Roosa, Wayne, "Signs of Consciousness: Pilgrimage and Presence in the Paintings of Joel Sheesley," in *Sheesley/Witkin: Fortitude and Forbearance*, Grand Rapids, MI: Center Art Gallery, William Spoelhof Center, Calvin College, 2001.

Roosa, Wayne, "Paradise Lost, Paradise Sublimated: The Suburban Paintings of Joel Sheesley," *The Sacred Art Exhibition Series*, Sacred Art Exhibition Committee, Millennium 2000, Cathedral Basilica of St. Mary, Minneapolis, MN: M and M Printing, 2000: 6–8.

Mahmoud, Ben, "'Shake the Coat': A Perfect Example of How Realism Should Be Done," *DeKalb Daily Chronicle*, November 19, 2000, section D: 1–2.

Walford, E. John, "Joel Sheesley: A Profile," *Image: A Journal of the Arts & Religion*, Issue # 4 (Fall 1993): 23–36.

2 Mary Fielding McCleary

Awards

2003 Honorable Mention, Assistance League of Houston Celebrates Texas Art 2003, Houston, TX

2001 Award, American Association of University Women

1988–89 Recipient of a Mid-America Arts Alliance/National Endowment for the Arts Fellowship

Exhibitions

2005 *A Broken Beauty*, Laguna Art Museum, Laguna Beach, CA (traveling)

2003 *Raid on the Inarticulate*, Adair Margo Gallery, El Paso, TX (solo)

2003 *Bread Upon the Waters: Pursuing the Art of Generosity*, Gallery W, Sacramento, CA (CIVA Traveling)

2002 *Sugar and Spice*, University of Maine at Presque Isle, Presque Isle, ME

2001 *Beginning with the Word, Constructed Narratives: 1985–2000*, Galveston Arts Center, Galveston TX (solo, traveling)

2000 *Word as Art: Contemporary Renderings*, The Gallery at the American Bible Society, New York, NY

2000 *Neo-Rococo*, University of Texas at San Antonio Art Gallery, San Antonio, TX

1999 *Texas IV*, Tyler Museum of Art, Tyler, TX

1999 *Thresholds*, Concordia University Gallery, Austin, TX

1998 *Scriptural References*, Amarillo Museum of Art, Amarillo, TX (solo)

1997 *Establishment & Revelation*, Dallas Visual Art Center, Dallas, TX

1996 *Arte Sagrado*, Concordia University, Austin, TX

1996 *CIVA Creates the Portrait*, Dordt College Art Gallery, Sioux Center, IA (CIVA Traveling)

1994 *50 for the 50th*, Temple Emmanuel Gallery, Houston, TX

1988 *Works by Women*, Gihon Foundation Collection, Peregrine Gallery, Houston, TX (traveling)

1988 *Texas Women*, National Museum of Women in the Arts, Washington, DC (traveling)

1981 *Salon d'Autome*, Blaffer Gallery, University of Houston, Houston, TX

Collections

Art Museum of Southeast Texas, Beaumont, TX

Gihon Foundation, Santa Fe, NM

Museum of Fine Arts, Houston, TX

The Pace Collection, New York, NY

San Antonio Museum of Art, San Antonio, TX

University of Oklahoma Art Museum, Norman, OK

References

Prescott, Theodore, editor, *A Broken Beauty*, Grand Rapids: William B. Eerdmans Publishing Company, 2005.

Romaine, James, *Objects of Grace: Conversations on Creativity and Faith*, Baltimore, MD: Square Halo Press, 2002: 50–63.

Willour, Clint, "An Obsession with Compulsion," *Artlies*, No. 35, Summer 2002: 8–11.

Goddard, Dan R., "Artworks Retell Bible Stories: College Professor's Updated Biblical Images Are Now on Display," *San Antonio Express-News*, October 9, 2001: 1D.

Wolfe, Gregory, "Mary McCleary: Constructing Paradox," *CIVASeen*, Vol. 1, 2001: 6–7.

Roosa, Wayne L., "A Fullness of Vision: Mary McCleary's Collages," *Image: A Journal of the Arts & Religion*, Issue # 23 (Summer 1999): 32–42.

Monfrini, Richard Joseph, "Recovering That Which Has Been Lost: A Brief Introduction to the Redemptive Art of Mary Fielding McCleary," *Corum Deo*, Vol. 3, No. 2, Summer 1995: 1–3.

3 Gregory King

Awards

2001 Harvey Fellowship, Mustard Seed Foundation, Arlington, VA

1999 Community Arts Assistance Program Grant, Chicago Department of Cultural Affairs, Chicago, IL

1998 Elizabeth Greenshields Foundation, Montreal, Quebec, Canada

1996 Arts Midwest/NEA Regional Visual Artists Fellowship, Arts Midwest, Minneapolis, MN

Exhibitions

2003 *Continuums*, Organization of Independent Artists, New York, NY (solo)

2003 *Brooklyn Underground Film Festival* (Public Discourse Program), Brooklyn, NY

2003 *The Best of Flicker Film Festival*, The Milky Way Lounge, Boston Film Revolution, Boston, MA

2003 *Improvised and Otherwise Festival* (film screening), WAX, Brooklyn, NY

2002 *Video Trade*, Infernale: International Student Film Festival, Universität der Künste, Berlin, Germany

2002 *Contemporary Doubles* (Fall Film Series Program), Consolidated Works Arts Center, Seattle, WA

2001 *In a Landscape*, Messiah College, Grantham, PA (solo)

2001 *Flicker Film Festival*, February and July screenings, Knitting Factory, New York, NY

2001 *Three Constants*, Barrington Center for the Arts, Gordon College Art Gallery, Wenham, MA (solo)

1999 *the last paintings . . .* The Butcher Shop, Chicago, IL (solo)

1999 *Alternating Between Details*, University of the Arts Gallery, Philadelphia, PA

1999 *Building Beauty*, North Park University Gallery, Chicago, IL

1998 *Three Arts Midwest/NEA Regional Fellows*, West Bend Art Museum, West Bend, WI

1998 *Sacred Arts XVIII*, Billy Graham Center Museum, Wheaton, IL

1997 *Articles of Faith*, Southern Ohio Museum, Portsmouth, OH

1996 *Reflections of Faith VI*, Kreft Center Gallery, Concordia University, Ann Arbor, MI

Collections

American Bible Society, New York, NY

Billy Graham Center Museum, Wheaton, IL

Messiah College, Grantham, PA

References

"The Apocalyptic Work of Gregory King," *Cornerstone Magazine*, Vol. 23, No. 105, 1995: 32–35.

Heilenman, Diane, "Art Reviews: Zephyr Gallery," *The Courier-Journal*, April 3, 1994, Section 1: 4.

4 Christine Huck

Exhibitions

2004 *Embodiments*, The Winds Cafe, Chicago, IL (solo)

2003 *Personifications*, Levis Faculty Center, University of Illinois at Urbana-Champaign, Urbana, IL (solo)

Collections

Henry Lee, Chicago, IL

Ben and Catherine Trapskin, Minneapolis, MN

5 George Wingate

Awards

2003 Juror's Prize, *Mixing It Up*, Lynn Arts Third Annual Mixed Media Show, Lynn, MA

1998 The Emile Carlson Prize, National Academy Annual Exhibition, New York, NY

1994 Award of Merit, National Academy Annual Exhibition, New York, NY

1988 First Prize, Creative Arts Workshop, New Haven, CT

Exhibitions

2004 *National Academy 179th Annual Exhibition*, New York, NY

2003 *Seeing Is Believing: Drawing as Insight*, Barrington Center for the Arts, Gordon College, Wenham, MA

2001 *Parlatorio*, Istituto San Ludovico, Orvieto, Italy (solo)

2001 *I Took a Trip*, La Galerie Basta!, Lausanne, Switzerland

2001 *Abstraction: The Power of Memory*, Gallery W, Sacramento, CA (CIVA Traveling)

1999 *Anacostia: A Place of the Spirit*, Union Station, Washington, DC

1998 *CODEX V: 20/20*, Aughinbaugh Gallery, Messiah College, Grantham, PA (CIVA Traveling)

1996 *CIVA Creates the Portrait*, Dordt College Art Gallery, Sioux Center, IA (CIVA Traveling)

1992 *Still Life: A Twentieth-century View*, Foxhall Gallery, Washington, DC

1991 *Works on Paper 22 x 30*, Aughinbaugh Gallery, Messiah College, Grantham, PA (CIVA Traveling)

1990 *Realism in Our Time: 1950–1990*, Joseph Keiffer Gallery, New York, NY

1989 *Small is Big*, Faculty Exhibition, Parsons School of Design, New York, NY

1988 *Christian Imagery in Contemporary Art*, The Rice Gallery, Albany Institute of History & Art, Albany, NY (CIVA Traveling)

1987 *Landscapes*, Katonah Gallery, Katonah, NY

1985 *Collecting in New York*, Museum of the City of New York, New York, NY

1984 *Painting in New York*, Museum of the City of New York, New York, NY

1980 *A Celebration of Landscape: Five American Realists*, Garrison Arts Center, Garrison, NY

Collections

Will Barnet

Art Buchwald

Ed Knippers

References

Herman, Bruce, "Looking Again, The Art of George Wingate," *Image: A Journal of the Arts & Religion*, Issue # 43 (Fall 2004): 103–9.

Dewey, David, *The Watercolor Book*, New York: Watson-Guptill Publications, 1995: 36.

Blake, Weldon, *The Artist's Guide to Using Color*, Cincinnati: North Light Books, 1992: 98.

6 Doris Hutton Auxier

Exhibitions

2004 *Manifest* 2004, Vancouver Arts Network, Vancouver, BC, Canada

2003 *Bread Upon the Waters: Pursuing the Art of Generosity*, Gallery W, Sacramento, CA (CIVA Traveling)

2002 *Red Tape*, Trinity Western University, Langley, BC, Canada

2000 *Evidence of Things Unseen*, Tyndale Theological Seminary, Toronto, ON, Canada

1997 Trinity Western University, Langley, BC, Canada (solo)

II God in the Mystery

7 Theresa Couture

Awards

1998 Full stipend offer, Lilly Fellows Program in Humanities and the Arts, Lilly Foundation in collaboration with Loyola-Marymount University, Los Angeles, CA

1992–1993 Artist residency, Center for Creative Imaging, Kodak Corporation, Camden, ME

Exhibitions

2000 *A Gathering of Light*, Visions Gallery, Albany, NY

1998 *CODEX III: Let This Mind Be In You* (CIVA Traveling)

1997 *New Art/New England*, Library Arts Center, Newport, NH

1994 *Gloria Wilcher Memorial Biennial*, The Currier Gallery of Art, Manchester, NH

References

Auxier, Doris Hutton, "Parting Shot," *Christianity and the Arts*, Vol. 6, No. 4 (Fall 1999): 71.

———, "With the Looker's Eye," *Face of the Deep: A Journal Exploring Art and the Spiritual Life*, Spring 1996: 36–48.

———, "Image as Praise," *Fellows Yearbook of the Graduate Theological Foundation*, 1995: 40–46.

8 Ellie Murphy

Awards

2002 Jerome Fellowship, Franconia Sculpture Park, Shafer, MN

1992 Susan Weadon Award, Yale University School of Art, New Haven, CT

Exhibitions

2003 *Percent for Art in Public Places*, Minnesota State Arts Board, St. Paul, MN

2002 *Jerome Fellowship Artist*, Franconia Sculpture Park, Shafer, MN

2002 *The Lunatics Have Taken Over the Asylum*, Works on Paper Gallery, Los Angeles, CA

2002 *Benefit*, Momenta Art, Berry Street, Brooklyn, NY

2001 *Selections*, Eyewash Gallery, Brooklyn, NY

2000 *Summer Reading*, Eyewash Gallery, Brooklyn, NY

1997 *Killing Time*, White Columns, New York, NY

1997 *The Art Exchange Show*, 67 Broad Street, New York, NY

9 Theodore L. Prescott

Awards

2001–2006 Distinguished Professorship, Messiah College, Grantham, PA

2000–2001 Exhibition Grant, Foundation for the Carolinas, for *Like a Prayer: A Jewish and Christian Presence in Contemporary Art*, Tryon Center for Visual Art, Charlotte, NC

Exhibitions

2004 *Metal, Wood, and Stone*, Elizabethtown College, Elizabethtown, PA

2001 *Abstraction: The Power of Memory*, Gallery W, Sacramento, CA (CIVA Traveling)

2000 *Elemental Things*, Roberts Wesleyan College, Rochester, NY

2000 Untitled, Evangel University, Springfield, MO (solo)

1999 *Theodore Prescott: Sculpture*, Hopkins Center for the Arts at Dartmouth College, Dartmouth College, Hanover, NH

1997 *Philadelphia Sculptors*, Washington Square, Washington, DC

1997 *Nature and Grace*, Messiah College, Grantham, PA

1996 *Art of the State*, William Penn Museum, Harrisburg, PA

1995 *The Florence Portfolio*, Pacific School of Religion, Berkeley, CA (CIVA Traveling)

1994 *Helen Figge Moss Memorial Exhibition*, The Stony Brook School, Stony Brook, NY (solo)

1990 *Sacred Arts IX*, Billy Graham Center Museum, Wheaton, IL

1988 *Christian Imagery in Contemporary Art*, The Rice Gallery, Albany Institute of History & Art, Albany, NY (CIVA Traveling)

Collections

Cincinnati Museum of Art, Cincinnati, OH

Evangel University, Springfield, MO

The Hammer Museum, University of California, Los Angeles (UCLA), Los Angeles, CA

The Vatican Collection of Modern Religious Art, Vatican City, Rome, Italy

References

Prescott, Theodore, "Beauty's Embrace: Recent Christian Contributions to the Discussion of Her Character," *American Arts Quarterly*, Vol. 20, No. 1 (Winter 2003): 9–16.

———, "Christ's Comeback in Art," in *One Incarnate Truth: Christ's Answer to Spiritual Chaos*, edited by Uwe Siemon-Netto, St. Louis, MO: Concordia Publishing House, 2002: 119–23.

———, editor, *Like a Prayer: A Jewish and Christian Presence in Contemporary Art*, Charlotte, NC: Tryon Center for Visual Art, 2001.

Eagleson, Hannah, "The Good, the True and the Beautiful," *World Magazine*, July 7, 2001: 54–56.

Daniel, Jeff, "Sculptor Reworks Symbols of Religion," *St. Louis Post-Dispatch*, May 21, 2000: F 6.

Prescott, Theodore, "Who do you say I am? Artist and Christian: Two Identities, One Person?" in *It Was Good: Making Art to the Glory of God*, edited by Ned Bustard, Baltimore, MD: Square Halo Books, 2000: 123–58.

10 John Reid Perkins-Buzo

Awards

2000–2001 Fellowship, Center for Interdisciplinary Research in the Arts and the Center for Art and Technology, Northwestern University, Evanston, IL

2001 Absolute eXcellence in Electronic Media (AXIEM) Award (Silver), Rapid City, SD, for the Sinsinawa Dominicans CD-ROM, *Where the Spirit Loves to Dwell*

2001 Communicator Award of Distinction, Arlington, TX, for the Sinsinawa Dominicans CD-ROM, *Where the Spirit Loves to Dwell*

Exhibitions

2001 *The Portal*, Block Museum of Art, Northwestern University, Evanston, IL

References

Perkins-Buzo, O.P., John Reid, "*Finding Nemo* and the Triune God," *Dialogue Australasia*, Issue 10 (September/October 2003): 20–21.

———, "Contemplation and the Moving Image," *CIVASeen*, Vol. 3, No. 1, 2002: 30–31.

———, "Film and Preaching," *Doctrine and Life*, Vol. 51, No. 1 (January 2001): 37–42.

11 Roger Feldman

Awards

1993 Artist Residency, Yaddo, Saratoga Springs, NY

1990 Connemara Sculpture Grant, Connemara Foundation, Dallas, TX

1989 Juror's Award, *Expressions of Faith III*, A.P. Tell Gallery, Grand Canyon University, Phoenix, AZ

1986 Individual Artist Fellowship Grant in Sculpture, National Endowment for the Arts, Washington, DC

Exhibitions

2004 *Building Wise: Northwest Biennial*, Tacoma Art Museum, Tacoma, WA

2002 *Exchange*, site-specific installation in Martin Square, Seattle Pacific University, Seattle, WA (solo)

2001 *Center*, site-specific installation in campus quad, George Fox University, Newberg, OR (solo)

2001 *Abstraction: The Power of Memory*, Gallery W, Sacramento, CA (CIVA Traveling)

2001 *Voice*, site-specific installation, Francis Schaeffer Institute, St. Louis, MO (solo)

2001 *Metanoia*, site-specific installation, Union University, Jackson, TN (solo)

2001 *Like a Prayer: A Jewish and Christian Presence in Contemporary Art*, Tryon Center for Visual Art, Charlotte, NC

2001 *A Presence Seen*, Haggerty Gallery, University of Dallas, Irving, TX (CIVA Biennial Conference Exhibition)

2000 *Inside Outsiders*, site-specific installation, University Gallery, Northwestern College, St. Paul, MN (solo)

1999 *Surface Understandings*, Concordia University, Irvine, CA (solo)

1999 *Library Sculpture Competition & Exhibition*, Concordia University, Mequon, WI

1998 *Cross Country*, Weaver Gallery, Bethel College, Mishawaka, IN

1997 *Probe*, site-specific installation, Roberts Wesleyan College, Rochester, NY (solo)

1997 *Unbuilt Southern California*, Guggenheim Gallery, Chapman University, Orange, CA

1996 *Crosshatch*, Azusa Pacific University, Azusa, CA

1995 *Roger Feldman: Recent Works, Drawings, and Maquettes*, Azusa Pacific University, Azusa, CA (solo)

1995 *Re-Manifesting the Sacred*, Badè Museum of Biblical Archaeology, Pacific School of Religion, Berkeley, CA (CIVA Biennial Conference Exhibition)

1993 *Site for Mixed Messages*, Biola University, La Mirada, CA (solo)

1993 *Fruit of the Spirit*, Artspace Gallery, Los Angeles Municipal Satellite Gallery, Los Angeles, CA

1992 *The Blind Will See*, Aughinbaugh Gallery, Messiah College, Grantham, PA (solo)

1991 *Roger Feldman Paintings*, Gallery W, Sacramento, CA (solo)

1991 *Works on Paper*, Aughinbaugh Gallery, Messiah College, Grantham, PA (CIVA Biennial Conference Exhibition)

1989 *Expressions of Faith III*, A.P. Tell Gallery, Grand Canyon University, Phoenix, AZ

1987 *Artists Build Art with Building Materials*, Pacific Arts Center, Seattle, WA

1985 *Sanctification Walk*, Seattle Pacific University, Seattle, WA (solo)

1984 *Open Dialogue: Time and Space*, Visual Arts Center of Alaska, Anchorage, AK

Commissions

1997 Roberts Wesleyan College Art Collection, Rochester, NY

1993 College Art Collection, Messiah College, Grantham, PA

1987–89 Renton Vocational Institute, Renton, WA

References

Botbyl, Eric, "Union Sculpture Walk," *Number 40: An Independent Journal of the Arts*, Vol. XVI, No. 1 (2002): 13–4.

Prescott, Theodore, editor, *Like a Prayer: A Jewish and Christian Presence in Contemporary Art*, Charlotte, NC: Tryon Center for Visual Art, 2001: 29, 56–7, 60.

Prescott, Theodore L., "Nature and Nature's God in Late Twentieth-century American Art," *The Cresset: A Review of Literature, Arts, and Public Affairs*, Pentecost 1998: 14–20.

Mulder, Karen L., "The Art of True Inquiry: A Profile of Roger Feldman," *Mars Hill Review*, Winter/Spring 1996: 41–7.

Anderson, Isabel, "Investigations," *Art Scene*, June 1996, Vol. 15, No. 10: 8.

Collison, Ellen S., "CIVA Profile: Roger Feldman," *Christians in the Visual Arts*, Spring 1990: 1–4.

French, Christopher, "Regional Pluralism," *Artweek*, June 18, 1983, vol. 14, No. 23.

12 Laurie Wohl

Awards

2003 Design Honor Award, Interfaith Forum on Religion, Art, and Architecture in conjunction with *Faith & Form* magazine

2003 Fellowship, American Artists Abroad, U.S. Department of State, Washington, DC

Exhibitions

2003 *The Art of Aging*, Hebrew Union College, New York, NY

2003 *Beyond Tradition*, Wisconsin Designer Crafts Council 79th Annual Exhibition, Marian Gallery, Mount Mary College, Milwaukee, WI

2003 *Life Forces: Contemporary Fibers*, Robert A. Peck Gallery, Central Wyoming College, Riverton, WY

2002 *Glory Be!* Johnson-Humrickhouse Museum, Coshocton, OH

2001 *Art Scene Chicago*, The Chicago Athenaeum, Schaumburg, IL

2000 *Living in the Moment: Contemporary Artists Celebrate Jewish Time*, Hebrew Union College-Jewish Institute of Religion, New York, NY and Cincinnati, OH

1999 *Contemporary Works of Faith '99*, Liturgical Art Guild, Schumacher Gallery, Capitol University, Columbus, OH

1998 *Visions and Revisions*, Catholic Theological Union, Chicago, IL

1996 *Why Is This Night Different . . .?* De Paul University Art Gallery, Chicago, IL

1995 *Recent Acquisitions*, American Craft Museum, New York, NY

1995 *Sacred Arts VX*, Billy Graham Center Museum, Wheaton College, Wheaton, IL

References

Wohl, Laurie, "The Art of 'Unweaving,'" *Preach: Enlivening the Pastoral Art*, January–February 2004: 23–6.

———, "Charles Nkosi," *Christianity and the Arts*, Fall 2000: 34–35.

Paine, Janice, "Profile—Laurie Wohl: Taking Time to Unweave," *Fiberarts*, September–October 1996: 25.

Paine, Janice, "Surface and Spirit: Three Artists Explore the Notion of the Sacred," *Surface Design Journal*, Fall 1996: 8–12.

13 David Blow

Exhibitions

2004 *Contemporary VI International Exhibition*, Period Gallery, Lincoln, NB

2004 *Arte Sagrado* 2004, Concordia University, Austin, TX

2003 *16th Annual McNeese National Works on Paper*, Abercrombie Gallery, McNeese State University, Lake Charles, LA

2002 *No Big Heads*, University of Alaska, Anchorage, AK

2002 *Art with a Southern Drawl*, University of Mobile, Mobile, AL

2001 State of the Art Gallery, Traverse City, MI (solo)

2000 Union Gallery, University of North Texas, Denton, TX (solo)

2000 *Viewpoints 2000*, The Art Center, Lewisville, TX

2000 Société Internationale des Beaux-Arts, Grand-Palais des Champs Elysées, Paris, France

1999 *International Digital Works on Paper*, University of South Carolina, Columbia, SC

1999 *Black & White*, The Boston Printmakers Exhibition, Federal Reserve Bank, Boston, MA

1999 *Ignite*, Biola University, La Mirada, CA (CIVA Traveling)

1993 Museum of Abilene, Abilene, TX (solo)

1991 Gallery X, Houston Center for Photography, Houston, TX (solo)

14 Bruce West

Awards

2000 Purchase Award, Springfield Art Museum, Springfield, MO

1999 Merit Award, Society for Contemporary Photography, Kansas City, KS

1998 Excellence Award, Society for Contemporary Photography, Kansas City, MO

1990 Artist Residency, The Appalachian Environmental Arts Center, Highlands, NC

1987 Fellowship Award in Photography, Mid-America Arts Alliance/National Endowment for the Arts

1977–1978 Fellowship, Ford Foundation for the Arts

Exhibitions

2004 *Only Skin Deep: Changing Visions of the American Self*, International Center of Photography, New York, NY

2004 *A Sense of Wonder: Photographs of Alan Brown and Bruce West*, Art and Design Gallery, Southwest Missouri State University, Springfield, MO

2002 *Photo National*, Lancaster Museum of Art, Lancaster, PA

2002 *A Delta Journey*, Sheldon Art Gallery, St. Louis, MO

2001 *A Question of Faith*, Gallery of Art, University of Northern Iowa, Cedar Falls, IA

2000 *MOAK 2000*, Springfield Art Museum, Springfield, MO

2000 *Recent Acquisitions*, St. Louis Art Museum, St. Louis, MO

1999 *Carried to the Heart: Faith and Doubt in Contemporary Southern Photography*, Millsaps College, Jackson, MS

1998 *Photographs by Bruce West*, Kirkland Arts Center, Millikin University, Decatur, IL (solo)

1995 *Biennial Juried Show*, Light Impressions Spectrum Gallery, Rochester, NY

1995 *Phototropolis*, San Diego Art Institute, San Diego, CA

1994 *Photography by Bruce West*, The Albrecht-Kemper Museum of Art, Saint Joseph, MO (solo)

1992 *Social Landscapes*, E.J. Bellocq Gallery, Louisiana Tech University, Ruston, LA

1991 *US Biennial*, Museum of Art, The University of Oklahoma, Norman, OK

1990 *Bruce West: Rural Architecture*, The Center for Metropolitan Studies, St. Louis, MO

Collections

The Albrecht-Kemper Museum of Art, Saint Joseph, MO

The Museum of Fine Arts, Houston, TX

Museum of Art, The University of Oklahoma, Norman OK

St. Louis Art Museum, St. Louis, MO

Springfield Art Museum, Springfield, MO

Victoria and Albert Museum, London, England

References

"[View] Point Makes a Point," *Artlogue: A Publication of the Missouri Arts Council*, Summer 2002: 3.

Bruce West, "Spiritual Adviser to the World," *Arkansas Review: A Journal of Delta Studies*, Vol. 32, No. 3 (December 2001): 207–14.

Bruce West, "The Last Look: Rural Church in Missouri" (photograph, 1999), *OzarksWatch: The Magazine of the Ozarks*, Vol. XII, Nos. 3 & 4 (1999): back cover.

Maude Schuyler Clay, "An Unseen Presence," *Image: A Journal of the Arts & Religion*, Issue # 24 (Fall 1999): 87–9.

Edgar Alben, "Profile of an Artist: Bruce West," *Springfield Magazine*, November 1988: 33–4.

III The Book

15 Michael R. Buesking

Awards

2000–2001 Dorothy L. Rollins Scholarship in Painting and Drawing, Art Department, University of Missouri, Columbia, MO

1999 Summer Research Grant, Evangel University, Springfield, MO

1996 Pew Summer Research Grant

Exhibitions

2000 *MOAK 2000*, Springfield Art Museum, Springfield, MO

1999 *For the Visual Arts*, Springfield Visual Arts Alliance, Springfield, MO

1997 *Sacred Arts XVII*, Billy Graham Center Museum, Wheaton, IL

1985 *Rickert-Ziebold Award Competition*, Southern Illinois University, Carbondale, IL

References

Palmer, Michael D., compiler and editor, *Elements of a Christian Worldview*, illustrated by Michael R. Buesking, Springfield, MO: Logion Press, 1998.

16 Ruth Dunkell

Exhibitions

2002 *In Search of Mary Magdalene: Images and Traditions*, The Gallery at the American Bible Society, New York, NY

2002 Goldman Art Gallery, Jewish Community Center of Greater Washington, Rockville, MD (solo)

2001 *Reach for the Moon: When Art and Medical Science Intersect*, Yeshiva University Museum, New York, NY (traveling)

1997 *Realm Between Realms: An Exhibition of Jewish Ceremonial Art*, B'nai B'rith Klutznick National Jewish Museum, Washington, DC

References

Kissel, Howard, "Magdalene Show a Blessed Event," *Daily News*, May 9, 2002: 46.

Josephs, Susan, "The Art of Salvation," *The Jewish Week*, June 29, 2001.

17 Paul Hebblethwaite

Exhibitions & Actions

2004 *Red Gallery: Spring Exhibition*, Campus House, West Lafayette, IN

2004 *Forest Communion on Foxridge*, Springville, IN (action)

2002 *Solid Rock*, The Bridge, Fresno, CA

1999 *Freeing Edward Weston*, West Lafayette, IN (action)

1998 *Art Rageous*, Cornerstone Festival, Bushnell, IL

1998 *Jumping Through Hoops*, Beelke Gallery, West Lafayette, IN

1997 *Least of These*, Christian Ministry Center, West Lafayette, IN (solo)

18 Makoto Fujimura

Awards

1990 Purchase Award, *Sacred Arts XI*, Billy Graham Center Museum, Wheaton, IL

Exhibitions

2004 *The Splendor of the Medium: Makoto Fujimura*, Kristen Frederickson Contemporary Art, New York, NY

2003–2004 *The Still Point*, Takashimaya Gallery, Tokyo and Osaka, Japan (solo)

2003 *Four Quartets*, Kristen Frederickson Contemporary Art, New York, NY (solo)

2003 *Contemporary Nihonga Artists: The Pioneers*, Okazaki Museum, Okazaki, Japan

2003 WATERwalks, ISE Cultural Foundation, New York, NY

2003 *Bread Upon the Waters: Pursuing the Art of Generosity*, Gallery W, Sacramento, CA (CIVA Traveling)

2001 *The Burning Bush*, Engstrom Galleria, Taylor University, Upland, IN (solo)

2001 *Makoto Fujimura*, The Henry Luce III Center for the Arts and Religion, Wesley Theological Seminary, Washington, DC (solo)

2001 *New York Work*, Barrington Center for the Arts, Gordon College, Wenham, MA (solo)

2001 *Like a Prayer: A Jewish and Christian Presence in Contemporary Art*, Tryon Center for Visual Art, Charlotte, NC

2000 *Altarpiece*, St. James Chapel, Union Theological Seminary, New York, NY (solo)

2000 *One Hundred Years of Nihonga*, Tokyo National University of Fine Arts and Music Museum, Tokyo, Japan

1999–2000 *Millennium Exhibition*, Cathedral Church of St. John the Divine, New York, NY (solo)

1999 *Art as Prayer*, Cooper Union Gallery, New York, NY

1998 *Makoto Fujimura*, Gallery You, Kyoto, Japan (solo)

1994 *The New Nihonga*, Koriyama City Museum of Art, Koriyama, Japan

1994 *Beyond the Nihonga: An Aspect of Contemporary Japanese Painting*, Tokyo Metropolitan Museum, Tokyo

1990 *Sacred Arts XI*, Billy Graham Center Museum, Wheaton, IL

1989 *Topos, Ethos*, IBM Gallery, Kawasaki, Japan (solo)

Collections

Roberta Ahmanson

Contemporary Museum of Tokyo, Tokyo, Japan

St. Louis Art Museum, St. Louis, MO

The Sato Museum, Tokyo, Japan

Tokyo National University of Fine Arts and Music, Tokyo, Japan

References

Fujimura, Makoto, *The Splendor of the Medium: Makoto Fujimura*, Korea: Poiema Press, 2004.

Lee, Booyeon, "Simple Truths: The Art of Makoto Fujimura," *International Herald Tribune*, November 1–2, 2003.

Roosa, Wayne, "A Three-Part Meditation on Makoto Fujimura's Triptych, *Gethsemane Altarpiece, on the Morning After Easter*," Exhibition Essay for The Eugene and Leona Olson Gallery, Bethel College, Saint Paul, MN, March 18–May 29, 2002.

Dyrness, William A., *Visual Faith: Art, Theology, and Worship in Dialogue*, Grand Rapids, MI: Baker Academic, 2001: 134–7.
Haggerty, Gerard, "Reviews," *ArtNews*, November 1996.

19 Dee VanDyke

Awards

1988 Fellowship, Southern Arts Federation, National Endowment for the Arts

Exhibitions

2003 *For Glory and Beauty*, The Lyndon House Art Center, Athens, GA

1999 *Francis, Greco, and VanDyke: Recent Works*, The Spruill Center for the Arts, Atlanta, GA

1999 *Souls Cast Shadows*, Zinc Contemporary Art, Bluewater Bay, FL (solo)

1993 *Cheekwood National Contemporary Painting*, Cheekwood Museum of Art, Nashville, TN

1990 *Charlotte National 1990*, Spirit Square Center for the Arts, Charlotte, NC

1989 *Birmingham Biennial V*, Birmingham Museum of Art, Birmingham, AL

1985 *3 + 1*, Museum of Arts and Sciences, Macon, GA

1984 *USA Volti del Sud*, Palazzo Venezia, Rome, Italy

References

"Malerin Dee VanDyke," *Lifestyle* (Düsseldorf, Germany), Spring 1992: 35.

"About the Cover Artist Dee VanDyke," *Journal of the Medical Association of Georgia*, Vol. 80, No. 7 (July 1991): 375.

McWillie, Judith, "Dee VanDyke," *New Art Examiner*, Vol. 17, No. 2 (October 1989): supplement following p. 36.

20 Helen Zajkowski

Awards

2000 Project Award, Stamford Cultural Center, Stamford, CT

1998 Connecticut New Art Annual Award, Stamford Museum, Stamford, CT

1992 Distinguished Fellowship Award, New Jersey State Council on the Arts, Department of State, Trenton, NJ

Exhibitions

2003 *Iron Works*, Anne Reid Art Gallery, Princeton Day School, Princeton, NJ and Rosenwald-Wolf Gallery, University of the Arts, Philadelphia, PA

2002 Zimmerli Art Museum, Rutgers University, New Brunswick, NJ

1999 *Grid Works*, Hera Gallery, Wakefield, RI

1998 *New Annual Art*, Stamford Museum, Stamford, CT

1996 Gallery Jag (UNESCO), Pulawy, Poland (solo)

1996 *Mary H. Dana Women Artists 25th Anniversary Retrospective*, Rutgers University, New Brunswick, NJ

1995 *Women's Work: Inherited Ideologies*, Myerson Hall Gallery, University of Pennsylvania, Philadelphia, PA

1994 *Connections*, The Elizabeth Ann Seton Memorial Gallery, New Brunswick, NJ (solo)

1994 *Silence*, American Center for Polish Culture, Washington, DC (solo)

1993 *Fellowship Exhibition*, Stedman Gallery, Rutgers University, Camden, NJ

Collections

Gallery Jag, Pulawy, Poland

Newark Public Library, Newark, NJ

Polish National Commission for UNESCO, Palac Kultury i Nauki, Warsaw, Poland

21 G. Carol Bomer

Awards

2004 Honorable Mention, *Alumni Show*, Dordt College, Sioux Center, IA

2002 First Place Painting and Best of Show, *Art Rageous*, Cornerstone Festival, Bushnell, IL

2001 Merit Award, *Festival One*, Union University National Invitational, Memphis, TN

2000 Second Place, *Exile*, Genema Gallery, Atlanta, GA

1998 First Place, *Sacred Arts XVIII*, Billy Graham Center Museum, Wheaton, IL

Exhibitions

2004 *East Tennessee Bank Show*, Reese Museum, Johnson City, TN

2004 *Alumni Show*, Dordt College, Sioux Center, IA

2004 *Sacrifice*, Grace Center Gallery, Asheville, NC (solo)

2003 *Appalachian Corridors*, Avampato Discovery Museum, Charleston, WV

2003 *Images of the Body*, Barrington Center for the Arts, Gordon College, Wenham, MA (CIVA Biennial Conference Exhibition)

2002 *Works of Substance, Works of Faith*, Mahady Gallery, Marywood University, Scranton, PA

2002 *Mourning and Dancing*, Columbia Theological Center, Decatur, GA

2002 *Art Rageous*, Cornerstone Festival, Bushnell, IL

2001 *A Presence Seen*, Haggerty Gallery, University of Dallas, Irving, TX (CIVA Biennial Conference Exhibition)

2001 *Arte Sagrado*, Concordia University, Austin, TX

2000 *Robes of Redemption*, Biltmore Gallery Downtown, Asheville, NC (solo)

1998 *Sacred Arts XVIII*, Billy Graham Center Museum, Wheaton, IL

1997 *Contemporary Works of Faith 97*, 15th Biennial, Liturgical Art Guild, Schumacher Gallery, Capital University, Columbus, OH

1997 *Sacred Arts XVII*, Billy Graham Center Museum, Wheaton, IL

1996 *Behold the Lamb: The Life of Christ*, Biblical Arts Center, Dallas, TX

1996 *CIVA Creates the Portrait*, Dordt College Art Gallery, Sioux Center, IA (CIVA Traveling)

1994 *Reflections of Faith*, Kreft Center Gallery, Concordia University, Ann Arbor, MI

1993 *Celestial Visions*, Biblical Arts Center, Dallas, TX

Collections

Concordia University, Austin, TX

Covenant College, Lookout Mountain, GA

Eastern Fine Paper, Charlotte, NC

University of North Carolina, Asheville, NC

Trinity Presbyterian Church, Asheville, NC

Westinghouse, Asheville, NC

22 Houben Tcherkelov

Exhibitions

2003 *Import/Export*, Sofia Municipal Art Gallery, Sofia, Bulgaria

2002 *AIM 22*, The Bronx Museum of the Arts, Bronx, NY

2002 *Looming Up*, Aspekte Galerie Gasteig, Munich, Germany

2001 *Supervision*, Contemporary Art Center, Moscow, Russia

2001 *Trendification*, <rotor> association for contemporary art, Graz, Austria

2000 *Cocoons*, XXL Gallery, Sofia, Bulgaria (solo)

2000 *Soziale Kunst aus Bulgarien*, Wittgenstein Palace, Vienna, Austria

1999 *Bacterium Bulgaricus Art*, Museum of Foreign Art, Riga, Latvia

1997 *A Home*, XXL Gallery, Sofia, Bulgaria (solo)

1997 *Lullaby*, Nexus Contemporary Art Center, Atlanta, GA (solo)

1994 *Freezing Up*, Museum of Natural History, Sofia, Bulgaria (solo)

23 David E. Levine

Awards

2003 Clement Award, University Art Museum, Albany, NY

1997 Honorable Mention, Institute for Contemporary Art, Boston, MA

1996 Janow Award, Artworks Gallery, Hartford, CT

1996 First Prize Painting, Hera Gallery, Wakefield, RI

1987 Arts Grant, Massachusetts Cultural Council, Boston, MA

Exhibitions

2004 *The God Show*, Newspace Gallery, Manchester Community College, Manchester, CT

2003 *Artists of the Mohawk/Hudson Region*, University Art Museum, Albany, NY

2003 *Toys and Games*, Anchorage Museum of History and Art, Anchorage, AK

2002 *Glory Be!*, Johnson-Humrickhouse Museum, Coshocton, OH

2001 *North American Print Biennial*, Boston University, Boston, MA

1999 *Selections from the Jewish Artists' Network*, Starr Gallery, Leventhal-Sidman Jewish Community Center, Newton, MA

1999 *Risking Art/Risking Faith*, Episcopal Divinity School, Cambridge, MA

1998 *Once Upon a Time*, Anchorage Museum of History and Art, Anchorage, AK

1998 *National Print and Drawing Exhibition*, Clemson University, Clemson, SC

1998 *What's So Funny? National Works on Paper Biennial*, University of Richmond, Richmond, VA

1998 *Homage to Picasso*, Marie Louise Trichet Art Gallery, Litchfield, CT

1997 *One Day 4 Arts*, Institute for Contemporary Art, Boston, MA

1997 *David E. Levine*, Cambridge Center Art Gallery, Cambridge, MA (solo)

References

Kiehl, David W., *North American Print Exhibition*, exhibition catalog for the North American Print Biennial (Boston University, Boston, MA), Fitchburg, MA: Friday Design, 2001: 14.

Sultan, Terrie, *New American Paintings*, Vol. 24 (February/March 2000): 106–9.

Cross, Sydney, David Houston, and Eleanor Heartney, *Clemson National Print and Drawing Exhibition*, exhibition catalog for the National Print and Drawing Exhibition (Clemson University, Clemson, SC), Wentworth Publishing, 1998: 17.

24 James Disney

Awards

2002 Individual Artist Award, Central Minnesota Arts Board, St. Paul, MN

1999 Best of Show, Christian Art Festival, Cross View Lutheran Church, Edina, MN

1998 Best of Show, *Sacred Arts XVIII*, Billy Graham Center Museum, Wheaton, IL

1998 Honorable Mention, Fine Arts, Minnesota State Fair, St. Paul, MN

Exhibitions

2003 *The Halo of Human Imagination*, The MacLaurin Institute Exhibit, Humphrey Institute, University of Minnesota, Minneapolis, MN

2003 *Images of the Body*, Barrington Center for the Arts, Gordon College, Wenham, MA (CIVA Biennial Conference Exhibition)

2003 *Votive Illustrations*, Gallery W, Sacramento, CA (solo)

2002 *Eggs, Camels, Whales, & Cowards*, Kellie Rae Theiss Gallery, Minneapolis, MN (solo)

2001 *A Presence Seen*, Haggerty Gallery, University of Dallas, Irving, TX (CIVA Biennial Conference Exhibition)

2000 *Icons and Phantoms*, Kellie Rae Theiss Gallery, Minneapolis, MN (solo)

1998 *Sacred Arts XVIII*, Billy Graham Center Museum, Wheaton, IL

1998 Minnesota State Fair, St. Paul, MN

1997 *You Are the Holy Ones of God*, Concordia University, St. Paul, MN (solo)

1996 *Reflections of Faith*, Kreft Center Gallery, Concordia University, Ann Arbor, MI

1996 *Behold the Lamb: The Life of Christ*, Biblical Arts Center, Dallas, TX

1996 *Icon Influences*, Visions Gallery, Albany, NY

1996 *CIVA Creates the Portrait*, Dordt College Art Gallery, Sioux Center, IA (CIVA Traveling)

References

Haack, Dennis, "Reformed Iconography: The Art of James Disney," *Critique*, Vol. 1, 2004: 8–12.

25 Anita Breitenberg Naylor

Exhibitions

2004 *Liturgical and Sacred Arts Exhibition*, Springfield Art Association, Springfield, IL

2003 *On the Edge*, Columbia Theological Seminary, Decatur, GA

2003 *Exhibiting the Spirit*, Old Town Hall, Fairfax, VA

2003 *Images of the Body*, Barrington Center for the Arts, Gordon College, Wenham, MA (CIVA Biennial Conference Exhibition)

2002 *The Purpose Driven Life*, First Baptist Church of Springfield, Springfield, VA

2001 *9/11 Pentagon Benefit*, Ritz Carlton, Tysons Corner, VA

2001 *Ancient Images/Modern Expressions*, St. Vincent's Gallery, Latrobe, PA

IV Faith and Healing by Grace

26 Erica Grimm-Vance

Awards

2002 Distinguished Alumnus Award for Professional Accomplishment, University of Regina, Regina, SK, Canada

2002 First Prize, Imago Juried Art Competition, Toronto, ON, Canada

1997 First Award of Merit, Seymour Art Gallery, Vancouver, BC, Canada

1996 Second Prize, Streff Gallery, Marylhurst College, Marylhurst, OR

1987 Grant, Saskatchewan Arts Board, Regina, SK, Canada

Exhibitions

2005 *A Broken Beauty*, Laguna Art Museum, Laguna Beach, CA (traveling)

2004 *New Work*, Kwantlen University College Gallery, Vancouver, BC, Canada (solo)

2003 *Imago New Heaven/New Earth*, Regent College, Vancouver, BC, Canada

2003 *Bread Upon the Waters: Pursuing the Art of Generosity*, Gallery W, Sacramento, CA (CIVA Traveling)

2002 *Mapping the Body*, Barrington Center for the Arts, Gordon College, Wenham, MA (solo)

2001 *Depth Maps*, Gallery Telpaz, Ottawa, ON, Canada (solo)

1998 *Liminal States*, Third Avenue Gallery, Vancouver, BC, Canada (solo)

1998 *Metaxu: Beauty is the Beginning of Terror*, Ameila Douglas Gallery, Douglas College, New Westminster, BC, Canada (solo)

1997 *Grace and Gravity*, Lookout Gallery, Regent College, Vancouver, BC, Canada (solo)

1996 *Image, Vision, and Voice*, Streff Gallery, Marylhurst College, Marylhurst, OR

1995 *Soil Rich as Blood*, Sunshine Coast Art Center, Sechelt, BC, Canada (solo)

1993 *Curator's Choice*, Doheny Fine Arts, Vancouver, BC, Canada

1991 *Body and Soul: Drawing Invitational*, Calvin College, Grand Rapids, MI

1983 *Emerging Saskatchewan Artists*, Assiniboia Gallery, Regina, SK, Canada

Collections

Calvin College, Grand Rapids, MI

The Estevan National Exhibition Center, Estevan, SK, Canada

Fackelbararnas Centrum, Holsby Brunn, Sweden

Billy Graham Center Museum, Wheaton, IL

Regent College, Vancouver, BC, Canada

Richmond Art Gallery, Richmond, BC, Canada

Saskatchewan Arts Board, Permanent Collection, Regina, SK, Canada

The Vatican Collection of Modern Religious Art, Vatican City, Rome, Italy

References

Prescott, Theodore, editor, *A Broken Beauty*, Grand Rapids: William B. Eerdmans Publishing Company, 2005.

Todd, Douglas, "Artist's Quest: To Try to Grasp the Ineffable with Human Hands," *The Vancouver Sun*, March 29, 2002.

Stockdill, Shirley, "The Art of Erica Grimm-Vance: Spirituality in Wax and Steel," *Topic: A Journal of the Anglican Church, Diocese of New Westminster*, Vol. 33, No. 2 (February 2002): 8.

Bascom, Tim, "A Beautiful Affliction: The Art of Erica Grimm-Vance," *Image: A Journal of the Arts & Religion*, Issue # 31 (Summer 2001): 26–35.

27 Stewart Luckman

Awards

Southwestern Minnesota Regional Area Council Award, Rochester, MN

Jerome Foundation, Foundry Workshop, St. Paul, MN

Artist's Fellowship, Minnesota State Arts Board, St. Paul, MN

Artist's Fellowship, Sculpture Space, Utica, NY

Exhibitions

1993 *Stewart Luckman*, Greenville College, Greenville, IL (solo)

1991 *Minnesota Metaphor*, Rochester Art Center, Rochester, MN

1990 *The Archaeology of Form*, Katherine Nash Gallery, University of Minnesota, Minneapolis, MN

1988 *Sculpture: Public & Private*, Aquinas College, Grand Rapids, MI

1988 *Collaboration: Eleven Artists*, Eugene Johnson Gallery, Bethel College, St. Paul, MN

1987 *Eighth Michigan Invitational*, Battle Creek Art Center, Battle Creek, MI

1986 *Three Sculptors: Collet, Luckman, Packer*, Muskegon Museum of Art, Muskegon, MI

1982 *Group Invitational*, St. Olaf College, Northfield, MN

1979 *Cornett, Luckman, & Milder*, Art Latitude Gallery, New York, NY

1977 *Crowell, Kielkopf, Luckman, & Randall*, The Minneapolis Institute of Arts, Minneapolis, MN

1968 *Stewart Luckman*, University Gallery, Hamline University, St. Paul, MN (solo)

1962 *North West Coast Abstraction*, Seattle Pacific College, Seattle, WA

Collections

Bethel College, St. Paul, MN

Greenville College, Greenville, IL

University of Minnesota, Minneapolis, MN

Stony Brook School, Stony Brook, NY

Tweed Museum of Art, University of Minnesota Duluth, Duluth, MN

Commissions

1997 Timberland Corporation, Stratham, NH

1997 Vancouver Ballet Company, Vancouver, BC, Canada

1993 Archdiocese of Minnesota, St. Paul, MN

1984 Wyoming City Hall, Wyoming, MI

1975 Bethel College, St. Paul, MN

1973 State of Minnesota Veterans' Memorial Competition, Governor's Residence Design Award, St. Paul, MN

References

Harris, Moira F., *Monumental Minnesota: A Guide to Outdoor Sculpture*, St. Paul: Pogo Press, 1992: 103–6.

Luecking, Steven, "The Archaeology of Form," *Sculpture*, May/June 1990: 94–95.

Art in America, Vol. 77, Issue 8 (August 1989): 122–3.

Art in America, Vol. 70, Issue 7 (August 1982): 134, 218.

Luckman, Stewart, *Process: A Public Sculpture by Stewart Luckman: October 1–November 15, 1981, University Gallery, University of Minnesota*, [Minneapolis]: The Gallery, [1982].

28 Edward Knippers

Awards

1990 Third Place, Virginia Prize for Painting, The Virginia Commission for the Arts

1990 Best of Show, The Ellipse Competition, Arlington, VA

1987 Fellowship Award, Virginia Museum of Fine Arts, Richmond, VA

1987 Juror's Award, Painting '87, Arlington Arts Center, Arlington, VA

Exhibitions

2005 *A Broken Beauty*, Laguna Art Museum, Laguna Beach, CA (traveling)

2003 *Bread Upon the Waters: Pursuing the Art of Generosity*, Gallery W, Sacramento, CA (CIVA Traveling)

2002 The Catholic University of America, Washington, DC (solo)

2001 Like a Prayer: A *Jewish and Christian Presence in Contemporary Art*, Tryon Center for Visual Art, Charlotte, NC

2001 *Anno Domini: Jesus Through the Centuries*, The Provincial Museum of Alberta, Edmonton, AB, Canada

2000 Urban Art Institute, Chattanooga, TN (solo)

1999 *Anacostia: Hope in the City*, Union Station, Washington, DC

1998 *CODEX V: 20/20*, Aughinbaugh Gallery, Messiah College, Grantham, PA (CIVA Traveling)

1997 *Passionate Grace: Recent Works by Edward Knippers*, Biblical Arts Center, Dallas, TX (solo)

1997 *Search for the Spiritual*, De Pree Art Center & Gallery, Hope College, Holland, MI (traveling)

1997 *Italian Influences: A Contemporary View*, Foxhall Gallery, Washington, DC

1995 *The Florence Portfolio*, Pacific School of Religion, Berkeley, CA (CIVA Traveling)

1994 *Prophet: Studies in Form*, Foxhall Gallery, Washington, DC

1991 *Works on Paper 22 x 30*, Aughinbaugh Gallery, Messiah College, Grantham, PA (CIVA Traveling)

1990 *Violence and Grace*, Fred Jones Jr. Museum of Art, The University of Oklahoma, Norman, OK (solo)

1990 *The Quick and the Dead*, Roanoke Museum of Fine Arts, Roanoke, VA (solo)

1986 *Spiritual Impact: The Paintings of Edward Knippers*, Virginia Museum of Fine Arts, Richmond, VA

1986 *Memento Mori*, Arlington Arts Center, Arlington, VA (solo)

1977 *Watercolor Invitational*, The Speed Art Museum, Louisville, KY

References

Prescott, Theodore, editor, *A Broken Beauty*, Grand Rapids: William B. Eerdmans Publishing Company, 2005.

Goa, David J., *Anno Domini: Jesus Through the Centuries*, Edmonton: Provincial Museum of Alberta, 2000: 97.

Hogan Albach, Susan, "No Offense Intended: Christian Artist Says Nudity in His Work Isn't Irreligious," *The Dallas Morning News*, September 16, 2000: 1G.

Knippers, Edward, "The Old, Old Story," in *It Was Good: Making Art to the Glory of God*, edited by Ned Bustard, Baltimore, MD: Square Halo Press, 2000: 89–111.

Mathewes-Green, Frederica, *Facing East: A Pilgrim's Journey into the Mysteries of Orthodoxy*, [San Francisco]: HarperSanFrancisco, 1997: 92–98.

Prescott, Ted, "Edward Knippers: A Profile," *Image: A Journal of the Arts & Religion*, Issue # 3 (Spring 1993): 24–36.

Verdon, Timothy, *Edward Knippers: Violence and Grace*, Norman, OK: The University of Oklahoma Museum of Art, [1990].

Brandt, Frederick R., *Spiritual Impact: The Paintings of Edward Knippers*, Richmond: Virginia Museum of Fine Arts, 1986.

29 Melanie Weaver

Exhibitions

2003 *Rise Above*, Azusa Pacific University Art Gallery, Azusa, CA (solo)

2003 *Toy Narratives*, Concordia University Art Gallery, Irvine, CA (solo)

2003 *War Stories*, A Shenere Velt Gallery, Los Angeles, CA

2003 *Contemporary Works of Faith*, Liturgical Art Guild, Columbus, OH

2002 *Glory Be!*, Johnson-Humrickhouse Museum, Coshocton, OH

2002 *The Healing Power of Art*, Lexington Art League, Lexington, KY

1998 *Passages of the Soul*, Cora Stafford Gallery, Denton, TX (solo)

1998 *B.A.G. Show*, Cora Stafford Gallery, Denton, TX

1994 *Searching for the Hidden*, C.S. Lewis Summer Institute, Queens College, Cambridge, England and Biola University Art Gallery, Biola University, La Mirada, CA

1993 *Passages of Healing*, Biola University, La Mirada, CA (solo)

30 Serge J-F Levy

Awards

2000 W.K. Rose Fellowship

1995 Hewlett-Mellon Presidential Grant for documentary photography, Vassar College, Poughkeepsie, NY

Exhibitions

2004 *Japan and New York City*, Leica Gallery, Tokyo, Japan (solo)

2002 *New York City Above and Below the Pavement*, The Half King, New York, NY (solo)

2002 *Religion in Prison Photo Essay*, Gen Art Summer Arts Festival, New York, NY

Collections

The Buhl Collection, New York, NY

Museum of the City of New York, New York, NY

References

Jennings, Peter and Todd Brewster, *In Search of America*, New York: Hyperion, 2002: 92–93.

Fitzgerald, Caitlin et al., *Turn Shake Flip*, New York: Eyestorm, 2001: 55.

31 Kathy Hettinga

Awards

2003 Scholarship Grant, Messiah College, Grantham, PA

2001 Scholarship Grant, Messiah College, Grantham, PA

1996 Grant, Houghton Institute for Integrated Studies, Houghton College, Houghton, NY

1988 Thimem Incentive Award, University of Colorado at Boulder, Boulder, CO

Exhibitions

2003 *The Practice of Hope*, Davison Gallery, Roberts Wesleyan College, Rochester, NY (solo)

2003 *Grave Images*, Dadian Gallery, The Henry Luce III Center for the Arts and Religion, Wesley Theological Seminary, Washington, DC (solo)

2003 *Bread Upon the Waters: Pursuing the Art of Generosity*, Gallery W, Sacramento, CA (CIVA Traveling)

2002 *Art of the State: 35th Annual Juried Exhibition*, Susquehanna Art Museum, Harrisburg, PA

2001 *Out of Darkness Into Light*, The Episcopal Church and Visual Arts, online exhibition: www.ecva.org/exhibition/light/pages/statement.html

2001 *A Presence Seen*, University of Dallas, Irving, TX (CIVA Biennial Conference Exhibition)

2001 *Like a Prayer: A Jewish and Christian Presence in Contemporary Art*, Tryon Center for Visual Art, Charlotte, NC

2000 *The Print and the Process*, The Albrecht-Kemper Museum of Art, St. Joseph, MO

1998 *CODEX III: Let This Mind Be In You* (CIVA Traveling)

1997 *Pyramid Atlantic International Book Arts Invitational*, Corcoran Museum of Art, Washington, DC

1996 *Sacred Arts XVI*, Billy Graham Center Museum, Wheaton, IL

1996 *Behold the Lamb: The Life of Christ*, Biblical Arts Center, Dallas, TX

1995 *Grave Images from the Mountain Desert of the San Luis Valley*, Day Missions Room, Yale Divinity School Library, New Haven, CT (solo)

1994 *Searching for the Hidden*, C.S. Lewis Summer Institute, Queens College, Cambridge, England and Biola University Art Gallery, Biola University, La Mirada, CA

1988 *Christian Imagery in Contemporary Art*, The Rice Gallery, Albany Institute of History & Art, Albany, NY (CIVA Traveling)

Collections

Grunwald Center for Graphic Arts, The Hammer Museum, University of California, Los Angeles (UCLA), Los Angeles, CA

Lutheran Theological Seminary, Gettysburg, PA

Murray Library, Messiah College, Grantham, PA

The New York Public Library, New York, NY

Arts of the Book Collection, Sterling Memorial Library, Yale University, New Haven, CT

References

Hettinga, Kathy T., "Grave Images©: A Faith Visualized in a Technological Age," in *Virtual Morality: Morals, Ethics, + New Media*, edited by Mark J.P. Wolf, New York, NY: Peter Lang, 2003: 237–58.

Prescott, Theodore, editor, *Like a Prayer: A Jewish and Christian Presence in Contemporary Art*, Charlotte, NC: Tyron Center for Visual Art, 2001: 24–25.

32 Michael Mills

Exhibitions

2004 *Currents*, Lieutenant Governor's Suite, Ontario Provincial Parliament, Toronto, ON, Canada

2003 *About Water*, Frederick Horsman Varley Art Gallery of Markham, Unionville, ON, Canada

2003 *Worship and the Arts Niagara*, St. Catherine's, ON, Canada

2002 *Evidence of Things Unseen*, Institute for Christian Studies, University of Toronto, Toronto, ON, Canada

2001 *The Next Generation: New Members of the Canadian Society of Painters in Watercolour*, John B. Aird Gallery, Toronto, ON, Canada

2001 *Body of Knowledge*, Tyndale College, Toronto, ON, Canada (solo)

2000 *Embodiment*, MacDonald Gallery, Dallas, PA (solo)

1999 *Covenant*, Delta Convention Centre, Regina, SK, Canada

1999 *Body Image*, Wilfrid Laurier University, Waterloo, ON, Canada (solo)

1998 *Works on Paper*, University of British Columbia, Vancouver, BC, Canada (solo)

1995 *Imago Dei*, Notre Dame Covenant, Hamilton, ON, Canada (solo)

V The Altarpiece and Book as Idea

33 Tyrus Clutter

Exhibitions

2004 *Prints & Paintings*, Union University Gallery of Art, Jackson, TN (solo)

2003 *The Blood of the Lamb: National Exhibition of Christian, Jewish, and Muslim Artists*, Time Warner Gallery, LynnArts, Inc., Lynn, MA

2003 *Bread Upon the Waters: Pursuing the Art of Generosity*, Gallery W, Sacramento, CA (CIVA Traveling)

2003 *Verses, Volumes, & Vision: Art and the Written Word*, Northbrook Public Library, Northbrook, IL

2003 *Art Rageous*, Cornerstone Festival, Bushnell, IL

2003 *Images of the Body*, Barrington Center for the Arts, Gordon College, Wenham, MA (CIVA Biennial Conference Exhibition)

2003 *Shadows: Interrupted Light*, Genema Gallery, Atlanta, GA

2003 *Cross Country III: A National Christian Art Exhibition*, Weaver Gallery, Bethel College, Mishawaka, IN

2002 *The Magic of the Woodblock Print*, David Young Gallery, Edinburgh, Scotland

2002 *Works of Faith, Works of Substance*, Marywood University Art Galleries, Scranton, PA

2002 *Sixth Annual Georgetown International Art Competition*, The Fraser Gallery, Washington, DC

2002 *Text Messages*, David Young Gallery, Edinburgh, Scotland

2001 *The Path I Tread*, Friesen Art Galleries, Northwest Nazarene University, Nampa, ID (solo)

2001 *Sixty Square Inches: 13th Biennial National Small Print Exhibition*, Robert L. Ringel Gallery, Purdue University, West Lafayette, IN

2001 *A Presence Seen*, Haggerty Gallery, University of Dallas, Irving, TX (CIVA Biennial Conference Exhibition)

2000 *Koinonia*, Friesen Art Galleries, Northwest Nazarene University, Nampa, ID

1999 *Ignite*, Biola University Art Gallery, Biola University, La Mirada, CA (CIVA Traveling)

1997 *12th Annual Small Works International Competition*, Amos Eno Gallery, New York, NY

Collections

Spencer Museum of Art, The University of Kansas, Lawrence, KS

The New York Public Library, New York, NY

Spring Arbor University, Spring Arbor, MI

34 Rosemary Scott-Fishburn

Awards

2000 Gordon College Excellence in Studio Arts, Wenham, MA

Exhibitions

2004 *Christ and His Saints*, The Preston-Cutler Gallery, Hamilton, MA (solo)

2003 *The Blood of the Lamb: National Exhibition of Christian, Jewish, and Muslim Artists*, Time Warner Gallery, LynnArts, Inc., Lynn, MA

2003 *Bread Upon the Waters: Pursuing the Art of Generosity*, Gallery W, Sacramento, CA (CIVA Traveling)

2002 *The Nicene Creed*, San Luis Obispo County Arts Council, San Luis Obispo, CA (solo)

2000 *Liturgy of the Hours*, Barrington Center for the Arts,

Gordon College, Wenham, MA (solo)

2000 *Introductions*, The Art Center, San Luis Obispo, CA

Commissions

2000 *Images of Creation*, San Luis Obispo County Arts Council, San Luis Obispo, CA

2000 Sustainable Harvest International, Portsmouth, NH

35 Bruce Herman

Awards

2003–2005 Lilly Foundation Fellowship, Center for Christian Studies, Gordon College, Wenham, MA

2000 Project Grants for *A Broken Beauty*: Fieldstead & Company; Council for Christian Colleges & Universities; Private Patrons

1993 Fieldstead & Company Grant (Florence, Italy, summer 1993)

1979 Philip Guston Traveling Prize, Boston University, Boston, MA

Exhibitions

2005 *A Broken Beauty*, Laguna Art Museum, Laguna Beach, CA (traveling)

2003 *The Body Broken*, Signs of Life Gallery, Lawrence, KS and Alva deMars Megan Chapel Art Center, Saint Anselm College, Manchester, NH (solo)

2002 *Return of Beauty*, Kristen Frederickson Contemporary Art, New York, NY

2002 *Fourdraw*, Southern California Baptist University, Riverside, CA

2001 *Saving the Appearances*, Messiah College, Grantham, PA (solo)

2001 *Abstraction: The Power of Memory*, Gallery W, Sacramento, CA (CIVA Traveling)

2000 *Recent Acquisitions*, DeCordova Museum, Lincoln, MA

2000 *Anno Domini: Jesus Through the Centuries*, The Provincial Museum of Alberta, Edmonton, AB, Canada

2000 *The Word as Art: Contemporary Renderings*, The Gallery at the American Bible Society, New York, NY

1999 *Building Beauty*, North Park University, Chicago, IL

1998 *Out of Ashes*, Grand Canyon University, Phoenix, AZ (solo)

1997 *Via Dolorosa*, Visions Gallery, Albany, NY (solo)

1997 *Searching for the Spiritual*, Hope College, Holland, MI

1996 *Sacred Fire*, St. George Cathedral, Jerusalem, Israel

1995 *The Florence Portfolio*, Pacific School of Religion, Berkeley, CA (CIVA Traveling)

1995 *Words & Images*, Calvin College, Grand Rapids, MI

1994 *Searching for the Hidden*, C.S. Lewis Summer Institute, Queens College, Cambridge, England and Biola University Art Gallery, Biola University, La Mirada, CA

1991 *Works on Paper 22 x 30*, Aughinbaugh Gallery, Messiah College, Grantham, PA (CIVA Traveling)

1991 *Invisible Cities*, Foxhall Gallery, Washington, DC

1983 *Contemporary Boston Portraits*, Boston University Art Gallery, Boston, MA

Collections

Calvin College, Grand Rapids, MI

DeCordova Museum, Lincoln, MA

The Frye Art Museum, Seattle, WA

The Hammer Museum, University of California, Los Angeles (UCLA), Los Angeles, CA

The Vatican Collection of Modern Religious Art, Vatican City, Rome, Italy

References

Prescott, Theodore, editor, *A Broken Beauty*, Grand Rapids: William B. Eerdmans Publishing Company, 2005.

Craven, Robert, "The Body Broken: New Paintings by Bruce Herman, Boston, MA," *Art New England*, June/July 2003: 32.

Goa, David J., *The Body Broken: The Art of Bruce Herman*, Manchester, NH: Alva deMars Megan Chapel Art Center [Saint Anselm College], 2003.

Goa, David J., *Anno Domini: Jesus Through the Centuries*, Edmonton, Alberta: The Provincial Museum of Alberta, 2000: 17.

Heller, Ena, editor, *The Word as Art: Contemporary Renderings*, New York: The Gallery at the American Bible Society, 2000: 1, 5, 22–23.

36 Robert P. Eustace

Awards

1999 First Place, *Images of Mary (Contemporary Variations)*, The Mariological Society of America, Dayton, OH

1988 Vermont Studio Colony Fellowship, Johnson, VT

1984 Fellowship Grant, New Jersey State Council on the Arts, Trenton, NJ

Exhibitions

2003 *Altarpiece Constructions*, Atelier Gallery, Madison, NJ (solo)

2003 *Images of the Body*, Barrington Center for the Arts, Gordon College, Wenham, MA (CIVA Biennial Conference Exhibition)

2002 *Works of Faith, Works of Substance*, Marywood College Art Gallery, Scranton, PA

2001 *A Presence Seen*, Haggerty Gallery, University of Dallas, Irving, TX (CIVA Biennial Conference Exhibition)

2000 *Arte Sagrado*, Concordia University, Austin, TX

1999 *Images of Mary (Contemporary Variations)*, The Mariological Society of America, Dayton, OH (traveling)

1997 *Works on Paper/Religious Art*, The Art Source Resource Center, Indianapolis, IN

1996 *Reflections of Faith*, Kreft Center Gallery, Concordia University, Ann Arbor, MI

1996 *Art Rageous*, Cornerstone Festival, Bushnell, IL

1995 *Re-Manifesting the Sacred*, Badè Museum of Biblical Archaeology, Pacific School of Religion, Berkeley, CA

1995 *Sacred Arts XV*, Billy Graham Center Museum, Wheaton, IL

1994 *Searching for the Hidden*, C.S. Lewis Summer Institute, Queens College, Cambridge, England and Biola University Art Gallery, Biola University, La Mirada, CA

1994 Greenville College, Greenville, IL (solo)

1993 *Women in the Bible*, The Biblical Arts Center, Dallas, TX

1993 *Sacred Arts XIV*, Billy Graham Center Museum, Wheaton, IL

1991 *It is Finished*, Biblical Arts Center, Dallas, TX

1988 *Christian Imagery in Contemporary Art*, The Rice Gallery, Albany Institute of History & Art, Albany, NY (traveling)

1985 *Art for the Church*, Billy Graham Center Museum, Wheaton, IL

Collections

Messiah College, Grantham, PA

Montclair State University, Montclair, NJ

Wheaton College, Wheaton, IL

37 James Larson

Awards

2001 Artist Fellowship, Blacklock Nature Sanctuary with funding from the Jerome Foundation, Moose Lake, MN

1994 Individual Artist Grant, East Central Arts Council/McKnight Foundation, Mora, MN

1987 Charles G. Shaw Memorial Scholarship Award, Brooklyn College, Brooklyn, NY

Exhibitions

2004 *Stations of the Cross*, House of Mercy, St. Paul, MN

2002 *New Work*, Louvin Gallery, St. Paul, MN (solo)

2002 *Confessionals*, Bell Tower Gallery, Minneapolis, MN

2001 *The Confessional Show*, Louvin Gallery, St. Paul, MN

2001 *Arts in Harmony*, Sherburne County Government Center, Elk River, MN

2001 *Image: East Central Regional Art Exhibition*, Cambridge, MN

1994 Eugene Johnson Gallery, St. Paul, MN (solo)

1987 Gallery 2147, Brooklyn, NY (solo)

References

Trachtenburg, Jordan, David Lantow, and Shannon Ketch, *Monster Trucks*, New York: Naked Eye Arts, 1994: 3.

38 Lynn Aldrich

Awards

2001 Third Prize in Sculpture, *Biennale Internazionale dell'Arte Contemporanea*, Fortezza da Basso, Florence, Italy

2000 Individual Artist Fellowship Award, J. Paul Getty Trust Fund for the Visual Arts, California Community Foundation

1999 City of Los Angeles (COLA) Individual Artist Fellowship Award

1999 Purchase Award, *Art Here and Now*, Los Angeles County Museum of Art, Los Angeles, CA

Exhibitions

2004 *Contemporaries*, REDCAT Gallery, Walt Disney Concert Hall, Los Angeles, CA

2003 *Research and Development*, Carl Berg Gallery, Los Angeles, CA (solo)

2003 *Post Cool*, Ben Maltz Gallery, Otis College of Art and Design, Los Angeles, CA

2002 *A Material World*, Irvine Fine Arts Center, Irvine, CA (solo)

2001 *Liquid Art*, Long Beach Museum of Art, Long Beach, CA

2001 *Biennale Internazionale dell'Arte Contemporanea*, Fortezza da Basso, Florence, Italy

2001 *The Permanent Collection: 1970–2000*, Los Angeles County Museum of Art, Los Angeles, CA

2001 *Like a Prayer: A Jewish and Christian Presence in Contemporary Art*, Tryon Center for Visual Art, Charlotte, NC

2000 *COLA 2000*, The Hammer Museum, University of California, Los Angeles (UCLA), Los Angeles, CA

1998 Art Affairs Gallery, Amsterdam, The Netherlands (solo)

1997 *Working Out the Kinks*, Künstlerhaus Bethanien, Berlin, Germany

1996 *Simple Means: Contemporary Sculpture from Los Angeles*, Montgomery Gallery, Pomona College, Pasadena, CA

1994 *Chasing Angels*, Christine Rose Gallery, New York, NY

1994 *Pagine Tessili*, Biblioteca Rispoli, Communi di Roma, Rome, Italy

1993 *Death and Resurrection of Nature*, Laband Art Gallery, Loyola Marymount University, Los Angeles, CA

Collections

Biola University, La Mirada, CA

Los Angeles County Museum of Art, Los Angeles, CA

Museum of Contemporary Art, Los Angeles, CA

Neuberger Berman, Inc., New York, NY

References

Harvey, Doug, "Stuff: The Sculptures of Lynn Aldrich," *L.A. Weekly*, November 7–13, 2003: 35.

Roosa, Wayne, "Re-Viewing Ancient Religious Texts," *ARTS: The Arts in Religious and Theological Studies*, 14/1 (2002): 11–17.

Duncan, Michael, "Reviews: Venice," *Art in America*, Vol. 88, No. 1 (January 2000): 127.

Greenstein, M.A., "The Meeting of Disciplines: Lynn Aldrich and Margaret Honda," *World Sculpture News*, Vol. 4, No. 3 (Summer 1998): 33.

Dyrness, William, "Whispers in Ordinary Time: The Art of Lynn Aldrich," *Image: A Journal of the Arts & Religion*, Issue # 19 (Spring 1998): 59–64.

Chattopadhyay, Collette, "Lynn Aldrich at Gallery LASCA," *Artweek*, Vol. 28, No. 7 (July 1997): 25.

39 Donald J. Forsythe

Awards

2002 Fellowship, Ballinglen Arts Foundation, Ballycastle, County Mayo, Republic of Ireland

1999 Messiah College Faculty Scholarship Grant, Messiah College, Grantham, PA

1999 Second Prize, Works on Paper, *Art of the State: Pennsylvania 1999*, The State Museum of Pennsylvania, Harrisburg, PA

1995 First Prize, Sculpture, *Art of the State: Pennsylvania 1995*, The State Museum of Pennsylvania, Harrisburg, PA

1995 Third Prize, Mixed Media, *67th International Juried Exhibition*, Art Association of Harrisburg, Harrisburg, PA

1990 Best of Show, *Sacred Arts XII*, Billy Graham Center Museum, Wheaton, IL

1989 Honorable Mention, *New American Talent 1989*, Texas Fine Arts Association, Austin, TX

Exhibitions

2004 *IMAGIO*, Marxhausen Gallery, Concordia University Nebraska, Seward, NE

2004 *Images from North Mayo*, Courthouse Gallery, Ballinglen Arts Foundation, Ballycastle, County Mayo, Republic of Ireland

2003 *Time Uncertain: Box Constructions, 1986–2003*, The Gallery at Penn College, Pennsylvania College of Technology, Williamsport, PA (solo)

2002 *Burning Lights*, Union University, Jackson, TN (solo)

2002 *Works of Substance, Works of Faith*, Mahady Gallery, Marywood University, Scranton, PA

2001 *Abstraction: The Power of Memory*, Gallery W, Sacramento, CA (CIVA Traveling)

2000 *Anno Domini: Jesus Through the Centuries*, The Provincial Museum of Alberta, Edmonton, AB, Canada

2000 *Art of the State: Pennsylvania 2000*, The State Museum of Pennsylvania, Harrisburg, PA

2000 *The Word as Art: Contemporary Renderings*, The Gallery at the American Bible Society, New York, NY

1998 *The Story of Christmas*, Visions Gallery, Albany, NY

1998 *CODEX V: 20/20*, Aughinbaugh Gallery, Messiah College, Grantham, PA (CIVA Traveling)

1997 *Art and Religion*, DOSHI Center for Contemporary Art, Harrisburg, PA

1995 *Art of the State: Pennsylvania 1995*, The State Museum of Pennsylvania, Harrisburg, PA

1995 *67th International Juried Exhibition*, Art Association of Harrisburg, Harrisburg, PA

1994 *Searching for the Hidden*, C.S. Lewis Summer Institute, Queens College, Cambridge, England and Biola University Art Gallery, Biola University, La Mirada, CA

1993 *Sacred Arts XIV*, Billy Graham Center Museum, Wheaton, IL

1990 *Sacred Arts XII*, Billy Graham Center Museum, Wheaton, IL

1989 *New American Talent 1989*, Texas Fine Arts Association, Austin, TX

1988 *Christian Imagery in Contemporary Art*, The Rice Gallery, Albany Institute of History & Art, Albany, NY (CIVA Traveling)

Collections

American Bible Society, New York, NY

Auburn Arts Association, Auburn, IL

The Bank of New York, Wilmington, DE

Edinboro University of Pennsylvania, Edinboro, PA

Rochester Institute of Technology, Rochester, NY

References

Goa, David J., *Anno Domini: Jesus Through the Centuries*, Edmonton: Provincial Museum of Alberta, 2000: 30–35.

Heller, Ena, editor, *The Word as Art: Contemporary Renderings*, New York: The Gallery at the American Bible Society, 2000: 4–6, 18–19.

Skillen, John, "The Reconstructive Art of Donald Forsythe, *Image: A Journal of the Arts & Religion*, Issue # 18 (Winter 1997–98): 75–88.

40 Christine A. Forsythe

Awards

2000 Third Prize, Crafts, *Art of the State: Pennsylvania 2000*, The Pennsylvania State Museum, Harrisburg, PA

1998 Faculty Scholarship, Messiah College, Grantham, PA

Exhibitions

2004 *Liturgical Art Exhibition*, Concordia University Nebraska, Seward, NE

2002 *Works of Art, Works of Faith*, Marywood University, Scranton, PA

2001 *Like a Prayer: A Jewish and Christian Presence in Contemporary Art*, Tryon Center for Visual Art, Charlotte, NC

2001 *Abstraction: The Power of Memory*, Gallery W, Sacramento, CA (CIVA Traveling)

2000 *Art of the State: Pennsylvania 2000*, The Pennsylvania State Museum, Harrisburg, PA

2000 *Artist Books*, Everett L. Cattell Library, Malone College, Canton, OH (solo)

1999 *Spirituality and the Arts*,

St. Michael's Lutheran Church, Harrisburg, PA (solo)

1999 *Arte Sagrado*, Concordia University, Austin, TX

1998 *CODEX V: 20/20*, Aughinbaugh Gallery, Messiah College, Grantham, PA (CIVA Traveling)

1998 *Meditations*, Aughinbaugh Gallery, Messiah College, Grantham, PA (solo)

1997 *Art & Religion*, Doshi Gallery, Harrisburg, PA

1995 *Mirror of Creation*, Billy Graham Center Museum, Wheaton, IL

1995 *Reflections of Faith*, Kreft Center Gallery, Concordia University, Ann Arbor, MI

1994 *Searching for the Hidden*, C.S. Lewis Summer Institute, Queens College, Cambridge, England and Biola University Art Gallery, Biola University, La Mirada, CA

1992 Greenville College, Greenville, IL (solo)

1990 *Sacred Arts XII*, Billy Graham Center Museum, Wheaton, IL

1988 *Christian Imagery in Contemporary Art*, The Rice Gallery, Albany Institute of History & Art, Albany, NY (CIVA Traveling)

Collections

Billy Graham Center Museum, Wheaton, IL

Rochester Institute of Technology, Rochester, NY

References

Prescott, Theodore, editor, *Like a Prayer: A Jewish and Christian Presence in Contemporary Art*, Charlotte, NC: Tryon Center for Visual Art, 2001: 24, 44, 54–55.

41 Sandra Bowden

Awards

2004 First Prize, Fourth Annual Festival of Christian Art, Woodbury, MN

2003 Festival Award, Cross View Christian Arts Festival, Edina, MN

2002 Best of Show, *VI Annual Sacred Art Exhibition*, Golden Isles Arts and Humanities Association, Brunswick, GA

1998 Honorable Mention, *Sacred Arts XVIII*, Billy Graham Museum, Wheaton, IL

Exhibitions

2004 *Printmakers of Cape Cod*, Cape Museum of Fine Arts, Dennis, MA

2003 *The Blood of the Lamb: National Exhibition of Christian, Jewish, and Muslim Artists*, Time Warner Gallery, LynnArts, Inc., Lynn, MA

2003 *Bread Upon the Waters: Pursuing the Art of Generosity*, Gallery W, Sacramento, CA (CIVA Traveling)

2003 *Under Cover: Book Arts*, St. Louis Art Guild, St. Louis, MO

2003 *Cross Country III*, Weaver Gallery, Bethel College, Mishawaka, IN

2002 *Small Works Show*, Foxhall Gallery, Washington, DC

2002 *Contemporary Works of Faith*, Liturgical Art Guild, Columbus, OH

2002 *VI Annual Sacred Art Exhibition*, Golden Isles Arts and Humanities Association, Brunswick, GA

2002 *Via Crucis: The Way of the Cross*, Istituto San Ludovico, Orvieto, Italy (solo)

2001 *Abstraction: The Power of Memory*, Gallery W, Sacramento, CA (CIVA Traveling)

2001 *Like a Prayer: A Jewish and Christian Presence in Contemporary Art*, Tryon Center for Visual Art, Charlotte, NC

2000 *Anno Domini: Jesus Through the Centuries*, The Provincial Museum of Alberta, Edmonton, AB, Canada

2000 *The Word as Art: Contemporary Renderings*, The Gallery at the American Bible Society, New York, NY

2000 *Spirit Infused*, Salisbury State University, Salisbury, MD

2000 *Arte Sagrado*, Concordia University, Austin, TX

1999 *Behold the Wood of the Cross*, Georgetown University, Washington, DC

1999 United Theological Seminary, St. Paul, MN (solo)

1998 *Nativity*, Biblical Arts Center, Dallas, TX

1998 *Art History 101: Icons of Western Art*, Wheaton College, Wheaton, IL (traveling)

1998 *CODEX V: 20/20*, Aughinbaugh Gallery, Messiah College, Grantham, PA (CIVA Traveling)

1997 *Art Rageous*, Cornerstone Festival, Bushnell, IL

1996 *Word as Image*, Bible Lands Museum, Jerusalem, Israel (solo)

1993 *Reflections of Faith*, Kreft Center Gallery, Concordia University, Ann Arbor, MI

1991 *Works on Paper 22 x 30*, Aughinbaugh Gallery, Messiah College, Grantham, PA (CIVA Traveling)

1990 *Sacred Arts XI*, Billy Graham Center Museum, Wheaton, IL

1988 *Christian Imagery in Contemporary Art*, The Rice Gallery, Albany Institute of History & Art, Albany, NY

1988 *Images of the Holy Land*, Calvin College, Grand Rapids, MI

1985 Vanderbilt University, Nashville, TN (solo)

Collections

Billy Graham Center Museum, Wheaton, IL

Haifa Museum, Haifa, Israel

Shaave Cedek Synagogue, Montreal, QC, Canada

The Vatican Collection of Modern Religious Art, Vatican City, Rome, Italy

References

Romaine, James, editor, *Word as Image: The Art of Sandra Bowden*, Baltimore, MD: Square Halo Books, 2005.

Heller, Ena, editor, *The Word as Art: Contemporary Renderings*, New York, NY: The Gallery at the American Bible Society, 2000: 10–11.

Prescott, Theodore, editor, *Like a Prayer: A Jewish and Christian Presence in Contemporary Art*, Charlotte, NC: Tryon Center for Visual Art, 2001: 23–4, 40, 59.

VI Last Things

42 Aaron Lee Benson

Awards

2000 Craftsman of the Year, Cumberland County Arts Council, Crossville, TN

1999 Innovative Teacher of the Year Award, Union University, Jackson, TN

1995 Georgia Individual Arts Grant, Southern Artists Federation

1995 Patterson Barclay Foundation Institutional Grant

1994 Churches Holmes Foundation Institutional Grant

Exhibitions

2004 *SUNY/Fredonia Sculpture Project*, State University of New York, Fredonia, NY

2004 Saratt Gallery, Vanderbilt University, Nashville, TN

2001 *Martyrs*, University of Arkansas, Little Rock, AR

2000 *The Word as Art: Contemporary Renderings*, The Gallery at the American Bible Society, New York, NY

1998 *Loose in the Fire*, Oxford University, Oxford, England

1997 Adam Gallery, Wheaton College, Wheaton, IL (solo)

1994 *The Courtyard Collection*, Portland Museum of Art, Portland, OR

References

Heller, Ena, editor, *The Word as Art: Contemporary Renderings*, New York: The Gallery at the American Bible Society, 2000: 8–9.

43 Peter Sheesley

Awards

2003 Prince of Wales Scholarship, New York Academy of Art, New York, NY

Exhibitions

2004 MFA Thesis Exhibition, New York Academy of Art, New York, NY

2004 *Illuminations*, Priority Associates, New York, NY

2003 *Landscapes*, Forbes Chateau, Balleroy, France

2003 *Borders to Bridges*, Kings College, New York, NY

2002 *Giving Thanks*, Bottom Feeders Studio Gallery, New York, NY

2001 *Chicago Art Open*, Chicago, IL

44 Guy Chase

Awards

1998 Purchase Award, *Sacred Art XVIII*, Billy Graham Center Museum, Wheaton, IL

1996 Honorable Mention, *Sacred Art XVI*, Billy Graham Center Museum, Wheaton, IL

Exhibitions

2004 Eastminster Presbyterian Church, Evansville, IN (solo)

2003 *Art with Text*, ArtCo Gallery, Minneapolis, MN

2003 *Really*, gescheidle, Chicago, IL

2001 *Not Flat*, Eugene Johnson Gallery, Bethel College, St. Paul, MN (solo)

2001 *Like a Prayer: A Jewish and Christian Presence in Contemporary Art*, Tryon Center for Visual Art, Charlotte, NC

2000 *Faith*, Dynamite Gallery, Grand Rapids, MI

1999 *Actual Things*, The Vault Gallery, Midtown Arts Center, St. Louis, MO (solo)

1998 *Sacred Art XVIII*, Billy Graham Center Museum, Wheaton, IL

1996 *The Really Big Kitsch Show*, St. Louis Design Center, St. Louis, MO

1996 *Still/Painting*, The Forum for Contemporary Art, St. Louis, MO (solo)

1996 *Sacred Art XVI*, Billy Graham Center Museum, Wheaton, IL

1995 *Re-Manifesting the Sacred*, Badè Museum of Biblical Archaeology, Pacific School of Religion, Berkeley, CA

1994 *Contemporary Visions*, Anderson Fine Arts Center, Anderson, IN

1991 *New Work: 14 St. Louis Artists*, Blue Moon Gallery, St. Louis, MO

1989 *13th Biennial Southern Illinois Artists' Competition*, Mitchell Museum, Mt. Vernon, IL

1989 *Icon and Object*, Urban Institute of Contemporary Art, Grand Rapids, MI

1989 *Seventh Biennial Watercolor Illinois*, Tarble Arts Center, Eastern Illinois University, Charleston, IL

1988 *Mid-America Biennial*, Owensboro Museum of Fine Art, Owensboro, KY

1988 *Christian Imagery in Contemporary Art*, The Rice Gallery, Albany Institute of History & Art, Albany, NY (CIVA Traveling)

1987 *Realism Today*, Evansville Museum of Arts and Sciences, Evansville, IN

References

Stein, Lisa, "What You See Isn't What You Get, 'Really,'" *Chicago Tribune*, May 16, 2003: 29.

Roosa, Wayne, "Re-Viewing Ancient Religious Texts," *ARTS: The Arts in Religious and Theological Studies*, 14/1 (2002): 11–17.

Bellos, Alexandra, "Paper Chase. Guy Chase: Still Painting," *St. Louis Riverfront Times*, June 19–25, 1996: 73.

Duffy, Robert, "White Light on Quicksilver," *St. Louis Post-Dispatch*, June 9, 1996: 4D.

Harris, Paul A., "Painting-by-the-Numbers Revisited," *St. Louis Post-Dispatch*, April 27, 1991: 6D.

Checklist of the Exhibition

Unless otherwise indicated, all works are collection of the artist.

Also, unless otherwise indicated, dimensions are given in inches as: height x width; or height x width x depth.

I. God in the Details

1 Joel Sheesley
Winter Conversation, 2003
Oil on canvas
30 x 45

2 Mary Fielding McCleary
Allegory of the Senses, 2002
Mixed media collage on paper
48 x 72⅞

3 Gregory King
4 or 5 Trees, 2002
Video

4 Christine Huck
Portrait # 32, 2003
Oil on panel
7 x 9½

5 George Wingate
Tangerine: Two States, 2002
Oil on board
5½ x 6¼

6 Doris Hutton Auxier
Solitude: First Temptation, 2004
Acrylic and mixed media on Baltic birch
30 x 30 x ½

II. God in the Mystery

7 Theresa Couture
Reflections on a Poet God, 2004
Between the Space and the Echo (l); *Kenosis* (c); *Between the Word and the Entry* (r)
Integrated digital media on fine paper
11½ x 29 (left); 15 x 11 (center); 11½ x 29 (right)

8 Ellie Murphy
"In the beginning was the Word … " (Binary Triptych), 2001
Clay, metal, wood, and cement
1⅓ x 6 feet; 1⅓ x 7 feet; 1⅓ x 8 feet

9 Theodore L. Prescott
Tabula Rasa II, 2003–04
Corten steel and Aflon marble
84 x 19¾ x 4
Private Collection

10 John Reid Perkins-Buzo
The Portal, 2004
Interactive multimedia video projection

11 Roger Feldman
Current, 2003
Pastel and mortar on wood
47¾ x 137¼

12 Laurie Wohl
Veil of Light: The Protecting Veil, 2001
Unweaving® mixed media: gauze fabric, acrylic paint, collage paper, modeling paste, and beads
79 x 19 (diameter)

13 David Blow
Lightness of Being, 2003
Digital Iris Giclee
25 x 30

14 Bruce West
Reverend Dennis's Golden Chair, MS, 2002
C-print
14 x 17
Entrance to Margaret's Grocery, MS, 2002
C-print
14 x 17

III. The Book

15 Michael R. Buesking
Ezekiel Scattering Hair, 2002
Oil on canvas
47⅛ x 38

16 Ruth Dunkell
Whose Glorious Beauty is a Fading Flower, ca. 2001
Pen-and-ink drawing
18⅛ x 24

17 Paul Hebblethwaite
Forest Communion on Foxridge, 2004
Photographs on inkjet prints
6 prints, 11 x 14 each

18 Makoto Fujimura
Eirenepoios, 2003
Installation with video
Eirene I, 2003
Azurite and malachite mixed with Hyde glue on Kumohada paper
60 x 83
Eirene II, 2003
Japanese vermilion mixed with Hyde glue on Kumohada paper
60 x 83
Precious Nard, 2003
Birch wood, Kumohada paper, Gampi paper, and azurite wash
48 x 90 x 19

19 Dee VanDyke
Anointed, 2002
Water-based media on canvas
216 x 18

20 Helen Zajkowski
Tower of Babel, 2002
Acrylic collage pop-up book
20 x 36 (open)

21 G. Carol Bomer
Global City Babel (Foundation), 2002
Mixed media on wood
30 x 30 (framed)

22 Houben Tcherkelov
St. Ioan, 2003
Glitter on wallpaper
17 x 19
Collection of William Petroni, New York

23 David E. Levine
The Breakfast of Champions, 2004
Manipulated photocopy
17 ½ x 12

24 James Disney
Through the Eye of a Needle, 2001
Watercolor
26 x 41

25 Anita Breitenberg Naylor
Revelation 3:5, 2002
Collage
48 x 48

IV. Faith and Healing by Grace

26 Erica Grimm-Vance
Binding Up, Healing Vision I, 2004
Graphite, encaustic, steel, and 23-karat gold
12 x 24

27 Stewart Luckman
Last Testament of Job, 2003
Marble
15 x 9 x 8

28 Edward Knippers
Ash Wednesday (Christ and the Demoniac), 2001
Oil on canvas
96 x 144

29 Melanie Weaver
Inhabiting / Flying, 2003
Mixed media sculpture
40 x 14 x 13

30 Serge J-F Levy
Faith from Inside — Religion in Prison: Oak Park Heights Super Maximum Security Facility for Men, Stillwater, MN, 2002
Silver gelatin print
15 x 20
Faith from Inside — Religion in Prison: Women's State Correctional Institution, Muncy, PA, 2002
Silver gelatin print
11 x 14

31 Kathy Hettinga
Chemotherapy Journey: Chemotherapy Patient, Gynecologic Oncologist Surgeon, 2003
Archival digital inkjet prints on Epson Smooth Fine Art Paper
44 x 65

32 Michael Mills
Hosts (Triptych), 2004
Digital photographs
20 x 62

V. The Altarpiece and Book as Idea

33 Tyrus Clutter
Altarpiece of St. Francis of L'Abri, 2001
Mixed media with oil and book pages
27 ¼ x 36 ¾ x 3 (open);
20 x 18 ¼ x 5 (closed)

34 Rosemary Scott-Fishburn
The Madonna and Child Enthroned with Angels and Saints, 2003
Copper relief drawing
4 x 7 feet

35 Bruce Herman
Annunciation, from the series *Elegy for Witness*, 2002
Oil, alkyd resin, and gold and silver leaf on wood
76 x 96
Collection of Mr. and Mrs. William R. Cross, Manchester, Massachusetts

36 Robert P. Eustace
Image: Seed of Divine Life, 2003
Altarpiece construction/combined process on wood and metal
25 x 19 x 3

37 James Larson
Stations of the Cross, 2004
Oil on paper
14 works, 8 x 6 each
On loan from various private collections

38 Lynn Aldrich
Baptistery, 2003
Gold leaf paint on pages from pool design books
78 x 140
Courtesy of Carl Berg Gallery, Los Angeles, CA

39 Donald J. Forsythe
Turf Painting / Ireland, 2002
Gouache, acrylic mediums, gold leaf, plaster, gesso, and County Mayo turf and turf ash over Bible pages on Arches watercolor paper
18 x 24

40 Christine A. Forsythe
Lenten Book: Book of Forty Number Three, 2004
Pages: handmade paper of various fibers and painted with gouache and metallic pigments, sewn with cotton and metallic threads; endpapers: Chiri paper and Thai soft Unryu; cover: bark cloth; binding: hemp and waxed linen
9 x 17 x 4 ½ (closed)

41 Sandra Bowden
Book of Nails, 2003
Mixed media with gold leaf
9 x 6 x 1 ¼ (closed); 9 x 12 x 1 ¼ (open)

VI. Last Things

42 Aaron Lee Benson
The Two Witnesses, 2004
Clay
9 x 8 x 2 feet

43 Peter Sheesley
Four Laws: I, II, III, IV, 2004
Oil on board
4 panels, 9 x 12 each

44 Guy Chase
Untitled (Ledger for Multiple Adjustments), 2001
Oil on panel
15 x 22

Credits